THE LETTERS OF
MAJOR
GENERAL
PRICE-
DAVIES
VC, CB, CMG, DSO

THE LETTERS OF
MAJOR GENERAL PRICE-DAVIES
VC, CB, CMG, DSO

FROM CAPTAIN TO MAJOR GENERAL, 1914–18

EDITED BY PETER ROBINSON
FOREWORD BY PROFESSOR JOHN BOURNE

First published 2013
by Spellmount, an imprint of

The History Press
The Mill, Brimscombe Port
Stroud, Gloucestershire, GL5 2QG
www.thehistorypress.co.uk

British Library Cataloguing in Publication Data.
A catalogue record for this book is available from the British Library.

ISBN 978 0 7524 8736 6

Typesetting and origination by The History Press
Printed in Great Britain

Contents

Introduction

Major General Llewellyn Alberic Emilius Price-Davies VC, CB, CMG, DSO[1]

These letters and diary entries reveal a unique testimony to one man's journey through the First World War, and a great insight into the changes that took place within the British Army at that time. The officer corps of 1914 was made up of people who were very familiar with each other, or, as the French might say, '*pays de connaissance*'. The letters reveal a great deal about the war into which they were thrust, seen through the words and thoughts of an officer steeped in the culture of the Old Army – Major General Llewellyn Alberic Emilius Price-Davies.[2] The diaries have been used to supplement the letters where they have been of interest.[3]

I have shown his career path up to the beginning of the First World War and his personal background in order to lay a foundation for what is to follow. The correspondence is almost entirely to his wife, Miss Eileen Geraldine Edith *née* Wilson, who was from an Anglo-Irish family of Currygrane, Edgworthstone, Ireland. They married on 6 August 1906. She was the sister of the future Field Marshal Sir Henry Wilson, who was later gunned down by Irish Republicans outside his house at 36 Eaton Place in London on Thursday 22 June 1922.

Major General Price-Davies VC went to the same school in Marlborough as his brother-in-law, and whereas Wilson joined the Rifle Brigade, Price-Davies entered King's Royal Rifle Corps. Price-Davies was also a student of Wilson's when he attended the Staff College Course at Camberley during 1908–09. Both served in South Africa, and were at the War Office when the First World War started.

I have been faithful in my rendition of both the diary entries and letters, and have not altered the text or changed the punctuation.[4] The letters are addressed to his wife, unless otherwise marked. I have tried to identify as many people mentioned therein as possible, and cross-referenced them in endnotes. I have done my best with the handwriting, but on occasion have been defeated, so any errors are mine and mine alone. I am grateful to Colonel Nick Lock OBE for information regarding officers of Royal Welch Fusiliers who served in the Great War. Finally, Major General Price-Davies VC was known by his contemporaries as 'Mary'; I have been unable to find the reason for this nickname or when it began, but it is in keeping with the period as so many officers did have curious epithets, often relating to their schooldays or service training.

Timeline

Llewellyn Alberic Emilius Price-Davies

Born:	30 June 1878, Chirbury, Shropshire
Educated:	Marlborough 1892–94
	Sandhurst
Nickname:	'Mary'
Regiment:	Kings Royal Rifle Corps
	2nd Lieutenant 23 February 1890
Promoted:	Lieutenant 1899
1899–1902:	South Africa. Price-Davies served in the
	following actions during the Second Boer War

Relief column for Ladysmith
Present at the Battle of Colenso, 15 December 1899
Served in operations in the Natal, 17–24 January 1900
Present at Spion Kop, 24 January 1900
Served operations in Natal, 5–7 February 1900 (present at Val Kranz)
Served operations in Natal, 14–25 February 1900 (present at Tugela Heights & Pieter's Hill)
Served in operations Natal, March–June 1900 (present at Laing's Nek)
Transvaal, January–August 1901
Served operations in Zululand Natal frontier, September 1901
Served Transvaal and Orange River, April–May 1902

Price-Davies was Mentioned in Despatches (MID) twice (*London Gazette* (LG) 20 January 1900 and 8 February 1901). He was also awarded the DSO for his services during the conflict (LG 19 April 1901).

During the latter part of the war, while serving in the mounted infantry, Price-Davies was wounded slightly on 17 Sept 1901. It was at Blood River Poort, a river southwards and to the west of Schurweberg in Natal, where General Botha defeated the column under the command of Lieutenant Colonel H. de la P. Gough. The citation for the award of his VC reads:

At Blood River Poort, South Africa on the 17th September 1901, when the Boers overwhelmed the right of the British column, and some four hundred of them galloping round the flank and rear of the two guns, riding up to the drivers (who were trying to get the guns away) and calling upon them to surrender, Lieutenant Price-Davies, hearing an order to fire upon the charging Boers, at once drew his revolver and dashed upon them in a most gallant and desperate attempt to rescue the guns. He was immediately shot and knocked off his horse, but was not mortally wounded although he had ridden to what seemed like certain death without a moment's hesitation.

(LG 29 November 1901)

Although he was severely wounded on 26 January 1902, he recovered to attend the presentation by Lord Kitchener on 8 June 1902, a fine day in Pretoria, in front of the government buildings:

Those to get the V.C's are on the left of it amongst the houses. The square is crowded with troops & civilians & all the windows are occupied. First of all 12 nurses get the Red Cross, then I have to go up leading the VC's Standing in front of K my deeds are read out & the K puts my VC on & rams the pin into me.[5]

Wounded:	Twice described as 'slightly and seriously' Captain, 7 January 1902
Decoration:	Queens South Africa Medal & 5 Clasps Kings South Africa medal & 3 clasps
Date of marriage:	Married Henry Wilson's sister, Eileen, on 6 August 1906
1906–7:	Adjutant 24 Battalion, Mounted Infantry School, South Africa
1908–9:	Staff College (psc)
1910 March – June:	Naval War Course, Portsmouth[6]
1910–12	Brigade Major Irish Command
1912–14	GSO 3, War Office, London
1914 August	GSO 3. France, BEF Liaison Officer, 2nd Division
1914 September – 1915 March:	GSO 2
Promoted:	Major, 1 September 1915 1915 March – November 1915. GSO 2
Promoted:	Lt Colonel (Brevet) 1 January 1916
1915 November – 1917 October:	Temporary Brigadier General, France GOC 113th Infantry Brigade, 38th (Welsh) Division
1917 October – 1918 March:	Brigade Commander Home Forces
1918 April 3 – 11 April:	Brigade Commander, France
Promoted:	Colonel (Brevet) 3 June 1918

	1918 April – November. Special Employed (liaison Officer) Temporary Major General
Mentioned in Despatches:	*London Gazette* 19/10/14; 1/1/16; 4/1/17; 11/12/17
1918–19:	President of the Standing Committee of Enquiry regarding Prisoners of War
Promoted:	Substantive Colonel 2 June 1919
1920–30:	ADC to King George V
1920–24:	Assistant Adjutant-General, Aldershot Command
1924–27:	Commanded the 145th Infantry Brigade
1927–30:	Assistant Adjutant and Quarter Master General, Gibralter. (acting Local Brigadier)
13 July 1933:	Hon. Major General
1933–48:	Member of the Hon. Corps of Gentlemen-at-Arms
1940–45:	Battalion Commander, Upper Thames Patrol (Home Guard)
Decorations:	Legion du Honour 4th Class; Order of St Maurice and St Lazarus, 3rd Class (Italy) 1914 Star and Clasp; British War Medal and Victory Medal, VC, CB, CMG, DSO
Date of death:	26 December 1965. Sonning, Berkshire

NOTES

1 LG 5 March 1900. Hugh Arthur Lewis Price-Davies serving in 14th Middlesex Regt was given permission to add Davies to the surname; his father had petitioned for this change in 1880. This officer also served as a captain in the Egyptian Campaign with the RWF (Royal Welch Fusiliers). Captain Charles Stafford Price-Davies served in KRRC (King's Royal Rifle Corps) in France and Belgium, and later in Macedonia and Turkey. He was awarded an MC.

2 I am grateful to the Trustees of the Imperial War Museum for permission to use this correspondence.

3 I am grateful to the Trustees of the National Army Museum for permission to use this correspondence and to Mr Nigel Steel who pointed me in the right direction.

4 Colonel R.J.L. Ogilby established the Army Museums Ogilby Trust in September 1954. Its purpose was to support regimental army museums by providing expert assistance. It was the stimulus of the trustees that lead to the foundation of the National Army Museum. I am very grateful to Professor Ian F.W. Beckett for the information about the existence of these diaries.

5 Diary entry for Sunday 8 June 1902.

6 I am grateful to Dr J. Moretz for this information.

One

1914

In the months leading up to the First World War, Price-Davies' diaries reflect the social life of a comfortable, married, middle-ranking officer. He and his wife go to the country and visit friends and relatives, and attend local point-to-point races. Tennis appears to be a passion and is played more as the year progresses, in particular with Henry Wilson at the Hurlingham Club.[1] Price-Davies attends the House of Commons in February to hear Lloyd George and records that he was 'quite brisk at times'. He dines with Heywood at King's Guard, St James' Palace and records: 'a great experience, introduced to Pryce Jones.'[2] They also go to Aintree for the Grand National in March, where they walk the course and bet on *Trianon III*, which came in second; 'they enjoyed it immensely.' In April, they go to 'Ponting's' lecture and cinematograph presentation of the 'Scott Expedition', which was 'most interesting one feels as if one might never complain of any hardships after what they have been through'.[3]

They attend church regularly on Sundays, although they vary attendance at Chester Square, the Brompton, Cranleigh Gardens and St Margaret's, Westminster. Price-Davies records in May that Thompson Capper has been promoted major general, 'at last'. At this time he writes, 'Henry went to the polo, an International Team was beaten by Hurlingham! So they are going to have a new team.' He returns to his old school for the funeral of a master, Mr Richardson, and records 'he was a good friend & a great loss to the school'. He attends the regimental dinner and sits between Prialux[4] and Saunders,[5] and stays with Stuart-Wortley.[6] During these months, Price-Davies and his wife go to the Albert Hall for concerts, attend the army tournament and the theatre. They see *Pygmalion*, which was 'excellent', as well as the *Land of Promise* (with Irene Vandebergh and Geoffrey Teale). In June they see Alexandra Carlisle in *Driven* and record her acting as 'splendid'.[7] Price-Davies also goes to see the Cavalry Club who were beaten by 'Old Cantabs' in the final of the Championship Cup. On Monday 22 June, a holiday for the king's birthday, he attends the Trooping of the Colour: 'had my photo taken.' Sport appears to be an important part of his life and he attends the Eton and Harrow game at Lords, and goes to Winchester to see the 60th (KRRC) play the Rifle Brigade. The Rifle Brigade have a 'Good side', and he enjoys listening to 'the Old Boys talking about old times' there. After dinner, 'Oxley,[8] Tavish[9] & I go up to the depot where we see Reggie Beauchamp, Gerald & others.'

Price-Davies, the man

Price-Davies was very much a Victorian who believed in service and duty for one's country, and joining the Army was a latent expression of this. He was educated at both Marlborough and Sandhurst, which reflects the social stratum from which he came. His time in South Africa before the outbreak of the second Boer War was one of routine interrupted by searching for a good polo pony. Although in this war he was both 'slightly and seriously' injured there can be no doubting his courage which was recognised by the award of the Victoria Cross. In 1906 he marries Eileen Wilson and leads a comfortable life of a young officer with posting to South Africa, Ireland and eventually the MOD in London. In these years he also passes the prestigious Staff College Course and attends the Royal Naval Command course. Both these events mark him out as a potential senior officer who was well connected both through his Regiment and his brother in law Henry Wilson.

During the war he undergoes a great deal of soul searching regarding the work that he undertakes and is deeply aware that having not commanded his own battalion that he lacks leadership skills. Once again while in command of his brigade during 1916–17 he shows time and again that he has the courage to be right where he should be commanding his men. However, after two years in command the stress undoubtedly has the effect of undermining his resolve and he received a home posting at his own request.

The last year of the war we see him agonising over his relationship with Lord Cavan where he acts as Liaison officer between him and the new CIGS Henry Wilson. Once again he has to lead a very diplomatic path which reveals how careful he has to be in resolving issues with much more senior commanders. His time spent with the Italians displays how charismatic they are and how temperamental to deal with. His working relationship reveals how he has been able to combine both his professional and social abilities and the same time passing back information gained from the Italians which ensued that the strategic plans were kept up to date with the current reality in theatre.

The Ulster Crisis[10]

Ulster[11] dominates the entries beginning in January 1914 with a reference about North Ulster; on 10 January Price-Davies discusses the matter with Henry Wilson, stating 'Doyle a sound man which pleases me I think we must not fight Ulster if we feel we ought not to, though fear the consequences of our actions.' By the 26th he records, 'Stapleton tells me that Plunkett has a plan to compromise Home Rule which he is trying to get accepted I hope he will succeed.' On 5 February he goes to a meeting chaired by Leo Maze: 'I never heard any speaker who impressed me as much with his earnestness. He clearly showed the feeling now existing in Ulster.' Henry Wilson goes off to Belfast and 'he is impressed with the earnestness of the Ulster people'. On 9 March Price-Davies records: 'A fateful day for the government as it announces their clauses for the Home Rule Bill which turn out to be each county can vote whether they wish to be excluded or not but only for 6 years. Unionist & Ulster will not accept this.' By 11 March 'Henry comes back after meetings at York & Leeds'. On the 12th he dines with George Cory at the Chatham Club with about sixty people where George Long addresses them on the Ulster Question, after which he takes part in a discussion 'but does not add a great deal to the controversy'.[12]

By 13 March: 'I walk with Henry things are very depressing Sir J French seems to have quite collapsed & given way to the politicians. Is there no end to this rotten state of affairs.'[13] On 21 March Price-Davies spends the weekend in Worcester and writes of 'Great excitement in the papers today. Reported resignations of Hubert Gough & other Officers at Curragh & Dublin & moves of troops.' By 23 March: 'Details of the resignations. The Government I think tried a bit of bluff but failed. This should shake them in their determination to use the army against Ulster.' On the 24th: 'George Cory to lunch who talks to us about the crisis & see Henry after lunch. War Office still rather excited about it but General Staff held together & helped Hubert Gough for all they were worth & won.' Later, however, there is a slight hesitation: 'fear that harm to the army over this crisis is great but the government is entirely to blame.' On 26 March Price-Davies records 'Henry tells us Sir J F & Ewart have resigned', but a day later he details:

> Sir J F & Ewart have not given their final decision about resigning I think the best is for them to resign & for the matter to end there. This army has shown it will not fight over Ulster & the fact that the government has repudiated the guarantee matters little to us except to those who gave in, Sir John Bryant, the less said the better.[14]

On Tuesday 31 March Price-Davies notes:

> What a surprise yesterday when it was given out that Asquith is to be new war minister. I walk to & from the WO with Henry. He seems in good spirits but thinks we have not heard the end of the business yet. Sir J French & Sir Ewart resigned yesterday I wonder who will succeed them.[15]

The following day: 'I walk home with Henry, Sir Charles Douglas is to be the CIGS I am glad as we might have had Nicholson or Ian Hamilton.' On 4 April: 'Henry comes in, no Adjutant General yet.' The next day, Saturday: 'General protest in the park I met J. Gough on the way up he was in a fearful rage at the way the government has handled Ulster & the Army. The meeting was most loyal & impressive.' By 10 April: 'The Ulster Council publish revelations regarding the Govt plan to coerce Ulster.' On Saturday 25 April: 'Another excitement Ulster have landed they say 70,000 rifles & 5,000,000 rounds of ammunition.' He then records on 8 May: 'Govt don't seem to know what to do?'

This record of entries regarding Ulster reflects the position of the pre-war army; whether his views reflect those of all officers is open to question.

On 5 May Price-Davies recorded that 'Budget means another £5 a year income duty off me', and on 27 May: 'I saw Hubert Gough for a short time J. G. has had an operation but is going on alright.'[16] By June, it appears that the crisis was over and he resumes his social life; playing tennis and attending various functions from regimental dinners to going to the theatre. He records that, at this time, Henry Wilson travels to France. On 11 June Price-Davies goes to Winchester for a Staff exercise: 'Up early & start at 7.15 with White, we have to run the 2nd Division. An interesting day.' And the following day, 'I get up at 2am & we have a busy time till the exercise finishes at 9am. Conference at 1.45pm.' On 20 June he attends the Staff college dinner: 'We had a great gathering of our term.' Come the end of July, they are in Spennymore, Durham: 'I go with Rex in their car to see Miners Demonstration, a great procession with many bands. Hear Richardson speak. Tennis in afternoon.'[17]

It is not until the 28 July that Price-Davies records:

> We go to London about 4.15 I make a call at the W.O. to hear if there is any further War News but Henry & Col Harper are out I went to Aldershot (Queens Hotel) at 8pm.[18] Harrington in Hotel, they go to a 'Ladies Farewell dinner' given by 1st Bn to General W Davies.

On 29 July:

> Went to 2nd Div HQ & I went with letters to Gen Perceval in afternoon. Had tea with Major Harrington. Come back after dinner with very bad War news the precautionary period has started. Henry is up he has no further news. It's thought that if Russia mobilizes it will bring in Germany France & England.

On the 30th, 'Go out to 2nd Div for today. War news still bad I go to Hawley', and the following day 'Got back at 4pm. Came back in motor with Sir A. Murray.'[19]

On 1 August Price-Davies was still at the Queens Hotel, Aldershot: 'Everyone talks as if we must have War. Gilly says they are all very pessimistic at the W.O. thinking the Govt means to back out of helping France if Germany sends an ultimatum to Russia & France.'[20] On 2 August: 'Germany declares war on Russia. France mobilizes. We return to London to find I had been wired for.' By 3 August:

> Events pass so quickly that it is hard to write today (Wed) what happened on Monday. There seems to be an absence of alarm & panic though some people are excited & laying in large stocks of food. Also bank holiday extended to Thursday (inclusive) we cannot get money. The Govt has appeared to us soldiers as weak & not to be behaving honourable towards France. They have a difficult task bothered as they are by a lot of peace at any price people. We do

not commence mobilization until Wed & even then it is not certain we go over to France. The effect is a gradual process rushing into War at once has undoubtedly been to consolidate the nation & to stop the Peace Party. I leave the W.O. on Wed.

London, 6 August 1914, Thursday: 'They say the Germans have been taken aback against Liege but one must not accept these rumours too readily. No news of the fleet.' On 7 August: '3rd day of mobilization. Go to Aldershot & form 2nd Div HQ. General Munro has taken over command.'[21]

Mobilization

The 2nd Division was part of the Aldershot command under Lt General Douglas Haig,[22] who received orders to mobilize on the afternoon of 4 August. The division was commanded by Major General C.C. Munro CB, which was part of 1st Corps. Mobilization proceeded rapidly with 6th Brigade being ready by midnight on 7/8 August. The following night the 5th Brigade and the 4th Guards, as well as Royal Artillery, Royal Engineers and the Divisional Train, also reported complete. Between 12–13 August the infantry brigades embarked for France from Southampton. At 6 a.m. on 15 August the Divisional HQ left Aldershot, reaching Le Havre between 16–18 August. The DHQ entrained for Wassigny, arriving early on the morning of 19 August. By 22 August, it had taken up a position on the line of La Longueville.

Price-Davies' letters and diary entries[23] begin at the start of this journey; he had taken up his post as staff officer grade 3 (GSO 3), with the 2nd Division.[24]

8.8.14

Queens Hotel

Seems to be alright about Liege & now we hear that the Germans have lost a cavalry division I seem to be busy all day in the office but seem to do little good.

10.8.14

Kitchener seems to be rubbing everyone up the wrong way at W.O.[25] His plan of taking Officers from the BEF to make another Army is madness.

11.8.14

Gen Perceval goes off with Advance party.[26] King comes round the troops who cheer him.

12.8.14

Got up at 1.30 and went to Farnborough to see some of the 6th Brigade off, saw 2 train loads of S Staffs & 3 of our own 1st Bn. Everything went alright &

I was relieved by Colonel White.[27] By coincidence a train containing ½ Bn of
2 Bn came along main line (entrained at Frimley) followed behind by ½ Bn
1st.

15.8.14

SS *Minneapolis*

Entrain 6, embark 2am Southampton & leaves 11.30am. Anchors off Le Harve
for night.

15.8.14
My own darling[28]

SS *Minneapolis*

This is a fine ship, it is a cattle boat but has 64 cabins. If the Germans get us
now there would be a howl! HQ of 2 Divs. And the Cavalry Div. We got
down about 8 but did not start till 11.30. Taking the taxis on board delayed
us a lot I don't know why but they are very dour about it. We nearly went
without lunch. Rothwell had to persuade the ships people to feed us.[29] It is
raining now and has been since 11am I wonder where we shall go to. Darling
I still see your little face as you said goodbye, may God give you strength to
stand this trial.

At the docks one large placard read 'I am commanded by the Lords
Commissioners of the Admiralty to tender to the men employed fitting and
coaling transports their Lords grateful thanks for their splendid work'.

16.8.14
My own darling

We have had a long day, reveille at 2.30am, breakfast 3.30am alongside at 4 &
busy till lunchtime to get wagons off. Arrangements might have been better
and it poured till about 10am. We delayed a long time because we had to wait
for a floating crane which took out taxis & wagons out and put them in a
lighter and they had to be taken out again on to the quay. Rather laborious
considering we were alongside at 12.30 the men manning the engine went to
lunch for an hour! The next thing was that the cavalry walked into the hotel
allocated to us for billets and we had to go to a very inferior place. In fact to
several places we are very scattered nearly a mile from our men & servants &
much further from where taxis are. The taxis are in the ASC store I have never
seen such a wonderful shed in my life very nearly a 1000ft long. The men are
in the cotton sheds. All day we have been running around in taxis. The trams
take us free.

I saw some of our men with local girls who were decorating them with
roses. I am in a room with Gort,[30] Col. White has been seedy & we feared it
was appendicitis.

17.8.14

My own darling

I have a censors stamp so with luck this won't be opened though of course I shall play the game. I am very fit & getting on alright so far but we shall be glad to get the Division together again. We are much scattered here when we landed & it is a difficult place to find ones way about. I go with the motor tomorrow which is very lucky. It is strange seeing our sentries walking alongside a French one.

Interpreters are a mixed blessing. Colonel White who is not well wanted a whisked egg in hot milk and brandy. The interpreter gave the order wrong I heard him but did not want to interrupt & he got no milk at all. Then a tiny jug was brought but in the end he got it all right.

Gort and I sleep in the same room. Very glad I brought my bath I had a good tub today. The general is full of energy & very fit. Put pyjamas on last night the general said I had not reached the age limit for wearing them!

18.8.14 (In the train)

Last night some of us dined in the club the British Consul was there, he was continually being sent for some reason or another. He had 3 fellows billeted on him & was told to take 3 more & had no place to put them. We tried to pay for our rooms in the hotel but we were told 'le ville' would pay. We were up at 4 & they got us coffee & off we went to the station. Henry may talk about his French friends if he likes but he may as well keep quiet about their railway arrangements as far as the transport of troops is concerned.[31] We had to entrain from the ground level using ramps. The horses were put in cattle trucks facing the engine one end of the train & with their heads facing inwards. It is not a good plan at all as it does not facilitate watering & feeding. Saddles and 2 men per truck are between the 2 rows of horses & the horses are kept from moving by their head ropes being attached to the rings in the roof. 3 horses fell off the ramp going up, my chestnut mare amongst them. She sat down violently & her tail looks badly bent & I expect she will be stiff.

The trucks and wagons have openings at the side no simple end boarding like we have at home and it is a job measuring the wagon. I superintended the work of putting wagons in, one truck was so rotten that the Major nearly went through the floor and we had to send in planks to put underneath. The men travel in the cattle trucks fitted with benches. We have 1st Class carriages 5 in this compartment.

All the French people are delighted to see us & little children come up and I shook one by the hand. We get very little news now the French papers are bad. We have just been cheered up a wayside station where the crowd of enthusiastic people gave us flowers, cigarettes etc.

18.8.14

Wassigny

Detrain at Wassigny 2.15am. A fine bit of country rather like England enclosed & prosperous.

20.8.14

I was very busy yesterday went on reconnaissance with a French officer. We went like the wind & killed a chicken. Rothwell has a dear old motherly lady looking after him. The last thing at night she opened a cupboard & took out a jerry remarking 'la vase de nuit!'

22.8.14

We have had little sleep since coming over. Last night I got 3 hours so as we got into our billets early I went to lie down at 3pm, but was woken up at 3.15 to go to meet Johnny G,[32] Col Carden,[33] Major Ready,[34] & I went in a Daimler & took a taxi to follow in case we had to do a reconnaissance. We took a wrong turn & had to pull up, whereupon the taxi rammed us & punctured our petrol tank & we had to work the pressure pump all the way. When we got there we were told we were to march at once! I had a chat with old friends in the 1st Div. Today. Poor Jourdain has gone sick with pleurisy & has to be left in a French house. The people here are wonderful I saw a woman with a basket of eggs today, giving them all away to the men and they run out of houses with wine and beer for them. So far I have seen no drunkenness at all.

22.8.14

Pont sur Sambe

March Longeville – Hargollie. Got a series of contradictory orders which are very harassing.

Sunday 23.8.14

March 3am to Genly & find 3rd Division in position. Go to billets but we are soon moved out again to take up position as the enemy was advancing. This was the Battle of Mons we were really hardly engaged as whole of 6th Bde were shelled but suffered no casualties Guards Bde had some.

24.8.14

Retreat commences at 4.45am. Infantry very tired & march discipline bad. Germans do not pursue vigorously.

25.8.14

Marolles

Return again 6th Bde rear guard. A scare in the afternoon that the Germans were between Wassigny & Landrecies & we are attacked at Marolles. Infantry under arms all night. What a splendid fight the Guards put up killing 800 Germans.

26.8.14

3.30am Retreat again Connaught Rangers got into trouble & lost a lot of men. Nothing but French troops everywhere cursing us & crowding all the roads I got lost & stay the night with some French soldiers.

27.8.14

Off at 4am again a critical day rear guard under pressure.

28.8.14

My hopes were frustrated as I was woken ¼ to 1 to be told we were to march at once. My friend the saddler with whom I lodged made me some coffee before starting. Since then we have been busy marching. We have seen a lot of French reserve formation. They seem to prefer to march through one village from both ends at once.

28.8.14

Cervies

March at 4 to Legunes where we hope for a little peace.

29.8.14

We have been very busy lately & 4 hours sleep is a long night you should see us writing orders were very sleepy it would make you laugh. Everyone very well and cheery. The men are wonderful they have done tremendous marches & even when quite exhausted & don't grumble & are quite civil when spoken to. Servants might like Players Navy Cut tobacco strong.

29.8.14

Cervies

A day of rest after 143 miles in 9 days.

30.8.14

Just resting under some trees. Had some coffee in a cottage & got to bed last night at 3.15 & up at 5.45 & all the time I was being disturbed by people being called. My horses are quite a success the chestnut mare a regular little lady & evidently has been a favourite. The second is stronger but greener but has a good mouth. The third is a wild beast when you get on and tries to leave the other horses and plunges forward to the great danger of all within reach. It has been a very hot day & the infantry felt it very much.

I have seen the little man twice & Hereward and the good battalion in the march there were many old mounted infantry faces.[35] We were told officially of the success of the fleet. How very plucky going into German waters.

Sunday 30.8.14

Cervies

Retreat order to beyond Soissons but the day was too hot & we could not get so far as Soissons.

31.8.14

Langone

Retreat over the Aisne.

Tuesday 1.9.14

Thury

March at 4. Fight at Village Cotterets in woods. Guards put up a good show. Very fine sight the guns being brought out of action under heavy fire.[36] General Scott Kerr & Coe hit, Colonel Thomas killed we hear.[37]

2.9.14

My own darling

A great date we rounded up 340 Germans. The Germans appear to have behaved well on the whole to the inhabitants but have absolutely ransacked deserted houses & have taken all the wine they can find. It is just 9 & we have not had dinner yet. We live a queer life. Reggie Ward & Bonham Carter were slightly injured today.[38]

3.9.14

My own darling

You know now I suppose how we pushed forward to Mons & how 5th Div got a rough time of it. We hardly fired a shot except the guns & lost few casualties. The 6th Brigade was under shellfire all afternoon and never lost a man. Then we turned and retreated, the Germans were not rigorous in their pursuit but it made us very tired going along like that till at last we got a rest day. But before that we had a show at Landrecies where the Germans attacked the Guards Brigade & 850 dead Germans were counted on the ground. That's the sort of stuff for them!

It is too sad seeing all the people fleeing from this country & and village after village is deserted. Col. Gordon had got a brigade and leaves us, Heywood is to be his Brigade Major I wonder how they will get on.[39] We have had some really scorching weather. How's K's Army getting on?

5.9.14

Colonel Gordon has gone to command 19th Bde.[40] We are to get Whigham instead.[41] 'Johnnie' has worked like a slave and does most of the general staff work but he is very irritable at times, gets quite excited. He is not the only one however, 'Arthur' has been very queer at times quite unhinges as Mrs Tim (Harrington) would say. The greatest disappointment has been 'Flower' who has really broken down & wants a rest badly.[42]

Our cavalry seem to be having show in this war & to be distinguishing themselves. An Officer in one regiment killed 3 Uhlans with his sword & there were many more stories but they have not gone madly charging about the country & have used their rifles a lot.[43]

5.9.14

Fontenay

Reach end of retirement. We are in a fine chateaux, have a bath, lovely peaches in the garden.

6.9.14

Rigny

Advance very slowly.

7.9.14

Col. Percival on reconnaissance at 5.30am but I was late & after 3 ½ hours never caught him up.[44] It was very annoying I was on duty last night and had to take orders out, got back at 12 & lay down but at 1am I had to go out again with orders, to bed at 2.30 & up again 5.30. This is the way we have to live.

I have not seen Hubert Gough yet though he has been quite near.[45] His Bde Major told us yesterday they were 'helping themselves to Germans'. Hugh said Henry was very tired I am sure many things have been a great disappointment to him.[46]

We have had excellent French wine during our travels even in small places. Nearly all or motors over here have gone bust. It is largely due to having to move at a walk in the columns. I should like to tell you about yesterdays little fight but must not I suppose. It was rather a good little fight in some ways. Today has been rather disappointing as we hung round a good deal but the news appears to be good. Dalton now is a Colonel and is here as Assistant Director of Medical Services rather funny having been in Dublin together.[47] We are waiting for orders it is now 11pm so I shall be late going to bed.

One of the prisoners was a waiter at the Savoy I forgot to tell you that the waiter was surprised by a sergeant whose sister is employed at the Savoy. Fancy them meeting like that. I had to go out to find a man a place to sleep in. We usually sleep in a barn or the floor of a room with straw. I have one or two tame fleas but we sleep soundly. Geoffrey Makins has arrived out here I saw him today.[48]

9.9.14

Domplan

A disappointing day cross the Marne at Charly & halt for a long time with 6th Bde in advance guard.

10.9.14

Clevillon

Fine capture of 340 by 6th Bde (chiefly by 1st Bn) at Hautevenes.

Saturday 12.9.14

Courcelles

Across the Vesle at Blaine. Bridge at Concelles broken. Get into billets late. We are in a fine chateaux. Heavy rain all night most depressing I am up all night delivering orders & we went to inspect the bridge at Pont Arcy & find it destroyed.

13.9.14

I hope Whigham will come out soon as Percival does not get enough sleep.[49] He drops off in the middle of writing orders. Last night we were in a fine chateau, tonight in a farmhouse. Taffy asks about German atrocities I think in these parts they have behaved fairly well. They have taken all the eatables & wine & ransacked empty houses but they have treated the people properly. There was a case the other day where 2 women were bayoneted & there was certainly a story at Mons. They put the inhabitants in front of them when they attacked us. The papers seem to be in the lowest depths of despair. I wonder what the Navy are doing? Isn't it extraordinary that we have complete command of the sea. I wonder is it true about the Russians.[50]

The General is naughty & will not sleep & I am anxious lest he should breakdown. Everyone is better since the retreat stopped. That retreat was humiliating to us in this Division as we had hardly been employed but we now know the reason for it but you can imagine what we felt like. The Germans did not press the pursuit & they try to do their battles with artillery. Our 1st Brigade had a little show the other day & came out of it very well. The Germans say our men are such good shots much better than the French.

Sunday 13.9.14

Viel Cucy

Crossed the Aisne with AG but Division remains on the south side.

14.9.14

Viermeil

Passage of the Aisne quite a battle. Guards Brigade on the left put up a good fight & we are repeatedly attacked. Enemy must have lost a lot of & we take about 150 prisoners and lose some of them after disarming them. We get a HE shell into the street close to our HQ which created great stir.[51]

15.9.12

We have been having a big battle yesterday & today & the troops have done splendidly. The 1st Brigade have their tails up. They say they can easily take on the Germans Infantry at 3 to 1. Yesterday 9 riflemen had a pile of 30 dead in front of them without losing one man. Now it is much quieter & I hope we get on. General Percival is splendid a fine soldier. One of my French attaches had a shell through both windows of his car yesterday rather a shock for him.

Move our HQ to a poultry farm. The enemy don't care much about attacking us again but we get a good dose of shell from him. We bombarded the enemy for half an hour in the evening.

17.9.12

The nights are getting cold now but the problem is that one seldom gets ones kit & one cannot carry a whole lot of stuff on ones horses. I cannot talk of casualties which have not appeared in the papers, very sad about George Morris.[52] I have not seen the little man in ages I wonder if there is any news of Stapleton? It is a great thing that the Goodlady is with you, thank her for her letter & tell her write again later.[53]

One French attaché has disappeared since his car was bust up. One fellow in the Guards was in a great state as he was reported killed though perfectly alright. Funny how these mistakes occur. No sign of Whigham, Cavan is to command the Guards brigade I think he is a good man.[54]

18.9.14

We are just waiting to move to our HQ to a more comfortable place. We are very short of accommodation especially for the officers. I had letters from Tim Harrington, he seems to be alright. I saw Beau Nesbitt today he has come out from home.[55] I have this beastly War Diary to keep which distracts me.

Sad poor Dalton getting wounded he got caught by shells & was rather bad. Lord Cavan arrived you remember he commanded Guards Brigade on manoeuvres last year.

19.9.14

We have had some good fighting here & German infantry won't face us at present they have had a good hiding. The 2nd Brigade had heavy losses poor Jackson, Bond,[56] Thompson & 4 others you don't know killed & 50 others wounded.[57]

Sunday 20.9.14

We had an attack today & there was a little confusion as some troops were driven back (Worcester & Connaught) but it all came right. Gilbean was killed I am very sorry he was a fine fellow. I go to Col. Westmacott.[58] General Haking was hit about 1pm.[59]

21.9.14

News is good tonight & we are in high spirits I really think our Division has done awfully well & the spirit of the infantry is wonderful. Rothwell telling stories tonight after dinner about a man in his regiment had one shot to go to hit the target to get his proficiency pay. He shut his eyes & pulled the trigger & the bullet ricocheted into spruce 'holy Jesus' said he 'look at my proficiency pay leaping down the range like a b....y kangaroo'. Another time a militiaman, the Captain had been lecturing on defiles & at the end of his ovation asked the Company if they understood what a defile was. They with one voice answered him that they did, so the Captain chose a man and asked to explain what a defile was 'Sure I don't know Captain unless it is two men from D Company' loud laughter. I saw young Brannon a day or two ago he seemed very well.[60]

21.9.14

I have had a busy morning starting at 6 & returning at 12.39 I went to 5th Bde, 3rd Bde (Welsh Regt) & to 6th Bde, & the Kings trenches. The enemy are shelling but there seems to be little rifle fire today. Round the Kings trenches is a mass of liquid mud. Most unhealthy I should say.

22.9.14

I was on duty last night & had a disturbed night but I had a wash and changed my underclothes for the second time since the War began! The mess has just got 1,000 cigarettes so you could stop sending cigarettes for a fortnight anyway. There is a conference on here now.

Whigham is here and very well I think he should run the show well. I saw Walter Down & Alan Paley just the same as ever.[61] General Munro very well & in good spirits.

The sappers have made wonderful bridges to replace the ones the French destroyed when they retired.

23.9.14

The R.B. 3rd Bn are here I tried to see them but had no time. Sherwood Foresters here. Royal Fusiliers here too. I saw Fowler Butler who commands them.[62] The same as ever I had a letter from Charles Deedes[63] asking for details of Jenkinson death I will send him a line.[64]

General Davies[65] has gone home to command some of 'K's' [Kitchener's] New Army I have lately been writing accounts of battles that is rather a business as one continually gets interrupted & sent on some job or other.

We all get on very well on staff. We have a great man to run the mess as mess Sgt. He came out as a chauffeur but when his car bust up he got a new car with French drivers & our mess Sgt went sick & we took this man in. He drives a motor badly but he is full of energy & enterprise & runs the mess well. I fear the price of messing will go up there is always that tendency in a campaign.

The spirit of the men is marvellous they know they can beat the German Infantry in spite of all the grousing about the superiority of the German rifle.

24.9.14

Such a day would you believe it both 1st & 2nd Bn's within 20 minutes ride from here I had tea with 1st Bn & found lots of 2nd Bn there so went back with them to their place. They seem to know that Jackson & Bond are both dead. They had a tremendous fight shooting away at 30 yds, it is very sad about the casualties I am so sorry for the poor wives. I saw Hereward today & he took a letter to post for me. He seemed cheery about the situation. We have been very quiet lately the Germans have had enough of us for the present. Eric Foljambe[66] well & in great spirits also Young, Brown well too, Williams, Kay, Curry, Leith, Chico & others.[67]

I do think it is too awful about Rheims cathedral & does seem a terrible thing to go & blow it up with shells like that. I expect our Hotel caught it too. Sullivan[68] our Provost Marshall is a queer card, he is a great musician & has played in concerts and played at the same place as Margaret Cooper, and conducted his regimental band in front of the King. We had lovely melons tonight from Paris. We live like fighting cocks.

Thursday 24.9.14
Had a long day in office writing accounts of the battle.[69] J. Gough told me Henry had asked if I could be spared to go to GHQ I must go if I am asked but it goes against the grain now that the regiment has lost so many officers & Kay & Williams have given up their jobs to go to the 2nd Bn.[70]

25.9.14
Irvine one of our Doctors came back today he has had an exciting adventure.[71] Captured by the Germans he escaped & for days had to dodge the German columns. At last he had to cross a railway every inch of which was guarded by sentries. There was nothing for but to walk boldly passed the sentries, which he did & was lucky as tow trains were at the level crossing & the sentries were talking to people on the train. Some of the guards looked after him as he went up the road, but didn't fire. He got to Lille where there was a hospital, they put him in a motor pulled the blinds put up a red cross flag & motored him to Dunkirk & he returned to London, a good performance.

26.9.14
We are all well Rothwell was hit in the leg this morning but it is not serious. I believe I saw Charles Grant. He had been hit twice in the arm but was alright & doing duty. Today we had a lovely morning dodging shells. Last night there was artillery fire ours & Germans at intervals all night but it takes a lot to keep me awake now I drop off very quickly.

27.9.14
Sir John French has been over here to see the men who got DSO's & DCM's. He made a great speech but his audience was only staff officers, our despatch riders, telephonists & our servants. No sign yet of Farmer Davies brother who is to relieve me. Looking through some old orders I see Johnson went to 19th Brigade as Bde. Major. As Heywood is BM of that Bde something must have happened. I have been hard at work at my War Diary to get it squared up for Davies.

Winston Churchill was here today, he wore Trinity House uniform, leather boots & a coat British warm.[72] You never saw such a sight I don't hold with these people coming out & treating the war as a show, sightseeing. Terrible thing those cruisers being sunk we must get level with the Germans somehow.

We caught two Germans today in a haystack where they had been living for a week or 10 days coming down at night. They did not look very bold warriors. General Munro says he gets fever if he sleeps too much! A queer notion I think. Most of the staff have a touch of mild fever, and colds so far I have been lucky.

28.9.14

We are just waiting for Seagrave[73] to come Cherry[74] has taken the car to Corps HQ to fetch him. Farmer Davies brother is not to come at all as he has gone back to brigade. I heard such a piece of news today I am to be liaison officer to Hubert Gough[75] I don't quite know all it means but I shall live partly at GHQ where I shall see Henry & partly with 2nd cavalry div. where I shall be with General Gough.

I see Capt. Berners was killed on the 12th the day the Brigade did so well.[76] General Perceval, was with them that day commanding the Guards brigade.[77]

I expect I shall be at GHQ tomorrow, my horses will go by road about 25 miles & I shall motor with my kit. Last night was a horrid night I was on duty when heavy firing began. Old Munro gets fussy as usual & had us all out including the paymaster & ordnance officer! Our kits were packed & put on the wagon. And there we were all standing in the road for 2 hours. Finally we went to bed when the firing ceased I went over to 1st Div. & found only George Paley up, he was on duty & all the time the firing was against the French some way on our right.[78]

Poor Green married that Camberley girl was shot dead today.[79] Very foolishly he exposed himself at RB trenches where the snipers are only 150x away & was hit just above the heart.

Colonel Stewart commands a battery here. In fact quite a lot of Staff College professors are here, the two Percivals, Whigham, J. Gough, Jeudwine, the latter two are at Corps HQ.[80]

They don't seem to be able to get a successor for me. First it was Farmer Davies brother then he asked to go back to his old brigade, & Seagrave was kicked out & came here & arrived last night I spent all day moving from 6.45–1200 taking him around. Then a wire arrived tonight timed at 8.30 to say Seagrave was to go to 17th Brigade as Brigade Major & we heard that Omanney was to come here.[81] Now another message timed at 8.30 to say that this was not settled. So I go to GHQ to spy out the land & post letters & come back here. My horses are well now. The mare is full of beans it is nice to feel her fit & fresh under me. Today I saw the RB they were very nice to me. I at last saw the great Jullundar.[82]

The old man got his foot run over by a runaway cart and is laid up. Alexander says Green was absolutely foolhardy, would not listen when they told him there were snipers about. The news seems to be good tonight but we cannot count on an advance for a bit. Charles Grant is Bde Major 3rd Brigade and Robin Gant is to be Bde Major of 5th Brigade.

1.10.14

I am not sure if I told you of my visit to GHQ or not I motored over to see what I could find out. I walk into a room and there they all were of the old W.O. the lot it seemed strange. Uncle,[83] Charles, Hereward, Evans, Bowdler,[84] Farmer, Kyshe, Hare and Ma Johnson.

Things have been very peaceful here lately, we have lovely wood fires in the Office & mess, and there is plenty of wood. The poor men must be very cold without blankets & some without greatcoats but they do what they can with straw.

2.10.14

Here I am in Henry's room. Very happy being with him just had dinner & champagne & off now on a night jaunt with Charles Deedes. So funny seeing Ernest bringing soup at dinner in uniform. I shall be very busy which is good Baker-Carr late RB is to be my chauffer.[85] Henry is off somewhere tonight.

3.10.14

Had a long talk with Tommy today he has such a bad cold.[86] We were all waiting for Henry to come back. I had to go off to Douglas Haig's & 1st & 2nd Div. Hereward is sampling some chewing gum, this gives us much amusement. Saw P.T. today just the same also Tavish.[87]

Henry was perfectly sweet when he came to dinner last night he said 'It is nice to see you Mary' & he has shown me all his usual consideration sending me off to his room to write to you. Charles Deedes and I went on a jaunt last night to see Hubert Gough. He was of course tucked away where we had a job to find him. I went to Gough this morning & I had a long talk with him. He is full of spirits & left all our generals without a shred of character or reputation.

I had a nice room allotted to me but when I was away fetching my kit a flying Officer came & bagged it. Now I am in 'la vieux mansion', the good ladies are very solicitous of my welfare but the room is not so nice as the other having no table. They were anxious to make all English & French soldiers comfortable.

Poor Uncle Edwards son Dick was killed in Pegasus, wasn't that the ship taken on by the German ship in Africa![88]

4.10.14

Fere en Tardenois

Last night came back through Compeigne & Soissons, the Germans have made rather a mess of the latter. The woods in these parts are lovely wish I could tell you all but I am afraid I cannot. Had a bath today & a shave in hot water. They made me 2nd grade which I presume increases my pay. Tommie will be over soon I have great difficulty in getting all the information I want to take out to Hubert I dare say I will get better at it.

5.10.14

Start at 9am & catch Cavalry Division at Thennes, south of Amiens & don't find Gough for a bit so do not start back until 4pm. Chain breaks just passed Montidier & a French ambulance charabanc driver comes to our assistance but it is dark before we start again having 60 miles to do. The road is full of lorries & two of them get stuck & blocked the road necessitating a detour.

6.10.14

Go to stay the night in rear with Gough or perhaps return tomorrow according to circumstance. We all appear to have had rather an adventure yesterday Baker-Carr suggested a certain road home I doubted whether we could use it but he assured me that Farmer Davies had been along it which was not the case. It appears the road runs between the French & Germans & BC assures me now that in one place the German trenches were only 150 yds away! But fancy the French allowing us to go along! I expect they thought it was quite natural of these mad Englishmen.

7.10.14

A long day up at 5, coffee, bread & butter then went back to GHQ calling at Gough's on way. Arrived at GHQ 10.30 & left again at 12.45pm. The other chain broke less than 3 miles from Gough's HQ about 5pm. Go back to my hotel at 9pm & had a great dinner. I must tell you about yesterday. We didn't leave GHQ till 2pm and got to Gough's at 6 & came to this town arriving at the Hotel de Ville 8.45pm & get our billet de lodgement. Baker-Carr & I. First the Commander of the Guard showed me into a room & left me there with 2 men. After a bit 3 more came in & said I must go to the 'other side'. I was conducted by a soldier who met a civilian. We wanted the best hotel of course but it was full. Our friend had to get someone else. Meanwhile a soldier came in with the same trouble. Then the town clerk arrived & our friend returned with a long story which appeared to be sad news that all the places were taken. There was however, the Hotel de Pomme but that was not a good hotel. I interposed to say that all we wanted was a bed & that the sooner we got it the better so we came here. It was a good hotel usually frequented by horse dealers! It is simple and clean & good omelettes & excellent brandy.

Hubert Gough is splendid & it is so grand being with him. On my return to GHQ I was ushered into Sir John French so you see I am a person of some importance. As a matter of fact I was lucky to get this job & I think it will suit me well but I do hope I will manage it properly.

8.10.14

Abbeville

A late morning go out to Gough in a French car. Lunch at Hotel du Rheim. See Cathedral start back with BC at 3.30pm. Hanging about Abbeville trying to get started to go to Gough again. Dinner Hotel du Boef at 10.30 Colonel Greenly comes so I don't have to go out.[89]

9.10.14

I saw Tim Harington today tell Mrs Tim he is very well & full of life.[90] Hereward and I had an excellent breakfast in a little café this morning, as our mess was not running. You ask me what my work is? I am backward & forwards in the motor taking information & orders & bringing back information I also take out letters & parcels & newspapers. Gough has got the 2nd Division. The only thing I want is a compass, there are some very nice ones, which float in a liquid & go in a case on ones belt, the latter is essential.

10.10.14

Abbeville

Gough at Fontes N of St. Hilare. I had to go & find out the situation of 2nd Corps for him.

11.10.14

Abbeville

From Gough in last night's billets then go to C. in C. at Bethune & then back to Gough S of Aire. Had to wait for him & started back after dark.

12.10.14

Abbeville

Baker Carr gone to Paris. Have another car allotted get to Gough beyond Hasbrouck at 1pm & then to C in C at Bethune. Some fighting going on but not very serious. Returning to Gough to see him take Mont des Gats.[91]

13.10.14

Some busy days Gough has been a long way from GHQ & so I have not been back till 8.45, the night before last & 9.15 last night. Then dinner, then we have to report to Sir John French after which it is 11pm & bed time as I get up at 6.30am. The weather has been perfect from my point of view if it had not been for the dust but it must be very cold at night for the men who have to sleep out. BC went to Paris yesterday to get some chains for motor & so I had a scratch lad to drive me. He drove me very well. I am very interested in my work but it is difficult sometimes Gough expects a lot of news & there is very often nothing. Weekly Times not coming now I only had one copy I think you might stop it & send one ordinary Times I can take it into Gough he always asks for papers.

I heard Burners was killed in a white flag business & am practically certain that is wrong. It may have happened in an incident which I shall now narrate.

The Guards Brigade captured 150 prisoners & in spite of what the Officers could do the men insisted on getting up and going to them. Whilst so engaged another German attack came up & fixed on the prisoners & all, it may have been at that time that Berners was killed. I shall try to find out when I can.

I had a job getting back from Gough. It was foggy I had a rotten map having mislaid my good one & lost my way & then was blocked by transport but I got back at 9.30. At 10 Radcliffe & Charles & I went to a little café & had an omelette & coffee quite a grand meal & people so nice only cost 2 francs each.[92] The big town where I had a job getting a billet was Amiens there can be no harm in telling you now. We were at the 'Hotel de la Pomme du Pine' such a name. Then we went to Abbeville where we were very comfortable of course I must not say where we are now though everyone must know. I should not worry about Zeppelins and invasions. It is unlikely they would drop bombs on London an undefended town & if they do it would be unlikely they would catch you with a bomb so don't worry anymore about it.

I came across the West Kent's the other day they were very pleased to see me & I had a chat with Colonel Martin who has sent a message to you.[93]

14.10.14

I struck out new ground today & went to see Rawly.[94] As I walked in one door Tommie [see fn.100] walked in at the other. He was quite pleased to see me the nice old thing. He says he is very well. The whole country was full of French Territorial's on my way home I thought I should never get through I can't make out how French soldiers get anywhere. Whenever I see them they are either halted with their arms filed in the middle of the road or elsewhere they are just shuffling about.

14.10.14

St Omer

Got out about 12 to Sir H. Rawlinson at Ypres a wonderful 14th century Cloth Hall there, 150yds long. Saw TC.[95] A German aeroplane was brought down at Ypres today. Many French troops on the road delay me coming back.

15.10.14

Nice letter from Mrs Percival I had no idea he liked working with me in fact I thought he looked upon me as a useless encumbrance. I saw Gen Munro & Whigham too. I don't know now if I am a liaison to Gough or Rawly. I have just been out with Charles Deedes & Bartholomew[96] for a walk I saw Tavish & Tim Harrington & Oxley all seemed fit. I got the refills for lamps alright, no cigarettes come yet I hope they will soon. Kay is wounded I hear. Went to see 4th Corps (Sir H. Rawlinson) at Poperinghe.

16.10.14

I told you I was not welcome in my billet. BC's room was not a good one & had so little hot water & no key to come in at night so we asked for another.

Apparently Thresher[97] sent his interpreter to the people to say we were uncomfortable & that we were not done better they would billet 2 NCO's in there. That night BC was in a good room Madame turning it out for him & I had a strip of carpet in my room. They were very upset we had not told them we were not comfortable I think it will be a lesson to them but as Thresher found us another we cleared out today. I hope to have a hot bath & it looks promising.

I was out with Rawly again today Deegan is his Provost Marshall. It is great seeing him again I have not seen Bungo yet, who is under Rawly but I hope to do so soon.[98]

You ask about our mess we are a cheery lot. Henry, Uncle, Evans, Radcliffe, Charles & Lock, Dawnay, Lynn, Shea (all liaison officers), Colonel Huguet & another Frenchman who speaks English perfectly.[99] They call us 'lizas' Lynn is a gunner Major rather a nice creature Col Huguet has the nicest place you ever saw. They get a little annoyed with Uncle sometimes for not doing things but he is very good as a whole. Henry went for a gallop today I think he is not so rushed now & that things are working smoothly I saw all 2nd Div staff today they were in great form. We hear no Russian news except what is in the papers they don't seem to get on much but I fancy the weather must be vile.[100]

17.10.14

I had a great day seeing Rawly, Tommie & Bingo who sent you messages & was very nice to you. Stewart[101] is with Tommie, Westminster is ADC to Rawly![102] He is quite pleasant to talk to, all the staff I come across are so nice to me. In some ways Herbert's staff are not so nice but they always rather busy & fussed & cavalry are always independent cusses & don't care much for people from the outside & object to senior commanders & staffs & such like. Great news we hear 4 German destroyers being sunk but sad about the Hawk.[103] I saw Commander Samson, a short thick set determined looking man.[104] Rawly thinks him wonderful. Young Bilger is with Bingo as an ADC so if you see Lady Stamfordham you can say he looks blooming.[105]

Morland has got 5th Div.[106] Bingo wants me as a Liaison officer!

18.10.14

I have had a miserable day and feel so ashamed of myself. If only I could tell you all that is going on in my poor brain. Also I have a confession to make I hope you won't be very angry I have not been very happy all the time because sometimes I have done so badly & I thought it over whether to tell you or not. Then I decided not to because I did not want to add to your troubles. I knew it was hard enough for you to bear but if on top of all you know I was doing badly & was miserable about it you would have been very unhappy. Now things are a little different as you have not the same anxiety about me & I must tell you. Well all that is gone now & it is no good making up for past troubles. It is today that really matters. It is the first chance of showing whether I am really worthy of my past or not & I have failed. And it is so sad because it was a simple thing really & anyone but an idiot would have done it. My darling I wonder if I can make you understand about it. It is part of my duties to see that orders are understood & carried out in the spirit that was intended I went out today fully expecting to find Rawly doing a certain thing & found him doing something totally different of course I ought to have told it was not what was required or if I had not done that I should have come back at once to report. How clearly I saw it then when it was too late! Instead I did not report until I had been out to see 'Tommie' & then it was too late for anything to be done. I don't know what bewitches me to do these things I don't really mind much for myself but it is you & Henry I am so sorry for. Murray was upset about it but was very nice in fact nicer than he ought to have been with me but it weighs very heavy on me just at present.[107] I have a mind to tear this up. Now baby I must sleep it off & I know no doubt I shall feel much better in the morning.[108]

18.10.14

St Omer

A bad day. I did everything wrong. The 4th Corps were not obeying orders in the spirit intended & I did not put them right I knew I had done wrong when it's too late. I usually do! Altogether I feel most miserable.

19.10.14

It is nearly 11.30pm I have had a better day today. Everyone is very nice to me but I still feel very sorry over yesterday. I know you will be happier to know this I had a talk to Charles about it & feel better.

Sir John very angry about yesterday not with me as he does not know probably what I did but it makes it unpleasant. Reggie Seymour is with the 2nd Battalion, Baker Carr saw him today.[109] We broke a chain again today so I got man to take me along. Luckily I met a naval motor to finish the journey & then got another car to take me home. Baker Carr fixed his chain up & had tea with 2nd Battalion. I am afraid I have distressed you with my troubles my sweetheart, I am better now just off to bed.

A better day. Sir John however still annoyed with the 4th Corps & the 3rd Cavalry & got quite angry about it. He really is unreasonable with it. Cavalry got some fighting & have casualties.

20.10.14

My own darling

Tony Boden is missing I am afraid I don't know whether he was killed or not but he was not brought in after he was hit.[110] I had no idea I was mentioned in despatches can't think what it was for?

21.10.14

I spent a very happy day today I don't know why but everyone is so awfully nice to me. It is really delightful with Rawly & Byng & TC. We had an interesting day

& things have gone well on the whole. The 4th Guards Brigade & 5th Brigade both in 2nd Div they got well into the Germans with machine guns.

The car I was in today was built for Russian roads & has extra strong springs it was simply excellent on these roads & we had a good run back I must take you to see Ypres one day. Did I tell you they call it Wipers, rather good. I attended an interesting interview today between John French and 2 French generals it was rather like some of the old prints with maps on the table & the thing about my job you can worm ones way into places like that.

21.10.14

St Omer

Germans appear to have attacked strongly without success. Hear poor Skaife is killed.[111] Attended conference between Sir J. French, Sir D. Haig[112] and General de Mitry,[113] and a General commanding a French Territorial Div, very interesting.

22.10.14

Things are going pretty well at the present but one cannot tell from day to day, for you know probably as I do that things have reached a state of deadlock along the front. However, we shall see what the next week brings forth I was out today with my people & went to see Makins, Jeffrey's brother commanding 6th Cavalry Brigade.[114] He was very nice & glad to get some soup & newspapers. Tommy so nice with me he had a chauffeur killed outside his HQ today by a chance shell. Poor Welsh Fusiliers have had a lot of officers killed Skaife, Kington,[115] Hoskins,[116] Lloyd.[117]

Belgians doing well. Things looking up today 1st Corps captured 400 prisoners & I saw 100 dead Germans. Old 2nd div doing well.

24.10.14

I am at Rawly's HQ waiting for him to come in so I can get away.

9.45pm I did not get far with this. Henry is in good spirits I think things are going well today & yesterday we hope tomorrow will be as well BC has taken the car to Paris to get his clutch replaced with leather as it was slipping.

Bad day for 7th Div, Wiltshire Regt copped most of it & Germans got into woods but were eventually driven out with aid of 5th Brigade.

25.10.14

Just finished dinner I was in late I am smoking a cigarette before going in to report to Sir A. Murray I thought I told you I was liaison to Rawly? 2 Div's did well today capturing 2 guns and some prisoners The 1st Corps excellent. Things are going well I think. You never saw anything like the weather quite hot even motoring. Hugh Dawnay has gone to command the Life Guards as the Colonel.[118]

Sunday 25.10.14

St Omer

Took Burton out with some plane tables for 4.7-inch guns. 2nd Div has some success capturing 2 guns. Went out to see T. Capper and saw 20th Brigade (Ruggles–Brise) get shelled.[119]

26.10.14

My days have been busy & are as follows, up at 6 and to the office to pick up the situation. Breakfast at 7.30 & 8 then round to the department for instructions, letters & report to C.G.S. get final instructions from Uncle & Henry & off about 9 or 9.30 motor for 1 & ½ hours and spend the day going to KTCJ, Bingo & perhaps one of the Brigadiers. Then lunch from our basket, tea from Rawly & start home 6 or 6.30 dinner 8 or 8.30. Report to C.G.S. or C in C. write a short report chat to a few people, write to baby & so to bed. It was nice getting a ride yesterday TC very anxious for me not to get his pony shot. Saw a terrible sight one of our aeroplanes shot at by our own troops, caught fire & 2 officers killed. Hopkins and Crane.[120]

27.10.14

Rawly is going home to teach 8th Div & 7th Div is going over to Douglas Haig.[121] Poor TC, I am sorry his Div has not had a better chance. Saw Max Earle today.[122] He seemed rather worn & has a cold otherwise he is alright & is resting now.

Tit Willow here with the Indian contingent.[123] I am sending home some relics & also things I don't want out here. Base of a shell that was fired at us at Villiers Cotterets, Sept 1st as it rolled up to me I stopped it with my foot and picked it up. The shoulder straps of a man that was killed on the Aisne. The postcard of Soupir it was a chateau in our line at the Aisne, which was used as a hospital. I am gravely situated again as the 3rd cavalry Div has been given to Allenby[124] and the 7th Div to Haig both of whom have liaison officers I shall still go to see them but I suppose no longer report to the C in C.

27.10.14

St Omer

7th Div. Saw Max Earle. Maurice of Battenberg killed a great loss as he was a fine fellow.[125]

28.10.14

I have not seen Henry's horses I am moving mine to Tommie's HQ I had a ride today which was good I am amused at being mentioned in despatches I think Munro mentioned nearly all his staff. F.E. Smith is with Tit Willow![126] He is furious about it.

29.10.14

Rather heavy fighting today but we have done alright I should say. Poor Max Earle has been severely wounded I hope he is not very bad.

'Leith' I saw coming along on a stretcher shot in the groin & legs but hailed me quite cheerily.[127] Saw old friends from the regiment & gave them choco- lates & cigarettes, one said he had been my servant in Cork for a short time. BC not back yet I had a car driven by a man who has been 16 years with the Daimler Company. He was their tester & demonstrator driver I think he called it & has been all over the world driving cars for princesses etc. Has been to Lisbon, Germany, Russia, USA etc. He speaks French, German & a few other languages. Nasty wet weather tonight I am told 'Chico' is wounded we have no details.

Heavy attack on 7th Div, 20th Brigade suffered heavily, Stuckley killed & many other casualties.[128] I think the Germans suffered a great deal & our artil- lery did well.

30.10.14

Such a day you never saw anything like the roads. When it is wet these narrow pave roads are a deuce as they have a camber & you slide off into the sides unless you keep in the middle. The result is when passing other things you may get bogged down & left. Returning home I came behind French lor- ries I counted 55 & found they had met another line coming in the opposite direction so I made a long detour. Poor Max Earle I am afraid there is little hope for him & they did not get him in last night because of the Germans. I feel very low about him & poor Mrs Earle. You can say the French are fight- ing well & their artillery is marvellous.

As regard the Germans they have of course rather surprised us with their reserve formations & with the amount of artillery they had up their sleeves. Saw Tommie today he seemed very cheery. Gen Montgomery[129] says you can send anything out by him.

Heavy fighting today attacks against 3rd Cav Div & 7th Div also against 1 Cavalry Corps. Very heavy shelling & rifle fire. Foch comes to see Henry at midnight.[130]

1.11.14

I get your letters regularly though Henry gives me 2 at a time. B.C back again now. Poor Colonel Burn his son has just joined the Royals & came out 2 days ago was killed yesterday.[131] Colonel Burn was to have gone out with me to see him tomorrow.

Go to see 7th Div in morning & in evening we go to French at St Eloi. Situation still critical.

2.11.14

My own darling
I had dinner early, as Henry was out to see Gen. Foch. I took Col. Burn out today to try to get news about his son's death. He was plucky I know he felt terrible but he was cheerful as he could be. People are wonderful at times. He married Lord Leith's daughter and as he was the only child, his son would

have come into the property.[132] I saw Gen. D'Urbal today such a nice cheery man & he chatted away to me.[133]

It is sad about Percival & Ommaney.[134] Munro is alright but had a severe shaking I don't suppose he has told Mrs M anything.[135] He was quite indignant when I said, 'I hope you are alright again' & he said 'I was never all wrong' I am delighted Henry is pleased with my work.

When I saw D'Urbal I had to speak French it was rather fun. I did not get to bed early last night after all as Swinton (another of the green crowd) pounced on me to make me tell him the doings of the day.[136]

2.11.14

St Omer

We go out to 1st Corp today to do Gilly's work as he has gone home to marry Miss Ruhe. The Corps has had a hard time. In the afternoon I went to J. Gough he looked very serious. The fighting is very critical I hope it will come out alright.

3.11.14

St Omer

Go to see 1st Division & TC. Things are quieter today Ypres was shelled & it is like a city of the dead.

4.11.14

St Omer

Fairly quiet day at D.H. HQ, shelled in evening Colonel Marker badly hit.[137]

4.11.14

Sir John is getting much more friendly now. Told me to be careful of my cold tonight & to lie up if I felt bad! Very nice of him I thought. It has been almost stuffy today & BC & I felt quite hot coming home. We have had bad luck with the car & get stopped with ignition trouble & with hot water and dust in the petrol and tonight a man ran into us (he said it was his fault). All these things delay us so & Uncle always pitches into to me & says I must get home earlier & so we have great fun. Henry has started a plan. He goes off to see Foch after dinner & so we wait till he comes back & don't get to bed till 12. Henry has been wonderfully cheerful but we have had anxious days but I think things are better now. TC is happier & more confident.

Beauchamp Seymour is badly wounded I fear.[138] I took TC & 2nd Div a cake each today & now Bungo wants sausages & butter! I didn't see General Perceval today but was told he was very well.[139] I was going along yesterday when I found a French artilleryman who wanted to catch up his battery I took him to Ypres & dropped him there. He was delighted when he saw German prisoners.

6.11.14

I get your letters every night Henry leaves them on the table. Tommie's div is out of the trenches now. He is very funny about it 'I don't quite like going back to the trenches' he said I am afraid the last two officers in Welsh Fusiliers have gone, isn't it awful Cardogan[140] and his adjutant Dooner[141] Sir Arthur Murray's brother in law killed or prisoner, no more news of Max. Lock does not altogether believe the Pilckem story but thinks it's as well Mrs Earle should do so. Yes, both Percival and Omanney were killed. The 1st & 2nd Div had their HQ's in the same building & 2 shells came along & killed them & Trench of 2nd Div, Paley of 1st Div wounded.[142] Lomax & Morris felt queer for a bit.[143] A bad business some of the accounts written by eyewitness in the Daily Mail & I think the Times & possible other papers emanate from me. We gave our stories of the days doing to Swinton & Percy & they send them in. Russian news is good.[144]

6.11.14

St Omer

Saw Capper in morning, he was shelled out of Ypres last night. In the afternoon went to see 7th Cavalry Brigade. They had been sent to restore the situation, as the French were the Division on Cavan's right.

7.11.14

My own darling

I saw a boy called Dowling who was slightly injured he says Beaumont Nesbit was very fit yesterday. It is so sad about Hugh Dawnay killed I felt he would soon be hit as I am sure he was a very gallant man.

I am so pleased at seeing Harvey again but my nice mare is wounded. Harvey did very well & took her off to the vet & left her in his care so I hope to get her back. I can't see why Henry should not go over for a day. Cavan's brother-in-law Eustace Crawley has been killed I hear.[145]

8.11.14

I met Bungo & he sent a message to Henry to say he did not approve of my being taken away from him. I was going to him as well as Tommy & now I am to do 4th Corps, i.e. Rawly & Tommie & 8th Division on top of that. Henry told Rawly that he might have to take me away from him. Rawly said he wouldn't part with me that I suited him very well etc., etc. Isn't that fine. They are both very kind to me. I came across Chico in a wood today nicely buried underground! He seemed quite well but sad at the loss officers. He had near shaves a cut across his chest & a wound on his finger. Saw Tim Harrington today very fit. Poor General Montgomery his son was in the Goodhope,[146] he has no news of him yet.

The 22nd Brigade (one of Tommie's) took 3 machine guns the other night very credible, as they are not as strong as one battalion. They lost all their officers I fear.

I certainly think Henry should be told about Cecil but I don't see how you can do it. Uncle says Henry could easily get away for a day or two but Uncle doubts whether Cecil is 'fit subject for an operation' and strongly advises expert opinion i.e. other than a surgeon.[147]

Henry seems in good spirits. We have a new gun that does great work she is called 'mother' & there are some small ones. I saw Bill Furse[148] today just as talkative & emphatic as ever also Brigadier Paget[149] both very well.

Farmer Davies[150] says he has seen Beauchamp & Reggie. The former called to him & seemed to be getting on grand only his face is a little paralysed. Reggie is getting on alright. The doctors say he was hit through the heart. I am very glad Henry has been told about Cecil & that is better.

Yes, Tommy was out east of Ypres. At first his Division was all alone on the very extended point & attacked by superior numbers. Then the rest of the Army came to his assistance I went with him today when he went to make a speech to the 20th Brigade. They consist of Grenadiers, Scots Guards, Gordon's & Borders. They are all very keen & smart looking & were all drawn up in a hollow square. He instructed the battalions separately & made a little speech to each calling attention to some incident in the fighting in which they had distinguished themselves. He then addressed the Brigade as a whole. He told them that they had been fighting for their country & that this was no game that they were playing. He told them the Division might well be proud of what they had done after losing 75% of their infantry. He told them they must work together & pointed out what the value of discipline was. It was a fine speech & I think the men were impressed & pleased with it.

9.11.14

St Omer

First to Merville, 8th Division Staff have arrived, General Davies,[151] Colonel Anderson,[152] Hordern, Blaine, Colonel Hoskins,[153] Uniacke, Alexander, General Holland (RA),[154] Colonel Meeker (RAMC), Rotherham (CRE),[155] Major Rennee & others. Then to 7th Division & 21st Brigade at Ploegstreet. Then to 4th Corps where I saw Bill Furse & Ralph Paget commanding cavalry.[156]

10.11.14

Great news Max is a prisoner at Courtrai but alas at the same time Jock hears that Lord Bernard Gordon Lennox has been killed.[157] Sir John said he wanted to see me, he was like a child & said he wanted me to take him out somewhere & show him something. He wanted to get away from everyone including his ADC's, 'We'll get out & just poke about just you & I!!' So now I have to think out what to do with him. He said I was Not to let anyone know as the 'Corps Commanders might be annoyed'. The difficulty is this flat country is to get any place for him to see from, which is not dangerous. I was out all afternoon looking for places. Isn't funny he talked like a child who wanted to hide from his nurse and it is difficult to let him know the true state of affairs.

I was so surprised today to be told that BC wants to go home to instruct people in machine guns. He was an instructor at Hythe.[158] It is unkind thing to say & I would not say it to anyone else but I think he has had enough of this. It struck me once or twice that he does not care very much about shells! I shall be sorry to lose him as he is a soldier & does not talk nonsense.

Lord Bobs expected here tomorrow.[159] TC has gone on with his staff. Ian Stewart says he has never been spoken to like TC does. It is very strange.

11.10.14

My own darling

We have moved our HQ to another house and we are more comfortable as Henry told the Camp Commandant to get carpets, armchairs etc. The liaison officers (or Liza's) are to each have a table to themselves & we have a room of our own I don't know how it will work because we have to go into the office part of the house to see telegrams & get all the news. However, I am writing there now, no letters from you tonight & Henry had some from Goodlady. But I have had lots of parcels, then a parcel of boots & coat arrived, the coat is grand it is my own.

There was heavy fighting today but I understand it has gone alright.[160]

Heavy attack on 2nd Corps. Things are very exciting now & heavy casualties.

12.11.14

Another vile day such rain coming home, in fact it rained almost all day. Things appear to have been fairly quiet today compared with previous days I cannot make out the truth of these Germans. They certainly attack very vigorously & frequently but only on a limited front & they suffer very heavily. We are told they were driven on by their Officers but I doubt that I expect it is just the German discipline, which extends even to civilians that does it.

So glad you are pleased with my being appreciated! Today General Montgomery put his hand on my shoulder & said, 'you know we are very fond of this little man' of course it was a chaff but it was very sweet of him.

TC has got Hoskins as 1st Grade GSO, now Colonel H. Montgomery[161] has gone so I hope things will run more smoothly. Bobs is due in our mess tonight so I must be ready sharp at 7.30. Yesterday & the day before were a little anxious but today the situation is easier. Henry in great form he has a quiet room in this house. He amused me very much with stories of Foch.

My landlady was delighted with my present & jabbered so fast about it she called it a 'petite souvenir de families'. General Carter commands one of the Brigades in 8th Division.[162] Do you remember him when we first went to Middleburg? I had tea with KOYLI,[163] the other day Colonel Withycombe commanding.[164]

Times still anxious. Lord Bobs comes to the mess; he is wonderfully well & sprightly.

7.50pm and no one came to dinner. The lists are terribly delayed when the fighting is on. I am afraid Lord Bobs is very ill indeed. The 1st battalion had about 300 captured I am told I am very distressed about it so far they have fought so well. No one knows what happened some say they must have fallen asleep! It happened in broad daylight I have not heard the casualties amongst Officers but will see if Hereward knows anything.[165] My Corps is going into the trenches now being complete.

9pm Finished dinner Henry never came in & I am afraid he has not had any. Probably with Lord Bobs who I am told is unconscious. You ask how the French fight I don't know but I know a lot of my officers think they are no good but I believe also that they have in many cases fought with desperate heroism I am sorry they have not done well near us as it would have a good effect. They have their recruits coming in now. The Germans put them in some time ago with only 10 weeks training. The French put them in this week with 3 months training, 250,000 should make a difference we shall see.

You ask how Tommie has done. His task was a difficult one you remember he landed at Zeebrugge and went to Ghent to cover the retreat of the Belgian Army. He then as he puts it, ran away without firing a shot & then came down & joined hands with us in front of Ypres. There he was isolated and took up a very extended front to cover Ypres. He got heavy pieces against him & suffered accordingly. More likely or not some of the trenches were in bad places as his troops were new to the game but it became the fashion that 7th Division was running away & Sir J was always impatient with them.

Gradually they got mopped up until he lost 75% of his infantry but even then they several times fought very well & TC did splendidly in maintaining his front. His staff did not really play the game by him. They were I think rather disloyal & worked against him instead of with him but there were faults on both sides. Billy Drysdale says he was mad![166] He says he used to come in & tell him something go away & comeback & tell him something again. Well you know his absent-minded way. He is a man the troops must know to appreciate & it was unfortunate that he should have got command of a scratch Division. Many a time he & I walked up & down together discussing things & he has always been perfectly rational. I have done nothing with Sir J yet I want to find a place but fear it is too dangerous. Then the little excitement of attacks come & Lord Bobs visit & bad weather I must see Henry about it again.

I don't think the taking of Dixmunde is very bad though of course regrettable. The taking of Ypres would be bad because though quite unimportant its loss would give us a 'better line' to hold, it has become a point of honour for us to hold it & for the Germans to take it & there is no doubt they have made great efforts to do so, our troops though they have lost a lot & have had men captured & hence fought very well indeed & done wonders with very small numbers.

13.11.14

St Omer

Again attacks on 1st Corps. The Germans are determined to take Ypres but we are equally determined that they shall not get it, nor will they. 4th Corps is now complete & is to go into the trenches. When Henry came back from Foch tonight he had the news that the French are to take over 4th Corps area.

14.11.14
A slack day & so I wrote a few letters. Go to 4th Corps. Little hope for Bobs.[167]

15.11.14
Another beastly day rain & windy all day awful for those in the trenches. The country I work over now is deadly interesting, quite flat & full of roads that turn about in every direction. This morning an Irish sentry said to me 'I beg your pardon sir, but a French Officer came up to me and said if I saw Baker-Carr would I telephone the French mission' I wonder now would that be a Baker car!! He evidently thought it was something like a studebaker. Nothing happened to speak of yesterday there were the usual attacks. I believe Saunders & Gough are missing. I did not know anything about the 1st battalion because it was so difficult to get at the truth & later I forgot to tell you. I suppose I shall never know what happened.

16.11.14
You ask what I think of the big German guns. Well they steal a march on us here. Their shells are extraordinarily local in effect, the explosion being upwards at a sharpest angle, so you can be close to a shell without being hurt but in a village they are very nasty indeed. And of course if they hit a trench they damage it as they make holes about 6 ft deep & 5 ft wide. They are very accurate shooting with them. The German machine guns are the other factor in which they have got the better of us, they are very well & boldly used. They are better than our guns because they are lighter & can be brought up quickly.

Reggie Oxley says Gough's[168] mother has had a letter from him & that he says that he & Saunders are prisoners.[169] Oxley also says that the strength of the 1st Battalion is 6 Officers & 160 men. When is my compass coming out? It will be useful in the country I am in now.

18.11.14
Frost overnight. More water in the petrol today which delayed us & then BC put the car in a ditch. I left him & someone else gave me a lift to 4th Corps where I got General Montgomery's motor & took back to 8th & 7th Divisions. There I got a horse & rode over to Lawford's HQ where I had lunch & found BC at 7th Division on my return.[170] There was an ammunition pack where he got into the ditch & they had a breakdown going & were delighted to set to work & pull him out. They had great work over it. I hope Henry will be come back soon! We are a little concerned over this rumour of a Russian defeat, which is in the Morning Post, I expect there is something in it but hope it is not as bad as it will delay matters.[171]

19.11.14

A horrid day today snow all this afternoon & I had to keep wiping the wind-screen all the way home so BC could see to drive. The Prince of Wales called on Rawly this morning. You never saw anybody so young looking. They say he is very tough & a fine runner.

The people one gets to know here is immense! Prince of Connaught,[172] Westminster[173] (I don't know where he is now) Dalmeny, he is very nice,[174] Ilchester is the Kings Messenger & we see him occasionally.[175] I was offered Sir Philip Sassoon, as a chauffeur for the day yesterday.[176] I find French's personal staff nice to deal with. They are none of them soldiers though some have been! Colonel Barnes late of the 10th Hussars,[177] Freddy Guest (much nicer than the one we know),[178] Colonel Brinsley Fitzgerald,[179] a stockbroker, Major Watt a yeoman who was one of the private secretaries at the WO.

I saw 2nd Division staff today all seemed well Whigham, Ready, & Brind.[180] The General was out. Sir Arthur Murray is to live in our mess now I wonder how he will like it.[181] He is always very kind to me & very calm when I go in to report. But he is not on the same footing with us as Henry & Uncle. Snowed all afternoon & froze at night. Very cold for those in the trenches.

20.11.14

I had lunch with General Pinney, he was at staff college after me, next term junior I think.[182] Got to TC rather late but got a horse ride, which warmed me up grand. Incidentally my horse stopped & fell flat down! Things have been quiet again here Hereward just back he seems to think Cecil is bad, I hope not.

I saw Geoffrey Shakerley & 1st battalion he seemed very well.[183] The iodine has arrived. I shall be glad when Henry comes back! I forgot to tell you an engine nearly ran into me on at a level crossing today, a most unusual occurrence for as a rule the French are very fussy & stop you passing again before the train comes. My chauffeur was so startled he ran into the gatepost?

21.11.14

These poor fellows in the trenches have had a hard time this weather. Can you send any warm gloves out to the RB (Rifle Brigade) they seem to be hard up for warm things & of course feel the cold coming from India. See that our 3rd & 4th battalions get warm things before coming if you can. I saw Chico today he is well I think but looks worried & appears to be overwhelmed with work. Today I had lunch with Burton (RB) who is Brigade Major to the 25th Brigade, he took me to the trenches where everything was peaceful I had tea with 8th Division. Henry is back you found out what the compass was to cost didn't you? Someone frightened me today by saying they cost £5. Hard frost still continues.

23.11.14

I stayed last night at TC's he had a headache from eating too many 'acid drops', he did not come to dinner. Up at 4 today & no hot water except what I heated on the stove. Went with TC & others everything very quiet, the men have suffered so much cold feet & frostbite. We came out of the trenches about 8am I had lunch with them & came home early about 5. Little man gone on leave I hear.

Monday 23.11.15

St Omer

Up at 4 & out to trenches with General Capper, Colonel Hoskins, General Watt[184] & Drysdale. Very quiet there, very cold. There have been a lot of cases of frostbite.

24.11.14

I have some sort of cold on me & feel very slack & heady so I am off to bed early. I went to see the Indian Corps as well as my own today as Shea has gone on leave. Uncle & Gilly have gone too. Saw Tit Willow full of beans, there is a thaw today & it was very raw. The Indians have done very well but have lost a lot of casualties. They took 100 prisoners, 3 MG's & 1 trench mortar.

25.11.14

Today was mild but it has turned to frost again I went for a ride in the afternoon but things are very quiet now. The 7th Division has started a great scheme now they provide baths for the men when they come out of the trenches and the men appreciate it very much. There is also a barber & they hope to start a laundry. I take out the American Military Attaché tomorrow I don't know what I shall show him.

26.11.14

London

Go out to 4th Corps taking Colonel Squire, the American military attaché.[185] Return in time to motor to Boulogne & catch 4pm boat & arrive Victoria 8pm & so home. The delight at getting home is indescribable.

Friday 27.11.14

London

Very restful. Do exactly what we like. I go to W.O. to see DMO, General Callwell,[186] de Brett,[187] Bayne, A.G. Stuart, Bryan Curling[188] & Colonel Worthy, Miss Boyne, and Miss Bernard.

29.11.14

Church at Brompton. General Gough gives excellent sermon. Lunch with Stuart Wortley. Walk to W.O. with letter for Henry & then home.

2.12.14

Saw Cecil Wray she seems better.[189]

3.12.14

St Omer

Leave London 8.30am. Very bad crossing, lost luggage on way over chiefly parcels belonging to other people. The rest has been very jolly & I expect it has done us both a lot of good.

4.12.14

We were all introduced to the King. Took out Colonel Williams, Adjutant General of Canada today, very cold wind.[190] Lunch with 8th Division, go with General Capper to Bedfordshire Regiment, still a lot of cases of frost bite, etc.

Sunday 6.12.14

Take Vesey out to see his brother & go for a ride after having lunch with RB (Rifle Brigade).[191] Forget all about Vesey & have to go back for him. My kit arrived yesterday & I took Montagu Stopford his coat.[192]

10.12.14

Go to the trenches of 24th Brigade near Neuve Chapelle.[193] A lot of them are along drainage ditches & are very muddy. The men are wonderfully cheerful.

Friday 11.12.14

Misty morning & wet evening. Had a ride & saw General Milne at 7th Division looking very well.[194] Got home at 5.30 as I had a letter for Sir A. Murray.

12.12.14

Go to 4th Corps then to 2nd Cavalry Division & 8th Division. Had lunch with General Porter saw 8th Division cyclists & saw Dick Crichton at Meant.[195]

13.12.14

Alexander drives me to 4th Corps, 33rd Brigade RFA East Lancs, 25th Brigade & 7th Division. Another vile night. The weather has been very bad lately.

Monday 14.12.14

Go out early to the reporting centre to here news of battle at lunchtime. 2 Battalions attack Royal Scots & Gordon's & do well capturing trenches & 60 prisoners but we all ask why don't we attack in force & we are rather down-hearted about it.[196]

15.12.14

Go out early to the reporting centre. Took Major Forbes out to his Regiment, R.S. Fusiliers.[197] Went to 35th Brigade RFA (Colonel Nicholson a friend of Reid's).[198] Tea with Rawly No news today attack appears to have been held up.

17.12.14

St Omer

Draft arrives for 4th Corps some are much too old & will be of little value. Go to Bailleul to reporting centre. Nothing doing. Tea with General Holland.

18.12.14

Up at 5 go to Merville to see Rawly then back to St Omer then out again. 22nd Brigade attack enemy trenches but were repulsed after a gallant fight. 1st Brigade (Scots Guards) took trenches & Devon's (8th) also took trenches. Scots Guards forced to retire by hand grenades about midnight.[199]

Saturday 19.12.14

West York's bombed out of their trenches about 9 so we have nothing left but 25 prisoners which Devon's took to show for our work. Still it did some good I think the men fought well.

21.12.14

A horrid day more shelling than usual. Indians got driven in yesterday & 1st division go to their assistance.

22.12.14

Attack on 1st Corps & Indians continues & their L.N. Lancs & Northampton get driven back.

24.12.14

A lovely day went for a ride. Saw Stoppy when I was going out to 4th Corps. Tea with Rawly.

Friday 25.12.14

St Omer

Frosty go to 4th Corps & Divisions, lunch with Rawly. Then to 4th Division see Charles, Captain Poe, Hunter, Tim Daley, Tavish, Prusaby & others also General Fortesque & Fayman.[200]

26.12.14

St Omer

Frost & rains in evening took out Major Benet lunch with TC. Went to trenches of 22nd Brigade with Fellows (RB).[201] There was a Christmas armestice to bring in the dead. Their trenches are very good ones. Tea with General Lawford. Henry goes to Chantilly.

Sunday 27.12.14

Took out Commodore Ramsden & his adjutant he runs the Naval school at Crystal Palace.[202] Bellairs RN drove his car which followed us. Rain most of the day.

28.12.14

A vile day, a gale on the way home. Saw testing of W.O. trench mortar, the black powder is a drawback & still does not detonate properly.

29.12.14

Said goodbye to 4th Corps very sad having to give up going to them. Took Rumbold (late Bays) out. A queer card talks a lot. Fearful storm last night country under water trenches full too. Both ourselves & Germans are too busy draining to do too much sniping.

30.12.14

St Omer

Had to go out to 4th Corps again with a letter, saw 3rd Battalion (Foljambe & Matren) & had tea with them.[203] Henry told me some interesting news. He is the most wonderful man as clever & enterprising as he thinks so little of his own achievement & values public opinion so little.

Friday 31.12.14

Go out to 4th Corps for last time, lunch with RB & bring Montagu Stopford back with me & leave him at Gen S. HQ. Rain again the weather is very disappointing.

NOTES

1　Major General Henry 'The Intriguer' Hughes Wilson CB, DSO (1864–1922). He was appointed Director of Military Operations, August 1910. *See* Keith Jeffrey, *Field Marshal Sir Henry Wilson* (Oxford, 2006).

2　Captain (later Brigadier General) Cecil Percival Heywood CB, DSO, CMG (1880–1936). In 1936 he commanded 3rd Div.; Captain (later Lieutenant Colonel) Henry Morris Pryce Jones DSO, MC, MVO (1878–1952). Both Coldstream Guards.

3　Herbert George Ponting (1870–1935). He was a professional photographer on Captain Robert Falcon Scott's *Terra Nova* expedition.

4　Captain Geoffrey Kendall Priaulx, 2nd Bn KRRC. The officer was appointed second lieutenant on the same day as Price-Davies (23 February 1898). He was wounded September 1914 and again at Loos, 1915. Killed in action as Lieutenant Colonel 11th Bn KRRC, 25 March 1918. Awarded DSO (LG 18 June 1917).

5　Lieutenant W.A.C. Saunders-Knox-Gore.

6　Major General Hon. Sir Alan Richard Montagu Stuart Wortley KRRC (1868–1949). Director of Movements at MOD 1914–17. GOC 68th Bde, 23rd Div. February 1917. Temporary GOC 19th Div. April–May 1917. GOC 32nd Div. until June 1917. DQMG Mesopotamia Campaign. Knighted 1918. Retired lieutenant general 1927.

7　Alexandra Carlisle (b. Yorkshire 1886, d. New York 1936).

8　Colonel Reginald Stewart Oxley CB, CMG, KRRC (1863–1951). Temporary Brigadier General 24th Bde, 8th Div. He was sacked during the Battle of the Somme for not holding Contalmaison, 1916. He held a number of staff appointments before he retired 1919.

9　Major General Sir John Humphrey 'Tavish' Davidson DSO, KRRC (1876–1954). GSO 2, III Corps 1914–15. Temporary Brigadier General GSO July–December 1915. MGGS GHQ

BEF January 1918. CB 1917. KCMG 1917. Left army in 1922. Conservative MP for Fareham 1918–31. Chairman of Bank of Australia 1937–45.

10 This took place at the Curragh Military Camp, in Kildare, Ireland during March 1916. It involved officers of the 3 Cavalry brigade, which was commanded at the time by General Hubert Gough. It was an attempt by the Government to force the Home Rule Bill on Ulster against the wishes of the Unionist opposition. In an attempt to impose this proposition, the Secretary of State for War had inferred it would use the Army as a means to obtain a political result. The officers concerned intended to refuse to do this and threatened to resign their commissions if asked to do so. Some have labelled 'mutineers', but as the question was never put this is misleading. Among those involved was Henry Wilson, who was at the War Office at the time and played a significant role in bringing the crisis to an end. However, there were casualties, one of whom was Sir John French who left the War Office and would as a result of this move lead the BEF to France in August 1916.

11 Sir Hubert de la Poer Gough (1870–1963). Commanded the 3rd Cavalry Bde in 1914 at the Curragh Camp outside Dublin. He was alerted for duty in the North, to impose the Irish Home Rule Act on resistant Ulstermen; he conveyed for Asquith's government the unwillingness of his officers to march. The 'Curragh Mutiny' procured the shelving of the Act. For a fuller appreciation of the crisis, see Professor Ian F.W. Beckett.

12 Major George Norton Cory DSO (1874–1968). Royal Dublin Fusiliers, GSO 3 at MOD in 1914. Later major general 1919.

13 Sir John Denton Pinkstone French (1852–1925). CIGS during this crisis but due to his actions resigned his position on 6 April 1914 to become, briefly, Inspector General of the army. He was later to be C in CBEF.

14 Lieutenant General Sir John Spencer Ewart (1861–1930). Adjutant General of the army since 1910, he resigned March 1914. GOC Scottish Command 1914–18; 'JF' refers to Sir John French.

15 Herbert Henry Asquith (1852–1928). The prime minister who, on the resignation of Sir John French, took over the post at the War Office. At the beginning of the war he would appoint Field Marshal Lord Kitchener.

16 'JG' refers to Hubert Gough's younger brother, Johnny Gough VC (1871–1915).

17 He may be referring here to Robert Richardson (1862–1943). A miner and later Labour MP for Houghton-le-Spring Division Durham, 1918–3.

18 Colonel George Montague Harper DSO (1865–1922). GSO 1 Military Operations at War Office 1911. Later GOC 51st Highland Div. and Lieutenant General GOC IV Corps.

19 General Sir Archibald 'Old Archie' James Murray (1860–1945). Chief of Staff to Sir John French in 1914. He later became GOC in C Egypt, 1916.

20 Major Webb Gillman DSO, RA (1870–1933). GSO 1, War Office. GSO 1, 13th Div., 1914. Brigadier General at Gallipoli. Major General Salonika Force 1916–17. GOC 17th Div. August 1917. Chief of Staff Mesopotamia Force. CMG 1915. CB 1917. KCMG 1919.

21 Major General Charles Carmichael Munro (1860–1929). GOC 2nd (London) Div., later evacuated troops from Gallipoli and was C in C India.

22 Lieutenant General Sir Douglas Haig, GOC I Corps.

23 Diary entries will have the dates on the left, and letters on the right.

24 *See* Everard Wyrall, *The History of the Second Division 1914–1918*.

25 War Office.

26 Brigadier General Edward Maxwell Perceval BGRA, later Major General GOC 49th Div. on the Somme 1916.

27 Colonel Wilfred Arthur White, Connaught Rangers, DAA & QMG, 2nd Div. 1914. Invalided home 18 August 1914.

28 I shall use MOD from here to shorten the text.

29   Captain William Edward Rothwell OBE, Royal Inniskilling Fusiliers, ADC to General Munro, wounded 26 September 1914. Awarded a DSO 1 January 1918.

30   Captain Viscount Gort MVO, ADC. *See* John R. Coville, *Man of Valour* (London, 1972).

31   Henry refers to Major General Henry Hughes Wilson.

32   Brigadier General Johnny Gough VC, CMG, ADC 1st Corp.

33   Lieutenant Colonel Derrick Alfred Carden, Seaforth Highlanders. Killed, 25 May 1915 aged 40 years. Buried Hazebrouck Communal Cemetery, Nord, France.

34   Major (later Major General) Felix Fordati Ready DSO (1872–1940). Lieutenant Colonel Whites' successor.

35   Major Hereward Wake Bt, DSO, KRRC (1876–1963). Serving at GHQ. Held various staff appointments during the First World War. Was appointed BGGS to the Supreme War Council at Versailles, December 1917.

36   The action at Nery took place this day where three men of 'L' Battery Royal Horse Artillery were awarded VCs.

37   Brigadier General Robert Scott Kerr, GOC 4th Guards Bde, 2nd Div., was replaced by Colonel G.P.T. Fielding and then by Brigadier General F.R., Earl of Cavan on 18 September 1914.

38   Lieutenant A.L. Bonham Carter KRRC.

39   Colonel Hon. Sir Frederick Gordon DSO (Gordon Highlanders). Brigadier General 19th Inf. Bde 1914–15. GOC 22nd Div. 1917. Greek Macedonia, Serbia, Bulgaria and European Turkey. CB 1915. KCB 1917.

40   19th Bde was an independent division attached to 6th Div.

41   Brigadier General Robert Dundas 'Whigwam' Whigham DSO (1865–1950). BGGS 2nd Div. Deputy CIGS 1915. GOC 59th Div. June 1918. GOC 60th Div. August 1918. GOC 3rd Inf. Div. 1919. Adjutant General 1923. GOC in Chief Eastern Command 1927. Retired 1931.

42   Lieutenant (later Major) Horace John Flower MC, DSO, KRRC (LG 3 June 1916).

43   'Uhlans' refers to German Lancers.

44   Lieutenant Colonel Arthur Jex Blake Percival DSO. GSO 2, 2nd Div., Northumberland Fusiliers. Killed Ypres, 31 October 1914 aged 43 years. Buried Ypres Town Cemetery Extension, France.

45   Brigadier General H. de la P. Gough CB, GOC 2nd Cavalry Div.

46   Major Hon. Hugh Dawnay DSO, 2nd Life Guards. Killed in action, 6 November 1914 aged 39 years. Buried Herlebeke New British Cemetery, Belgium.

47   Lieutenant Colonel Charles Dalton, ADMS to 2nd Div. Mentioned in despatches (MID). Died of wounds, 18 September 1914 aged 48 years. Buried Viel-Arcy Communal Cemetery, Aisne, France.

48   Captain Geoffrey Makins MVO, 3rd KRRC. Killed by sniper, 23 August 1915 aged 37 years. Buried Merville Cemetery, Nord, France.

49   Colonel R. Whigham took over the post 14 September 1914.

50   The Austrian General Dankl was defeated at the Battle of Krasnik on 10 September. On 12 September the Battles of Grodek and Rava Ruska ended with the total defeat of Austrian Forces. On 13 September the Russians defeated the Germans at Srednike.

51   HE: high explosive shell.

52   Lieutenant Colonel Hon. George Henry Morris, Commanding Officer 1st Bn Irish Guards. Killed at Villers-Coterrets, 1 September 1914 aged 42 years. Buried Guards Grave, Villers-Coterrets, Aisne, France.

53   This is a reference to Price-Davies' mother-in-law, Mrs Grace Wilson.

54   Brigadier General 'Fatty', Earl of Cavan, 4th Guards Bde.

55   Captain Frederick George Beaumont-Nesbitt (1893–1971). Grenadier Guards. ADC to GOC XI Corps 1915–16. GSO 3, Fourth Army 1917–18. Brigade Major, 3rd Guards Bde

1918. MGGS British Army Staff, Washington DC 1941–43. MGGS Middle East, North Africa and Italy 1943–45. Retired 1945.

56 Lieutenant Robert Harold Bond KRRC. Killed, 14 September 1914 aged 32. Buried Vendresse British Military Cemetery.

57 Captain R. W. Jackson and Lieutenant C.S.R. Thompson; all others with 2nd Bn KRRC.

58 Brigadier General Claude Berners Westmacott (1865–1948). Worcestershire Regt, Commanded 5th Bde, 2nd Div. He had a breakdown in his health and was invalided home from France. Awarded CBE 1919, retired 1920.

59 Brigadier General Richard 'Dicky' Cyril Berne Haking (1862–1945). Hampshire Regt. GOC 5th Bde. GOC 1st Div. December 1914. Later XI Corps Commander.

60 Captain R. A. Bannon, 1st Bn KRRC. Wounded, 15 May 1915.

61 Lieutenant Colonel Alan Thomas Paley RB, GSO 1.

62 Lieutenant Colonel Richard Fowler-Butler (1865–1931). GOC 3rd Bn RB.

63 Lieutenant Colonel Sir Charles Parker Deedes CMG, DSO (1879–1969). He was also awarded the American DSM. He retired in 1937 with the rank of general.

64 Captain John Banks Jenkinson RB. Died, Monday 14 September 1914 aged 33 years. Buried Vendresse British Cemetery, Aisne, France.

65 Major General Richard Hutton Davies, a naturalised New Zealander, left 6th Inf. Bde to command 20th (Light) Div. Committed suicide, May 1918 aged 57 years.

66 Major Herbert Francis Fitzwilliam B. Foljambe 'B' Company 2nd Bn KRRC. Killed in action at the Battle of the Aisne, 14 September 1914 aged 42 years. Commemorated La Ferte-Sous-Jouarre, France.

67 Brown, Williams Kay, Curry, Leith, Chico: all officers of the 2nd Bn KRRC.

68 Captain G. A. Sullivan, DAPM.

69 2nd Div. took part in the Battles of the Marne and the Aisne as part of I Corps at this time.

70 Captain William Algernon Ireland Kay KRRC (1876–1918). Later Brigadier GS. Killed, 4 October 1918 aged 42 years. Buried Vadencourt British Military Cemetery, Massiemy, Aisne, France.

71 Captain Arthur Edmund Stewart Irvine RAMC, 5 August 1914 attached 1st Div.

72 Winston Spencer Churchill was First Lord of the Admiralty at the start of the war.

73 Captain W. W. E. Seagrave DSO. GSO 3, 2nd Div. On 12 September 1914 went to 17th Inf. Bde as brigade major.

74 Captain R. G. Cherry. ADC 2nd Div., on 19 December 1914 went to Royal Flying Corps.

75 Major General H. de la P. Gough CB. GOC 2nd Cavalry Div.

76 Captain Hugh Hamilton Berners, No. 3 Coy, 1st Bn Irish Guards. Recorded as [dead?], 14 September 1914 aged 32 years. Buried Soupir Communal Cemetery, Aisne, France.

77 Brigadier General Edward 'Perks' Maxwell Perceval (1861–1955). CRA 2nd Div.

78 Major George Paley. GSO 1st Div.

79 Major Arthur Dowson Green DSO. Worcestershire Regt, Brigade Major 17th Bde, 6th Div. Killed, 29 September 1914 aged 40 years. Buried Soupir Communal Cemetery, Aisne, France.

80 Colonel Hugh Sandham Jeudwine KRRC (1862–1942). GSO 1, I Corps. Later Major General 55th (West Lancashire) Div.

81 Captain Rupert Ommaney did become GSO 3, 2nd Div., but was killed when 2nd Div. HQ was shelled at Ypres, 13 October 1914. He had been on the same staff course at Camberley with Price-Davies in 1908.

82 Lieutenant Colonel Ramsay Harman Alexander, GOC 3rd Bn RB.

83 Lieutenant General Sir George 'Uncle' 'Daddy Harper' Montague Harper (1865–1922).

84 Major Basil Wilfred Bowdler Bowdler RE, GSO 2, Lieutenant Colonel DSO 1916, CMG 1919; Major Robert William Hare DSO (Norfolk Regt) (1872–1953), GSO 2. Later Brigadier General, CMG 1919.

85   Christopher D'Arcy Bloomflied Saltern Baker Carr (1878–1949). Wrote *From Chauffer to Brigadier* (London, 1930). KRRC 1898–1906. Lieutenant Colonel Tank Corps 1917. Brigadier General 1918–19.

86   This refers to Major General Sir Thompson-Capper, GOC 7th Div. Mortally wounded when up with his troops at the Battle of Loos, 27 September 1915 aged 51 years. Buried Lillers Communal Cemetery, Pas de Calais, France.

87   Major General Sir John Davidson, GSO III Corps; Captain(later General) Sir Walter William Pitt-Taylor 'PT' (RB) Staff Officer (1878–1950).

88   HMS *Pegasus* was an old light cruiser that was sunk off Zanzibar by the *Konigsberg*.

89   Lieutenant Colonel Walter Howorth Greenly DSO (1875–1955). 12th Lancers, GSO 1, 2nd Cavalry Div. GOC 2nd Cavalry Div. 1916 to April 1918. Head of British Mission to Rumania 1918–20. CMG 1915. CB 1919. Retired 1920. The 'Greenly Boot' was named after him.

90   Major Sir Charles Harington Harington (1872–1940). GSO III Corps. Later General and Deputy CIGs under FM Sir Henry Wilson. Later Governor of Gibraltar during the Spanish Civil War 1933–38.

91   Major General Hubert Gough. GOC 2nd Cavalry Div. was involved in Battle of Messines 12 October to 2 November 1914. The First Battle of Ypres was to begin on 19 October 1914.

92   Major Percy de Blaquiere Radcliffe RA, GS (1874–1934). Later major general who replaced Sir Frederick Maurice at the War Office in 1918 as Director of Military Operations. GOC 48th Div. 1923, GOC 4th Div. 1926. GOC in Chief Scottish Command 1930 and Southern Command 1933. He died from a fall from his horse in 1934.

93   Colonel Arundel Martin, 1st Royal West Kent's, 13th Bde, 5th Div., II Corps.

94   Lieutenant General Sir Henry Seymour Rawlinson (1864–1925). KRRC, GOC IV Corps. GOC First Army 1915 and Fourth Army 1916 at the Battle of the Somme.

95   Major General Sir 'Tommie' Thompson Capper (1863–1915). GOC 7th Inf. Div.

96   Lieutenant Colonel William Henry Bartholomew (1877–1962). GSO 1, 4th Div. BGGS XX Corps 1917–18. BGGS Egyptian Expeditionary Force 1918. Retired a full general 1940.

97   Colonel James Henville Thresher RB, Town Commandant.

98   Major General Hon. Julian 'Bungo' Hedworth George Byng CB, MVO (1862–1935). GOC 3rd Cavalry Div. Later XVII Corps and Third Army commander. He was corps commander of the Canadian troops when they captured Vimy Ridge. He was later Governor General of Canada and raised to the peerage, taking the title of Ist Viscount Byng of Vimy.

99   Colonel V. Huguet represented the French Republic at the funeral of Field Marshal Lord Roberts of Kandahar.

100 Between 15–23 October, the First Battle of Warsaw was taking place.

101 Major Ian Stewart (Scottish Rifles) GSO 2, 7th Div.

102 The 2nd Duke of Westminster, High Richard Arthur Grosvenor, Cheshire Yeomanry (1879–1953).

103 HMS *Hawke* was sunk by U-boat.

104 Commander Charles Rumney Samson DSO, RN (1883–1931). Remained in Flanders with his armoured cars after the Royal Marines withdrew from Ostend. This officer had a very full interesting war and was awarded a DSO & Bar, CMG and AFC. He eventually became an air commodore in the newly formed RAF. He resigned his commission in 1919.

105 Lieutenant Colonel Arthur John Bigge DSO (1849–1931). 1st Lord Stamfordham was then King George's Fifth Private Secretary.

106 Major General Thomas Lethbridge Napier Morland DSO, KRRC (1865–1925). Took over 5th Div. 18 October 1914. Lieutenant General GOC X Corps and one of Plumer's corps commanders at the Battle of Messines. XIII Corps Commander 1918 and C in C British Army of the Rhine. He retired a full general in 1923.

107 [Author?] *Official History of the War, Military Operations 1914*, [publisher?] Vol. II, p. 116: 'About midday a GHQ liaison officer arrived at 7th Division. HQ, and the misunderstanding with

regard to the interpretation of the order to move was discovered.' For a fuller picture see Ian F.W. Beckett, *Ypres: The First Battle 1914* (Longman, 2004).

108 This incident occurred during the Battle of Yser. [author?] *Military Operations, France and Belgium*, [publisher?] Vol. 2, p. 115–16: 'About midday a liaison officer from GHQ arrived at 7th Division HQ and the misunderstanding with regard to the interpretation to move on Menin was discovered.'

109 Lieutenant Colonel William Walter Seymour, RB (1878–1940). After the war he fought in the North-West Frontier, India and gained the honorary rank of brigadier.

110 Major Anthony Drummond Boden, 3rd RB. Killed in action, 24 September 1914 aged 43 years. Commemorated La Ferte sous Jouarre Memorial, France.

111 Captain Eric Ommanney Skaife RWF (Royal Welch Fusiliers) was in fact wounded on 19 October and taken prisoner 20th. He was repatriated 11 November 1918 and promoted to major. Awarded an MBE and Temporary Lieutenant Colonel GSO, War Office 1920. Later he commanded both 1st and 2nd Bns RWF. Military attaché Moscow 1933–37. Colonel of Regt 1948. Nominated a CB in 1952, and knighthood in 1956, the year he died. I am indebted to Colonel Nick Lock OBE, for all the biographical details of officers who served in the RWF during the First World War.

112 Lieutenant General Sir Douglas Haig, GOC British I Corps.

113 General de Mitry, II French Cavalry Corps, 4th, 5th, 6th French Cavalry Divs.

114 Brigadier General Ernest Makins DSO (1869–1959). Taken sick 7 November 1914. Colonel 1st Royal Dragoons 1931–46. Honorary Brigadier KBE, CB.

115 Captain William Miles Kington DSO, 1st Bn Royal Welch Fusiliers. Killed at the Battle of Langemarck, 20 October 1914 aged 38 years. Buried Ypres Menin Gate Memorial, France.

116 Lieutenant Edwin Cecil Leigh Hoskyns 1st Bn RWF. Killed, 20 October 1914 aged 24 years. Buried Ypres Menin Gate Memorial, France.

117 Captain Meyricke Entwistle Lloyd 1st Bn RWF. Killed, 20 October 1914 aged 34 years. Buried Ypres Menin Gate Memorial, France.

118 Major Hon. Hugh Dawnay went to command 2nd Life Guards.

119 Brigadier General Harold Goodeve Ruggles-Brise MVO (1864–1927). Grenadier Guards, GOC 20th Bde. Wounded 2 November 1914. Later a divisional commander and military secretary GHQ. CB 1915. KCMG 1919.

120 There were two officers killed on 18–19 September 1914: Lieutenant C.E. Crane 1st Bn Duke of Cornwall's Light Infantry (aged 22 years) and Lieutenant Herbert Leslie Hopkins RAMC (aged 27). Both are buried at Vailly British Cemetery, Aisne, France.

121 General Rawlinson left with some of his staff to UK to superintend the training and organisation of the 8th Div., which, when sent to France, was to constitute with the 7th Div. the new IV Corps. *See* O.H. 1914 Vol. 11, p. 254.

122 Lieutenant Colonel Max Earle DSO (1871–1953). Grenadier Guards. Wounded and captured 29 October 1914 at Gheluvelt. After the war, received CMG 1918 and CB. Gave the Lee Knowles lecture at Cambridge 1922–23.

123 Lieutenant Colonel Hon. Charles John Sackville-West (1870–1962). Wounded twice during the war. Attached GHQ and in 1919 Supreme Wear Council.

124 Lieutenant General Sir Edmund Henry Hyman Allenby CB, GOC Cavalry Corps.

125 Lieutenant Prince Maurice Victor Donald of Battenberg, 1st KRRC. He was the youngest grandchild of Queen Victoria. Killed in action Ypres Salient, 27 October 1914 aged 23 years. Buried Ypres Town Cemetery, France.

126 Frederick Edwin Smith MP, 1st Earl of Birkenhead (1872–1930). Was posted to France as a staff officer in the Indian Corps with temporary rank of major. Solicitor General 1915.

127 Captain Alex Robert Leith, KRRC.

128 Major Humphrey St Leger Stucley, Grenadier Guards. King's Company 1st Bn. Killed, 29 October 1914 aged 37 years. Buried Zantvoord British Military Cemetery, Belgium.

129 Brigadier General Robert Arundel Kerr Montgomery CB, DSO (Born 1862). GS IV
    Corps. Professor staff college 1906–09. KCMG 1919 as major general.

130 General Foch, French Commandant le Groupe des Armies du Nord (1851–1929).

131 Second Lieutenant Arthur Herbert Posden Burn, 1st (Royal) Dragoons. Killed, 29 October
    1914. Commemorated Panel 5, Ypres (Menin Gate) Memorial, France.

132 Colonel Charles Rosdew Burn MP (1859–1930). Married Ethel Louise Forbes-Leith 1891.
    ADC to King George V 1910–26.

133 General D'Urbal took over command of French forces in the north.

134 Captain Rupert Ommanney RE, attached GSO 3, 2nd Div. Staff (aged 36); Lieutenant
    Colonel Arthur Jex Blake Percival DSO, Northumberland Fusiliers, GSO 1, 2nd Div. (aged
    43). Both killed 31 October 1914. Buried Ypres Town Cemetery Extension, France.

135 During the battle for the Gheluvelt both 1st and 2nd Div. set up their HQs at Hooge
    Chateaux. On 31 October the HQ was hit by shellfire killing and wounding a number of
    the staff of these divisions.

136 Earnest Dunlop Swinton (1868–1951). He was working as an Official War Correspondent
    in France November 1914. He was later a major general and was heavily involved in the
    development of tanks.

137 Colonel Raymond John Marker, Coldstream Guards. AA & QMG I Corps advanced HQ
    was near the Menin Gate. Marker had been ADC to Lord Kitchener in South African War.
    Mortally wounded, died of wounds 13 November 1914 aged 47 years. Buried Gittishem
    St Michael, Churchyard, Devon, UK.

138 Captain Beauchamp Seymour KRRC. Survived the war, retired as a major.

139 Brigadier General Edward Maxwell Perceval was BGRA 2nd Div. and in 1915 Deputy
    CIGS, GHQ France. Major General 49th (West Riding) Div. (TF) until wounded.

140 Lieutenant Colonel Henry Osbert Samuel Cadogan, Commanding Officer 1st Bn Royal
    Welsh Fusiliers. Killed, 30 October 1914 aged 46 years. Buried Hooge Crater Cemetery,
    Belgium.

141 Captain Alfred Edwin Claud Toke Dooner, RWF, Adjutant 1st Bn. Killed in action,
    30 October 1914 aged 22 years. Buried Hodge Crater Cemetery, Belgium.

142 Major George Paley RB, GSO. Was in fact killed and not wounded, aged 42 years. Buried
    Ypres Cemetery Extension, France.

143 Lieutenant General Samuel Holt Lomax, GOC 1st Div. Was severely wounded and died,
    14 April 1915 aged 59 years. Buried Aldershot Military Cemetery. In all, six officers were
    mortally wounded and two died of their wounds at a later date.

144 The reference may be referring to Percival Philips who was a reporter for the *Daily Express*.

145 Major Eustace Crawley, 12th Royal Lancers (Prince of Wales's). 2 November 1914 aged
    46 years. Commemorated Panel 5, Ypres Menin Gate, France.

146 HMS *Goodhope* was sunk on 1 November 1914 at the Battle of Coronel with the loss of all
    hands. Lieutenant Lancelot Alexander Montgomery, Portsmouth Naval Memorial, UK.

147 Sir Henry Wilson's wife Cecil was suffering from gallstones at this time. *See* Keith Jeffrey
    p. 139.

148 Colonel William Thomas Furse DSO (1865–1953). GS 6th Div., he was also on the staff at
    Camberley when Price-Davies did the staff course in 1908. Later Master General Ordnance
    1916.

149 Brigadier General Wesley Lynedoch Henry Paget CB, CMG, MVO, CRA 6th Div. Died,
    10 June 1918 aged 60 years. Buried North Cheriton Cemetery, Somerset, UK.

150 Lieutenant Colonel Henry Rudolf Davies CB (1865–1950). 6th Inf. Bde, 2nd Div.

151 Major General Francis John Davies (1864–1948). Grenadier Guards, GOC 8th Div. 1914–15.
    KCB 1915. Military Secretary 1916–19. KCMG 1916. KCVO 1919. Lieutenant General
    GOC in Chief Scottish Command 1919–23. Retired 1923.

152 Lieutenant Colonel W.H. Anderson, GSO 1.

153 Lieutenant Colonel Arthur Reginald Hoskins DSO (1872–1942). AA & QMG. CMG 1916. Later Major General KCB 1919, GOC 46th Div. Palestine. Retired 1923.

154 Brigadier General Arthur Edward Aveling Holland DSO (1862–1927). BGRA July 1915, GOC RA VII Corps. September 1915 GOC 1st Div. CRA Third Army June 1916. GOC I Corps February 1917. Lieutenant General 1919. CB 1915. KCB 1918. KCMG 1919. Retried 1920. MP for Northampton 1924–27.

155 Lieutenant Colonel Walter Henry Rotherham CRE. Taken sick 19 February 1915. Survived the war, retired as a colonel.

156 Major Albert Edward Sydney Louis Paget MVO. 11th (Prince Albert's) Hussars. Later Lieutenant Colonel GSO 1, 3rd Cavalry Div., IV Corps. Died, 2 August 1917 aged 38 years. Buried Wandsworth Cemetery, London, UK.

157 Major Lord Bernard Charles Gordon Lennox, 7th Duke of Richmond. 2nd Company ,2nd Bn Grenadier Guards. Killed in action, 10 November 1914 aged 36 years. Buried Zillebeke Churchyard, Belgium.

158 Hythe, Kent was the School of Army Musketry.

159 Field Marshall Frederick 'Bobs' Sleigh Roberts, 1st Earl Roberts (1832–1914).

160 This was part of the great German attack on the front from Messines to Polygon Wood. The date 11 November 1914 officially known as "Battle of Nonne Bosschen (Nuns Copse)". OH Vol 2, Ch XVII.

161 Colonel Hugh Maude de Fellenburg Montgomery RA (1870–1924). GSO 1, 7th Div. until 12 November 1914. Staff duties 1914–18. CB 1918. CMG 1919.

162 Brigadier General Francis Charles Carter CB (1858–1951). Northumberland Fusilier, 24th Bde. Went sick 16 March 1915 after 8th Div.'s First Battle of Neuve Chapelle.

163 KOYLI: King's Own Yorkshire Light Infantry.

164 Lieutenant Colonel William Maunder Withycombe (b. 1869). Commanded 2nd Bn KOYLI, 13th Bde, 3rd Div., II Corps. CMG 1915. DSO 1918.

165 During the Battle of Gheluvelt the 1st Bn moved forward to the Menin Road on the night of 1 November with orders not to retire. The defensive position was poor and led to it being enfiladed, surrounded and then overrun. Nine officers and 437 men of the battalion were killed or captured by the Germans. *See* Major General Sir Stuart Hare, *The Annals of the KRRC* ([Publisher], 1932) Vol.V, p. 61–62.

166 Captain William Drysdale, Royal Scots, Brigade Major 21st Bde until 17 February 1915. Killed commanding 7th Bn Leicestershire Regt, 29 September 1916 aged 39 years. Buried Caterpillar Valley Cemetery, Somme, France.

167 Earl Roberts died 14 November 1914 of pneumonia. He was given a state funeral and buried at St Paul's Cathedral, London, UK.

168 Captain G.V.H. Gough, 1st KRRC, POW at Nonne Bosschen. He survived the war.

169 Lieutenant Alan Morley Saunders 1st Bn KRRC, POW at Nonne Bosschen.

170 Brigadier General Sydney 'Swanky Sid' Turing Barlow Lawford (1865–1953). GOC 22nd Bde, 7th Div. Later Major General 41st Div. After the war he went to India as a lieutenant general. He left the army due to marital scandal and divorced his first wife. His son by second marriage was Peter Lawford, the actor.

171 On 14 November the Germans halted the Russian advance into East Prussia and launched a powerful offensive along the Vistula from Thorn. The Russians retreated and took up defensive positions from Gombin to Lodz. On 16 November the Germans overran the Russian rear guard at Kutno and Vlotslavek. There was heavy fighting around Plotsk.

172 Prince Arthur William Patrick, Duke of Connaught (1850–1942).

173 The Duke of Westminster was an ADC on General Rawlinson's staff.

174 Lord Dalmeny, Albert Edward Harry Archibald Primrose (1882–1974). Grenadier Guards (temporary Lieutenant Colonel) was AMS, BEF. He was later ADC and Military Secretary to Lord Allenby in Palestine. also a first-class cricketer.

175 Giles Stephen Holland Fox-Strangeways, 6th Earl of Ilchester, Coldstream Guards
(1874–1914).

176 Sir Philip Sassoon was Haig's private secretary, an aesthete, politician and millionaire, and
described as a 'semi oriental figure like some exotic bird of paradise against the sober
background of GHQ', Robert Blake (ed.), *The Private Papers of Sir Douglas Haig 1914–1919*
(London, 1952), p. 30.

177 Lieutenant Colonel Reginald Walter Ralph Barnes DSO (1871–1946). 10th Royal Hussars
(Prince of Wales's Own). Temporary Brigadier General 111th Bde 1915, Major General
GOC 32nd & 57th Divs 1917–19. CB 1916. KCB 1919.

178 Frederick Arthur Guest (1875–1937). 1st Life Guards. He was an MP at the outbreak of
the war and returned to service. In 1914 he was ADC to Field Marshal Sir John French. In
1916 he was awarded a DSO in the East African Campaign, where he was invalided through
illness. He returned to politics in May 1917 and he was Secretary of State for Air 1921–22.

179 Colonel Brinsley Fitzgerald, Private Secretary to C in C, Field Marshall Sir John French.

180 Major John Edward Spencer Brind DSO, RA (1878–1945). DA & QMG 2nd Div. 1914.
GSO 2, X Corps 1915–16. GSO 1 56th Div. December 1916. GSO 1 First Army 1917.
BGGS 1, Eleventh Army Corps. CMG 1918. GOC 4th Div. 1933–35. Awarded KCB, KBE.

181 Lieutenant General Arthur James Murray CIGS, BEF, 5 August 1914–January 1915.

182 Brigadier General Reginald John Pinney (1863–1943). Royal Fusiliers. GOC 23rd Bde, 8th
Div. Major General 35th Div.; after the Somme, 33rd Div. CB 1917. KCB 1918.

183 Major Geoffrey Charles Shakerley DSO. He would take over command of the 1st Bn in March
1915 after Colonel E. Northey went to command 15th Bde. Killed in action at the Battle of
Festubert, 15 May 1915 aged 46 years. Buried Rue-Petillon Cemetery, Fleurbiax, France.

184 Brigadier General Herbert Edward Watts (1858–1934). GOC 21st Bde. Later Major General
GOC 7th Div. and Lieutenant General XIX Corps.

185 Lieutenant Colonel George Owen Squier (1865–1934). He was the military attaché in
London at this time and was especially interested in military aviation. Later in the war he
was a major general and chief signal officer during. He was also a businessman and scientist.

186 Major General Sir Charles Edward Callwell, DMO 1914 (1859–1928).

187 Major Harry Simonds de Brett DSO, RA. GSO 1, MOD 1914. GSO 2, 28th Div. until
August 1915. GSO 1, 3rd Div. until November 1916. Brigadier General RA Heavy Artillery,
Mesopotamia Expeditionary Force until July 1918. AAG at War Office September 1918.
CMG 1917. After the war he became managing director and chairman of Simmonds Farson
Ltd, a brewing Company based in Reading. He retired in 1950.

188 Captain Bryan James Curling KRRC. Staff Captain, Adjutant General Office, MOD 1914.
DAA & QMG 29th Div. Mediterranean Expeditionary Force until December 1915. GSO
1 26th Div. until August 1916. GSO 1 65th Div. Home Forces. GSO 1 42nd Div. June 1917.
Brigade Commander 189th Bde, France, September 1918.

189 Cecil Wray was the maiden name of Sir Henry Wilson's wife.

190 Colonel Arthur Victor Seymour Williams (1867–1949). Adjutant General of Canada
1912–14. Later he commanded the 8th Canadian Inf. Bde, 3rd Canadian Div. On 3 June
1916 he was severely wounded and captured by the Germans at Mount Sorrell. He returned
to Canada on a POW exchange in 1918.

191 Major Charles Edward Gore Vesey RE (1880–1958). 8th Div. CRE 5th Div. to April 1916.
CRE VII Corps 1917–18. MID on two occasions.

192 Brigadier General Lionel Arthur Montagu Stopford (1860–1942). Irish Guards. GOC 82nd
Bde, 27th Div. Taken sick 9 January 1915. Commandant of RMA Sandhurst 1916–19.

193 Part of 8th Div.

194 Brigadier General George Francis Milne (1866–1948). CRA 4th Div. Later field marshal
and CIGS, where he supported the mechanisation of the British Army. Became 1st Born
Milne 1933.

195 Lieutenant Colonel Henry Colin Mansell Porter. Army Cyclist Corps, later 9th (S) Bn KRRC; Lieutenant Colonel R.E. Crichton RE, GSO 3 Meerut Div. Brigade Major 61st Inf. Div. until December 1915. GSO 2 GHQ until May 1917. GSO 1 GHQ 1918. Served in Italy April–November 1918.

196 This was an attack by Lieutenant General Smith Dorrien's II Corps on Wytschaete. It was led by 3rd Div.

197 Major Athol Murray Hay Forbes, 1st Bn RSF.

198 Lieutenant Colonel Graham Henry Whalley Nicholson, GOC 35th Bde RFA 6 November 1914–21 July 1915. CMG 1915. Brigadier general 1915.

199 Rouges Bancs – Well Farm attack (IV Corps).

200 Officers of KRRC. Captain Charles Vernon Leslie Poe, Captain Alan John Hunter (4th Bn) KRRC.

201 Lieutenant Ronald Townsend Fellows (1886–1936). 2nd RB. Later Captain Acting Lieutenant Colonel 1st RB 1916–18. DSO (LG 18 July 1918), MC. 2nd Baron Ailwyn of Honiton. Died from wounds received in the First World War.

202 The School at Crystal Palace was used to train Royal Naval divisions and navy signallers at this time.

203 Lieutenant Colonel Foljambe. The battle arrived back in England in November 1914 and landed at La Havre 21 December 1914. Became part of 80th Bde, 27th Div.

Two

1915

The second year of the war is more recognisable to the reader, as it has settled down into the trench warfare that would consume the forces of the belligerent countries for most of the next three years. As a Corps liaison officer, his work now incorporates both cavalry and infantry divisions. Although he still rides between various HQs, he also travels by car and illustrates these adventures with numerous anecdotes. The letters also reveal the social side of the war in France, painting a picture of how small the regular army was at this time and how the positioning of various officers was changing. They also recall the loss of friends with whom he had served, and how the war was hardening the spirit of those chosen to lead it.

By early March he had moved on to be a liaison officer with the newly arrived 46th North Midland Division. It is a territorial division formed in 1908 and commanded since 1913 by Major General E. J. Montagu Stuart-Wortley. As an officer from the same regiment, Price-Davies knows him well and his letters reflect how this division was settling in to the new type of warfare. Throughout this period he takes note of the way the war is growing and what influence allies like Russia are having. He also notes the weather and how that is affecting the way in which the Army is coping by visiting the forward positions of his division and checking on its progress.

At the end of July, the division is heavily attacked at Hooge; the fighting is very fierce and the losses are very heavy. By October the division attack the Hohenzollern Redoubt during the Battle of Loos; it was a catastrophe and despite desperate efforts, they fail to take their objective. The losses of officers and men was no reflection on the quality of the division as they had tried to achieve an impossible task set by the Corps commander, Lt General R. Haking.

Major Price-Davies' time with this division ends in November when he was told that he was to command the 113th Brigade, 38th Welsh Division.

1.1.15

My own darling

I have been in search of a dentist. First in the office of the DDMS.[1] They put me to a Doctor and I went to his home. No, he was at the hospital but if I went there he would give me treatment. I found an English orderly outside the hospital and he said there was a dentist attached to No 9 Clearing Hospital who had 'taken out 5 teeth for a chap yesterday'. Then to No 9 Clearing Hospital but the dentist had gone away so back to the French Hospital where I found the Doctor. He said his English assistant would be at his home at 11.30 so I should go off there. I want to get this little thing put right whilst I have a chance.

Of course the dentist would do nothing today. They never will. He dug a hole with his little instrument & I am to have done tomorrow at 9am I think it will be rather tender.

Henry & Uncle have gone out shooting today it is cold & windy so they won't have much of a day. I shall go later to see the 7th battalion.[2]

I went out this afternoon to see the 1st Battalion I thought Northey looking rather drawn & not in good form, they say he is depressed.[3] I left him and went to see some of the others, even Willan quite pleased to see me, Bonham Carter there also.[4] Shakerley's brother, a lot of young boys & some fellows who were promoted from the ranks.[5] They were living in a little Inn & were in the same room as customers, farm hands, road menders etc. It was very queer we had tea & I produced a cake, Gwen sent me & we made a good hole in it. Evans says that the 1st battalion were partly let in by the Coldstream who relieved & one of them apologised for it all & thought that our company should have got away.[6]

1.1.15

St Omer

Horrid weather in the afternoon high wind & rain. Nothing settled about me yet so I take a day off to go to the dentist. After lunch motor to Locon (N of Bethune) & see the 1st Bn, Northey, Williams, Carter, and others.

2.1.15

The little dentist described it as a 'decent sized county in there' and he showed me the cotton wool that came out of it. He did not hurt me but it was very tender, now I cannot bite on it. It was a good job getting it done it cost me 20F. I went out to 4th Corps today & found out how the wet is affecting their trenches. It is beastly country & all full of water. Yes we are holding the line we have held for a long time. Attacks are useful in order to keep the Germans firing away. Rex attack was to retake trenches we had lost I don't know the facts but I think it would have been useless to throw in more men on top of Rex's battalion. The mistake was to put them in at night to attack over ground they did not know, I think it one of those fights that is best forgotten, but of course I may be wrong.[7] Anyway that is the general impression of course the men have lots of stories I have no doubt the men of the 1st Battalion could easily explain whose fault it was that we lost 3 companies.

I think the Russians are doing all right & that the Austrians have had a pretty hard knock. I hardly ever see Sir John now. I had tea with Rawly tonight.[8] My batman produces the most marvellous things to eat. I suppose it is the usual French plan but they have great industry. Evidently at his home in the south of France they make wonderful sausages from pigs which keep for many years & are very good sort of German sausages. Then they kill about a hundred geese a year & each goose is boiled & has things done to it & put in a jar and sealed up. The livers are taken out & 'pate de foire gras' is made of them & they are tinned. He produced one today & it was awfully good & he says it is not rich like the ones you buy.

Everyone seems to be going away Henry & Murray on leave, Gilly & Smyth are also going I believe so I shall start on the Cavalry soon.[9] A.G. Stuart is here he is a great addition to the mess. He is pleased with the way the Ulster people have played up. He said the bigoted prods say why do they want to fight a protestant country with RC's as our allies & he says the Orange Lodges are financed by German money!

January 1915

St Omer

Get tooth stuffed not a great success at present. Went to 4th Corps to find out how their trenches were affected by the wet. They were flooded out in many places. Saw 20, 23, 24th Bde.[10]

3.1.15

I have been busy writing out things connected with the Cavalry in my note-book & am going to try to see Charles & the 4th Battalion at lunch time but I don't know whether they pay any attention to Sunday or not. Hereward has gone on leave, Gilly has gone too.[11]

A cake has arrived addressed by Goodlady very many thanks to whoever sent it I am afraid my cakes don't last long as I produce them at meals. Smyth has had his orders now & I start with the Cavalry tomorrow I am afraid it will be dull work but that can't be helped. Henry goes off tomorrow I believe. No of course I don't agree with you taking the pledge because we want to have one glass of port together on Sunday nights.

Went out to see Charles got stuck in mud on way but got help to push us out. Had lunch with 4 Bn HQ (Tim, Majendie & others).[12] Took Charles for a drive & called at Stoppy's HQ I saw Follett but Stoppy was out.[13] Henry goes on leave tomorrow, Gilly & Hereward went today.

4.1.15

I feel very tired tonight I don't know why I have begun my duties with the Cavalry and am pleased to have a proper job again. I am not quite sure what to do about my tooth. The tooth had a hole in it but did not ache. I then had it stuffed with gold but found it was so tender I could not bite on it. I went to the little man today & he was most anxious to put it right but could not see what is wrong. He then took an electrified wire, which became red-hot with which he proceeded to fire my gums. This made them rough & a little sore but so far has had no effect. He says if the tooth does not get well I am to go back in 2 days time & he will see if the nerve is alright he also said he would look at the canals. Now what I want to know is should I let him go on to see what is wrong or should I go to a good man in Boulogne or should I leave it alone & eat on the other side of the mouth & get it seen by Farmer later on? I don't fancy having the stuffing taken out again as it takes time & is a bother.

Henry went off this morning but stays in the lines of communication for a day at a time. I met Wilfred Jelf he seemed very well.[14] I went to 4th Cavalry Bde they were very nice and pleased to see a visitor & I had a long chat with them (& some old Brandy) I then went to 1st Bde but only saw the Bde Major Captain Osbourne, he did not impress me with his wisdom but I dare say he is alright. After that we got stuck in the mud, the metalling of the road suddenly ends & we sank in & the silencer rested in the mud. We had some very nice people in a farm who lent us a horse & pulled us out. About ½ hour afterwards a motor lorry passed us & we got into the mud & stuck again. They went on & did not stop in spite of my shouting at them. However by dint of pushing & manoeuvring we got through all right.

4.1.15

St Omer

I now take liaison to Cavalry Corps. Went to 4th Cavalry Bde (Gen. Bingham) I found them very pleasant, also went to 1st Cavalry Bde got stuck in mud again & had to get a horse to pull us out.[15]

5.1.15

It is very sad my teeth do not seemed to get right & I have slight neuralgia nothing to speak of. The weather continues to be beastly. We went our rounds today I always do the same to start with de Lisle, Bungo, & then to Gough, this takes me to about 12, then we go off & at 12.30 we pull up somewhere & have lunch in the car then after a smoke we go to a Brigade or two & end up with the Cavalry Corps again where we get letters to bring back.[16] Today I went to 7th & 8th Cavalry Brigades where no one was in. The difficulty is that people are usually out. They usually have comfortable quarters. At 7th Bde there was a man in the 11th Hussars I am sure we must have met I must think it out. I saw Stoppy yesterday, he had a cold & said he was very ill!! I also saw Blair the other day he is on the staff of 27th Div I thought he looked very changed in fact I could not think who it was till the next day.[17] I had an invitation to shoot from 6th & to hunt from 7th Cavalry Bde I don't know if either will materialize.

Coming back I picked up a man who drives one of the 2nd Div cars. He was coming in here to try & join the Flying Corps, when we got here they told him he should have gone somewhere else. I hope you will see a lot of Henry when he is at home & that he will take a good rest.

6.1.15

Lazy night, the tooth is a bother but I have slight neuralgia & headaches. Gilly is GSO 1 of 13th Division.[18] The Russian news is excellent the knock the

Turks have had should make them feel sorry they began but of it is a long way from Constantinople. The French seem to be fighting like the deuce. We are not doing very much our end. My cavalry are all resting & have made some sort of thatched stables, which give the horses more shelter. Fancy poor old Stapleton being sent round Germany as a show.

We are all fixed up here now, Charlie Grant 1st Army, Lynn 2nd Army, A.G. Stuart, Indian Cavalry, Tim Holland, French 8th Army (Urbal).[19] We are all here and then we have Captain Spears, French 10th Army (de Maud'huy) Sydney Clare, Colonel Hudson & C.B. Thomson (all with Joffre).[20] Today I struck a nice crowd & had lunch with them. Glenn Campbell commanding 6th Cavalry Bde.[21] Boyd Rockfort is there & seemed very well.[22] Glen Campbell is very interesting & a thoughtful soldier. They seem simple folk & this suited me. I went to see 2nd Bde Mullens he was very pleasant but not as clever as Campbell I should say.[23] Tit Willow is going home to some job I understand he lives at Downton Hall.[24]

7.1.15

At least the weather was nasty, rain all last night & rain & winds all today. Col Bruin came out today he is a charming companion but I found talking all day in addition to guiding the car through unknown country some of it is, rather a strain! Royals are in a nice chateau with a lovely old barn knocker on the door & rather a nice old oak bureau. Then we went to 3rd Bde where we found Kearsley, Bde Major.[25] Do you remember we met his father somewhere but I have a sort of idea it was during the Irish crisis, perhaps at Tom Notts? Then on to 5th Cavalry Brigade HQ. The man I thought we had met is Drake, where was it we met him?[26] Then we came home after picking up letters at Cavalry Corps HQ. Barrow is leaving to command Indian Cavalry Bde.[27] He was in Cavalry Corps Staff. Col Hudson has gone home now, as there were too many lyiza's with Joffre.

Tim Holland said he is going to CGS, who said he had some Gillette safety razors to give away, so away I went too & got a lovely razor in a neat little case silver gilt. Also some shaving soap & some tobacco from fatty & some chocolates so I did well. Fatty was in a bad temper today. The weather perhaps & then we had to pass Stoppy's Brigade & then there more lorrys coming in the opposite direction & all that irritated him.

8.1.15

Dreadful rain last night, regular torrents & some of the roads are under water & large fields are now ponds. One of my Brigades has had to move to a dryer spot, Fatty was in better temper & the morning was lovely today but he does not think Friday is a good day & things went awry. First of all water got in where it was not wanted & stopped the car. Then a man upset some stones in the road with a clatter which frightened a man's horse so much that it sat on the radiator & other Officers nearly fell off. We had a hard chase after Tip but eventually ran him to ground. He is very well & cheery & enjoying life immensely. Coming home we nearly had an accident & would have had but for Fatty's presence of mind. We were going through Hazebrouck when we saw a wagon coming down the road, which would not pull over though there was plenty of room, it then become evident that it was coming right into us & Fatty put his brakes on & skidded his car round just cleared the wagon whilst we crashed into a cart that was standing (without a horse) in the street. We only broke the tip of the shaft, it appears that the wagon was running away. The driver was very frightened when we went to him. The man who owned the cart was annoyed but Fatty startled him by cursing him for leaving the cart in a public road & said that if it had happened in the French area he would have been run in!

I seldom see Bungo, Biggs or Hubert, they are always out when I call. Allenby commands the Cavalry Corps, Bulkeley-Johnson commands 8th Cavalry Bde.[28]

8.1.15

St Omer

Fine till evening, country very wet I saw Tip, went to see Jardine but he was out.[29]

9.1.15

Who was asking you for Indian Expeditionary Force stamps? I think I can get them as Stuart has found them & I am buying two sets, we will keep one. We had rotten day today the car broke down & poor Fatty got his feet in a fearful state of mud trying to find out what was wrong. He got the engine firing once but it stopped I got rather damp too trying to help him. Then I had my lunch & started to walk to 2nd Div HQ but luckily found a car round the corner & an old ASC friend I had not seen since South Africa. We were in the same column & in hospital together I got a lift to 2nd Cavalry Div & got a car to tow us in there. It cleared up in the afternoon but the rain was awful this morning. Charlie Grant fills his room with friends F.E. Smith & Dalmeny's brother.[30] I saw Edmund Talbot a little tub of a man, my introduction was a first, as he had not heard of me or you. I thought him a beast not to have heard all about you.[31]

9.1.15

St Omer

A bad day, very heavy rain. Car broke down & got it towed to 2nd Cavalry Div then got another. Car punctured wheel put another on – tyre flat. Got another car from Cavalry Corps to get us home. Got my tooth seen to in the morning. Had stuffing out & it was found nerve was exposed. Now being put right by killing nerve.

Sunday 10.1.15

St Omer

Lovely fine morning but rain again at night. Saw Hubert Gough he is not in good form. Go to Bethune to see Lea who is in hospital but I found he had gone. Go to see 2nd Div only 2 Officers left of the Staff who came out originally. Tea with Bungo.

11.1.15

St Omer

Lovely day rain in evening. My car was not ready to go yet. Saw Benson 7th Lancers, Lord Tweedmouth, Blues. Tea at 2nd Cav Div (Bingham).[32] Brought home an Officer of the 20th Hussars who was going to the Musketry School here he was very interesting.

12.1.15

St Omer

Went to 7th Bde, but they were out. Lunch with Tip, should have gone yesterday! Went to 7th div to pick up my saddle as Harvey moved to Corps HQ today. Saw TC in good form. Country very wet great floods everywhere. TC hinted that I had done liaison work long enough, said it was a job for a wounded or sick man.[33]

13.1.15

St Omer

Go to dentist he finds another piece of nerve. Go to 2nd Army (Smith Dorrien) as well as Cavalry Corps.[34] Visit II & III Corps & Cavalry Corps. See Gough in his new quarters.

14.1.15

St Omer

In addition to usual round went to see 27th Div & then to tea with 3rd Bn. There have been a lot of cases of frostbite trouble in the Division. The trenches they took over from the French appear to be bad. Henry comes back.

15.1.15

St Omer

Fine but windy. Lynn goes to II Army today. I rode from Cavalry Corps HQ to Hindeghem (& 7th Cavalry Bde). Then to 2nd Cavalry Div & got back early & had a chat with Henry. Things are rather gloomy I think.

16.1.15

St Omer

Lunch with Grey & Cavendish, Burnten & Featherstonehaugh (3rd Cavalry).[35] Then to Rognetaire & Terronanne & then home. Philip Howell in for dinner.[36]

Sunday 17.1.15

St Omer

Took round Queen Alexandra's presents to 10th Greys, 4th DG's, 3rd DG's & Carabineers. Tea with Greys where I met Crombie who I had not seen for 15 years. Loch & Bulfin came to dinner.[37] 28th Division is arriving.

18.1.15

St Omer

Snow. A horrid day. Took the presents to the Bays & 5th DG's. Home early. Something must be done to car, got stuck twice, Essex Yeomanry pulled us out. Henry going off to look at French lines.

19.1.15

St Omer

Bad day the car went wrong again. Tried to go to 4th Bn but got a wrong road. Had tea with General Fortesque.[38] Car got stuck on way home & we got some Royal Scots to help us out. Heard Lady Edwina Lewin has a son.[39]

20.1.15

St Omer

Henry goes off. Went to see 4th Bn. They were cheerful in spite of the handicaps they have been through in the trenches. Tea with Philip Howell 4th Hussars.[40]

21.1.15

Feel rather lively, go for a ride & lunch with 4th Corps. Rawly out but lunch with Dalles, Bagshot, Lumsden & Amery there.[41] Go to 4th Cavalry Bde General Vaughan there but Bingham out.[42]

23.1.15

Bright frosty morning but mild in evening. Got back about 2pm & Uncle, Baring, Charles Deedes & I motored to other side of Clainmaras & walked back 6 miles at a good pace.[43]

Sunday 24.1.15

Frost gone & rainy day. Walk with Bungo from his HQ to Corps & back. Lunch with Bungo. Tea with 5th Cavalry Bde (Chetwode) at Fangnembugers.[44]

25.1.15

Hear of naval success sinking the Blucher.[45] Robertson becomes the CIGS.[46] Attack on Givenchy by the Germans at first successful but they were driven back & 2 Officers & 51 others taken prisoner.

26.1.15

St Omer

General Perceval comes as sub chief, Henry to be Chief Liaison Officer I understand.[47] Very intriguing business doing this in Henry's absence. I had tea with 3rd Cavalry Div & saw Charles Rankin.[48]

29.1.15

St Omer

Henry comes back. I go round to see Sir A. Murray to say goodbye as he has been very nice to me. Saw Archie Chapman. Brooke, Mallinson, Loch & de Brett & Hutch in for dinner.[49]

30.1.15

Henry saw Robertson yesterday but Sir J is in bed! Took Hutch out to his Corps. The days are frosty & bright & today not cold. Got back early & walk with H for over an hour.

31.1.15

Filthy day, snow. Went to 1st Bde & I went with General Bungo & Osbourne to see some horses in 11th Hussars, Bays & 5th DG's. They all looked very fit in spite of being in the open (some were under shelter). Had a chat with Henry his affairs are all right. He is to be made a temporary Lt General.

4.2.15

St Omer

Go back to Ypres a great change since I was there last. Cloth Hall all burnt out & battered by shells & Cathedral also. Most of the town is knocked about & burnt out but there are people living there & shops open etc.

7.2.15

Slight muddle as to who is to go where this morning but we keep to original plans except that DG goes to 2nd Cavalry Div I go to 3rd Cavalry Div amongst others.

9.2.15

St Omer

A rainy day go to Cavalry again & got home early Henry overtook me & I got into his car.

10.2.15

Hereward & Evans say I must stay in, took a walk in afternoon & go to the old fort with underground passage. Evans to go to 3rd Div, Morris to come here also Hutch.[50]

11.2.15
Uncle goes to 17th Infantry Brigade we are sorry to lose him from here.[51]
Fine day again but cold go out to Ypres.

12.2.15
Lunch with Briggs. Go to Ypres. Cavendish not at all well. 2nd Div relieves the reserve in Ypres. Bother with lights on way home.

Saturday 13.2.15
Simmonds drives me again but his spring breaks & I have to wire for another car. Lunch at 2nd Cavalry Bde with Hamilton Grace.[52] Nothing going on in Ypres, Gough relieves Byng tonight.

14.2.15
Very wet day went to 2nd Army as well as Cavalry. 28th Div (Archie Chapman's Bde) lose some trenches & counter attack fails.

16.2.15
Get my rounds done early & go to 2nd Cavalry Div about 12 they had settled to take me to the trenches but I have to go alone. Go to 4th Cavalry Bde HQ & then to communication trench nearly up to my knees in water, change before coming home. Cold bad on my chest so Henry says I am not to go out tomorrow.

19.2.15
Russian news appears to be very bad as they are getting a nasty knock in East Prussia.

Saturday 20.2.15
I go for a walk in the afternoon. Harper comes to see me with his Legion of Honour on.

22.2.15
Misty day take Major Murray out. Poor J. Gough died a great loss.[53]

Tuesday 23.2.15

St Omer

17 YEARS SERVICE

26.2.15
Took out Cyril Hankey, always a pleasant companion & we had a busy round. 3rd Cavalry Div, 2nd Army, Cavalry Corps, 2 Cavalry Div, 2nd & 3rd & 3rd Div, 1st Cavalry Div, & 5th Corps. Broke down George Cary sent us a car to carry us in & at Steenvorde I picked another for GHQ.

2.3.15

Go into the 18th Hussars trenches with Armstrong, some shells fell in Ypres. Hear 4th Bn had a fight & lost Poe & Eden killed, Bircham & Bailes wounded.[54] 16 killed & 30 missing probably killed, 60 wounded.

3.3.15

Go to see 4th Bn in addition to my usual round. Bircham did splendidly well Tim told me in fact 4th Bn appear to have done well but could not accomplish what they were ordered which was to clear 600yds of trench.

4.3.15

Saw French XX Corps on the road (or parts of it) an inspiring sight in their new blue uniforms. Cavalry leave the trenches today being relieved by French 9th Corps.

5.3.15

Went to see the 2nd Bn at Hinges after delivering my letters. Saw Chico, Rudolf, Featherstonehaugh, Algy, Upton. On the way home had tea with Philip Grange & found John Orghe there who has come out with 4th Corps.

Saturday 6.3.15

St Omer

Lunch with Bungo & came home early. Walk with Henry for an hour & got very hot. We are going through critical times.

8.3.15

St Omer

Took Hindskip out, had lunch with Daddy Martin, he is Brigade Major to Hasler 11th Bde.[55] Then on through Armentieres to Uncle Harper who is in bed but not bad. Tim & I went to see farmer Davies in hospital a gloomy place.[56]

9.3.15

St Omer

Got much delayed today as North Midland Division are on the move. We start fighting tomorrow.[57]

10.3.15

Hazebruck

Start at 6.45 & go to Hazebruck. In afternoon I go to 7th Division. The attack goes in pretty well & about 1,000 prisoners are taken in or near Neuve Chappell.

11.3.15

Sailly

Go to 4th Corps in morning & then find attack is held up by machine guns, which cannot be dealt with. After lunch CGS says I am to go off to be GSO 2nd Grade North Midlands Division.[58] I go to St Omer to get my kit & then out to my new job. The Division get in late to billets luckily it is dry & warm.

12.3.15

Sailly

Go over to Vieuse, Belgium with General Shipley & others to see General Gough.[59]

Saturday 13.3.15

Sailly

I am afraid we shall not progress much more in this battle I rode over to see the troops & also take a walk with Dansey in evening.[60]

14.3.15

Fearfully heavy artillery fire heard towards Ypres after dark & there is some more during the night. We are to move tomorrow.

15.3.15

Sailly

Start our move then get orders to remain. Finally we get orders to move tomorrow.

17.3.15

Merries

Dansey & I have to go & see about moving some of the troops into new billets. Saw Tim Harington & Montague Pryce have been wounded.[61]

19.3.15

A horrible day, driving snow at intervals. Rode with Rothesay S.W. in morning saw N & D Brigades.[62]

Saturday 20.3.15

Some of our troops are being attached to the 6th div for instruction. Things are quiet. H over for tea with the General.[63] I went to Bailleul & back with him. Hargreaves getting on well but has had a foot off. Took Bridge over to 6th Div to arrange attachment of gunners.

22.3.15

Went to see N & D Brigades at work in a wood but had to come away before work began. Another fine day, dinner at Generals. Guthrie arrives but there is no job for him at present.

24.3.15
Go into 16th Infantry Brigade trenches with General Ingoville Williams &
Headlam.[64] The best trenches I have yet seen.

26.3.15
Lynn goes home to have a tooth done, Harvey hears his son is dead & goes off
home. Go out with General round Battalions of Staffs Bde in morning. See L
& L Bde march off to form 4th Division. Hear V.29 is sunk.

Sunday 28.3.15
Church parade – perished. After lunch went off with Gathorne to 4th Div
& then to 11th Bde. Daddy Martin took us into trenches.[65] Tea with him &
Haslar.[66]

29.3.15
Out with General round Notts & Derby's Bde & 5th Leics, call at 7th div in
afternoon after seeing the Staffs Bde digging. Then on to see 4th Div 'Follies'
excellent in Armentieres under 5,000 xx from the trenches. Dinner with 4th
Div in Nieppe.

30.3.15
Had a good ride in morning to Steenweck & back, Bishop of London
preaches at the service in evening.[67] One Battalion had 5 miles to march but
600 of them volunteered to go.

31.3.15
Sudden orders to go & take over the trenches of 5th Div, N.E. of Bailleul.
Staffs Bde start off in afternoon. All attachments cease & all troops come back
to us.

Thursday 1.4.15
A busy day, go with Abadie to see 83rd Bde & make arrangements.[68] In evening go with Lynn to 5th Div HQ move progressing.

2.4.15
Lynn & I go with Dillon round part of ground in rear of new line. We took
out Colonel Feetham to command Staffs Bde.[69] Tea with 8th Div.

3.4.15
Rode my new horse quiet a success. After many days dry wind we have rain.
We are continuingly having to alter our moves to suit other people.

Sunday 4.4.15
Went to see 1st & 4th Bn. Lunch with Hereward (1st Corps) & General
Morris. General inspected 1st & 2nd Bn. Shakerley, Burnham, Carter &

Dennison with 1st. Chico, Upton, Rudolf, Algy Hasler with 2nd. Dudley & Horden came in at tea & also General Haking & Westmacott.[70] General seedy.

6.4.15

St James Cappell

Move to our new quarters, rather a business getting hold of our new circumstances. This trench business needs a lot of supervision & attention. General seedy again.

8.4.15

Went out with Col Feetham had breakfast & then down to his trenches. The communication trench was very wet but not wet in the trenches. Got back & had lunch feeling quiet weary.

10.4.15

Tried some proper waders in communication trench but my toe went through on the way back. Water still up to the knee. Went into trenches of 5th Lincs & some of Notts & Derby. Busy in office in afternoon.

11.4.15

After lunch go out with General to Sherpenberg a fine view as the day was clear. Fitzgerald appeared bringing Curzon with him & we had to take them to Kemmel, which spoilt our day.[71]

12.4.15

After lunch I went to Locre & saw Colonel Goodman & Burhin commanding 6th & 7th N & D.[72] They seemed very cheery. Then went to Kemmel where I remained with Colonel Levenson Gower.[73]

Saturday 17.4.15

In afternoon I go with Lynn riding as far as Lindenhorst. He goes off then & I walk down to the trenches I get into E.2 & walk all the way to H.4 the left end of the line. Very active snipers who have one or two at me but I am pretty careful! Whilst there our St Eloi attack (5th Div) commences & as I came away our demonstration began. One or two bullets came near me as I came here (after dark) & one of our shrapnel burst near me.

18.4.15

Go out with Wignall to see about getting some T.M's, which we manage to do.[74] The N & D Bde want them. Fearful influx of visitors at all hours today. 3rd Div continue their little success.

19.4.15

Go out in afternoon & see Colonel Jones 5th Leics & meet Lynn at Lindesbrock & see 5th N & D, 5th Lincs (Col Sandell) & 4th Lincs (Col Jessop).[75]

20.4.15

Go into trenches 11, 11b, 10A, 9 & 8 & so finish all I have not seen except E1, + 3 + 4 which are at present difficult to access. I met Colonel Ragmen commanding the 5th Leicester's. In evening Lynn & I took a walk, we saw Germans shelling Hill 60 I hope we manage to hold it but I hear they had a bad time of it.[76]

21.4.15

Lynn & I went up to the new com trench (Pall Mall) & into F.6 & so along F.4 + 5. The N & Derby have done great digging. Fine weather continues.

22.4.15

Went into trenches with Wyncoll.[77] Furze & his brother, Bishop of Pretoria to lunch.[78] A sad blow in the evening to hear of the French being driven in N of Ypres & left of Canadians. It seems to have been a flight on the part of the former & latter behaved well. They say there were asphyxiating gases. This will upset all our plans, I am afraid.

23.4.15

Lots of gunning today but we remain quiet. Troops are being rushed up but nothing much seems to have been accomplished. Heavy gunfire at night again.

24.4.15

Some of our trenches were fired in by T.M. & 8th N & D lost 14 killed & 14 wounded. I went to see the trenches this morning with Wyncoll. E.1 was very nasty with corpses sticking out of the ground. Heavy bombardments can be continually heard N of Ypres our attack does not appear to progress much.

Monday 26.4.15

Went into G.1. trench & others they are rather dominated in that trench by the Germans. The 8th & 9th N & D had heavy casualties from minenwerfers. Fighting N of Y seems to be still very heavy & we don't make much headway.

27.4.15

Went out in afternoon & met Colonel Maynard & A.G. Stuart in Shepenberg later had Russian Officers in toe.[79] Very little news from Ypres. Lynn & I went into trench 13 with Colonel Knight.[80]

28.4.15

Long morning, went up new communication trench to G.F. with Johnson Adjutant 6th N & D got home 3pm.[81] Rumour Italy has declared war but cannot get confirmation. Little news from Ypres.

30.4.15

Took Dansey into the trenches met Burnett 2nd in Command of 5th South Staffs (Col. Rayner) took us into a snipers post but could see very little.[82] The turnips between the lines have flowered & their height is a nuisance. One new T.M. firing 50lb shell got to work tonight & appeared to be a success.

Saturday 1.5.15
Lynn & I rode to Boeschepe to see Colonel Annesley who has some kites.[83] He is a maddening & magical man & I don't think we shall get much good out of him. We had a very jolly ride. Heavy firing round Ypres & somewhere down south.

2.5.15
A long morning out, started with Lynn & Granby in car & saw L & L HQ & N & D HQ. Then up new CT to G4 & along trenches & out down Pall Mall & so home about 4pm. The General saw some men in Hospital poisoned by gas, he says it was a terrible sight.

3.5.15
Lynn & I went into E valley great improvement there I rode home. This is the night of the retirement from Ypres salient is to take place very sad but I am afraid inevitable. Rain in night. More news of asphyxiating gas, the Germans are awful brutes.

4.5.15
St James Cappell
Very hot today, went to Crow's Nest farm & had a look at Germans trenches also looked at Piccadilly which is now dry nearly all the way, a lot of has had to be done there.

6.5.15
Went into trenches this morning with Captain Scorer, 5 Lincs.[84] Very hot everyone is much exercised with schemes to deal with gas attack.

7.5.15
Guthrie & I rode into Bailleul to see some bombs being made, after tea Lynn & I went in again to see General Furse.

8.5.15
Went into trenches with Colonel Knight 5th North Staffs, lovely day. In evening got orders to extend our front by 1 Bn northwards.

Sunday 9.5.15
St James Cappell
Got up at 5.15 a lot of news in. Very hard fighting round Ypres but we appear to hold our own more or less. The French attack progresses but our attack at Neuve Chappell way does not seem to.

10.5.15
Took General Furse to the trenches. A lovely day little news.

11.5.15

St James Cappell

Went into the trenches, they are not nice, we have taken over from 3rd Div & the communication trench is bad & trenches not too safe.

12.5.15
Went onto some of the K trenches with Johnson Adjutant to Sherwood Foresters. They are not too good & CT very wet.

13.5.15
Long time in office. Rode to Kemmel. Tea with 6th Sherwood Foresters took some officers of the 5th Bn into the trenches. Back 7pm. Heavy fighting began in night. Germans firing trench mortar bombs & shells at G.1.

14.5.15
Rode with Lynn to Kemmel & went into trenches & saw where G.1. had been smashed by shell & saw the dead Germans in the trench. General goes to Paris, as his neck is bad with neuritis, General Campbell comes to command in his absence.[85]

Sunday 16.5.15
Spent most of the day in office. I went round to see General Clifford[86] & had tea with General Feetham[87] & went with him to Wolveringham. There I met Guthrie & Dansey to see the French howitzers fire. They made good practice.

18.5.15
Damp day, walked with General Shipley in afternoon round our 2nd line trenches.[88] Had tea with Colonel Jones & Broomfield (5 Leics).[89]

Friday 21.5.15

St James Cappell

Went to Wolveringham with Smithson to arrange for employment of his trench howitzers they found amongst enemy trenches opposite B trench. T.H. made good practice afterwards. General Snow came to dinner.[90]

22.5.15

St James Cappell

Lovely day went with Roberts looking for wire in Staffs area. Heavy firing from South after dinner & by midnight there was a terrible commotion in progress. Earlier there appears to have been German counter-attacks against the Canadians, which were driven off.

Sunday 23.5.15

A great day up at 5.45, went round trenches with Colonel Abadie I went to see 3 + 4th Bn's. 4th Bn came out of last fight with 3 Officers & 10 men. 3rd Bn were 27 days in the trench on end. Saw Gosling Tim, Linger, Harte & Hordern.[91]

24.5.15

Took Captain Stewart ASC into trenches in the <u>pm</u>. Heavy fighting going on round Ypres & more gas attacks reported which is beastly.

28.5.15

Went to see some experiments with incendiary shells, which did not come off. 3 & 4th Bn arrived for instruction. Saw 7 & 8th RB & 8th KRRC. Verdant, Billy Seymour, Greg Campbell, Wreakin, Maurice, John & Moore.

Sunday 30.5.15

Lynn & I went to see 3rd Bn to arrange for them to take over additional trenches. 6 Sisters came to tea also. General Pulteney & his ADC's Pathey played tennis.[92]

31.5.15

A lot of fellows from 3 & 4 Bn's to dinner, Gosling, Makins, Ponsonby, Majendie & Cherks. Went out with CRA to see some subsiding line with Furse & General Heath.[93]

1.6.15

CRA & I went with Howard to show him where to dig. After dinner CRA & I went out to see Battalion of New Army at work. They dug very well & get back at midnight.

3.6.15

St James Cappell

A long day walked round new trenches we have taken over & met the horses at Dickenbusch at 7.30 & ride home. After dinner went with CRA to see Bn's digging.

4.6.15

I hear the Germans have captured Premzsyl.

Sunday 6.6.15

Very hot, went round trenches. Band played at tea. The Duchess of Sutherland[94] was to have brought some pretty nurses to tea but it fell through.

7.6.15

Went with Lynn & Guthrie to Armentieres to see Newton & his workshop.[95] Very hot indeed today. Colonel Allen turned up.[96]

9.6.15
Duchess of Sutherland & General Makins[97] came to dinner Colonel Lecky there. Afternoon went to 138th Bde.

10.6.15
A.G. Stuart & 2 correspondents came to lunch I went with T in <u>pm</u>.

13.6.15

St James Cappell

Lynn & I go out into 5th South Staffs. Tea with Bennett, Poaching. Peake. Conference Brigadier Generals after lunch.

16.6.15
General Short came to lunch & I took him to the trenches to try some artillery tests.[98] They did not do very well.

17.6.15
Went to 139th Bde trenches. When I came back found we had orders to move & hand over our trenches to 28th & 50th Div's. A very good thing for us to be shaken up.

18.6.15
Went with Lynn in afternoon to see 50th Div (General Lindsay) about their coming over here.[99] Hake & Grogan came to lunch & went into the trenches that 28th Div are taking over.

Sunday 20.6.15
Went to lunch with Horden (50th Div) & then into trenches we are to take over. Went through Ypres it is an awful sight nearly all flat & burnt out. A long walk to trenches and back.

22.6.15

St James Cappell

Lynn & I go over to see 13th Bde & 5th Corps in morning. We take a walk in evening & after dinner go to see 138th Bde on march.

Thursday 24.6.15

Basselboom

We change our HQ, in office in afternoon.

25.6.15
Went with CRA 3rd Div.[100] We went to Hooge & into stable of a Chateau there. Everything blown down but there are some wonderful underground places made by the French.

26.6.15

A lot of walking making improvements for work near Littlebebe. Then dinner with Colonel Levensen Gower & then with Wynn to Zillebeke with stores got to bed 1 am.

6.7.15

Basselboom

A long day up at 5 go out to trenches got back 3.45pm to bed after 12.

7.7.15

Folkestone

General Clifford & General Allen & I start off to motor to Boulogne. Breakdown 5 miles from St Omer. Get a lift & then on in a car from GHQ. Saw Hutch, Charles Deedes, Clark, Grant, Perks. Very rough crossing, very sick.

12.7.15

Basselboom

I get 4.30 Boat & ends a very happy holiday I meet General Clifford & Allen & we motor back together. We are to take over more trenches.

13.7.15

Office work, order comes for Lynn to go as BGGS 7th Corps & Dansey as A.A. & Q.M.G 10th Corps.[101] Philip Grove to come in Lynn's place.

14.7.15

Lynn goes off at 10am very sad losing them. I go to trenches round Hill 60 in afternoon.

16.7.15

Conference in morning a lengthy business – issuing op orders. Start for trenches at 5pm & go to 8th Sherwood Foresters got home 11pm. Wet night.

Sunday 18.7.15

Went out in morning to Kinestraat Ajeres. Philip arrives for lunch & we go out together & see the 3rd Bde progress.

22.7.15

Making arrangements for attachment of 17th Div. Tea with Colonel Hudson & Humphrey's & then on to make arrangements with Porter (50th Bde).[102]

23.7.15

Went to meet General Campbell & walked with him & Fuller & Compton and General Allenby in trenches.[103] Verdant given the left & I went & saw him, walked back with Allenby & Shipley. Very windy & stormy day.

Saturday 24.7.15
Went with Cavan to see German mine crater made last night. We reconnoitred and found we could turn it to our account.

25.7.15
Went up in morning to see what work had been done during the night. An unlucky mortar bomb had killed one & wounded 20. On my way up I met a working party that had been shelled, very unlucky. German aeroplane brought down at Maple Cross & 2 killed in it.

29.7.15
A long day off to Ypres 7.30 to see about wagons unloading bricks for road over bridge 14. Had a good look at Hill 60.

30.7.15
Attack today on 41st Bde & counter-attack by them which did not succeed. Heavy losses in Regiment 7th, 8th, 9th Bn – 9th Bn took some trenches. Went to 14th Div in afternoon (General Couper & Isacke) in Ypres.[104]

Saturday 31.7.15
Went with General to see General Campbell & General Shipley. Things quieter today. In evening went out to Maple Cross met Addison got back 1am.

2.8.15
Off to Zillebeke with Addison & General Clifford & then with former to trenches, got wet coming back. Dinner with 138th Bde.

4.8.15
Met General Feetham in trenches & had a look at Verbrandmolen trenches, then out to collect Colonel Knight & back about 10pm as I had dinner with 139th Bde.

6.8.15
Got up to trenches & had a look at the line on our left where the trenches were lost. Got shelled coming home because some of 6th Div exposed themselves in the communication trench.

Sunday 8.8.15

Maple Cross near Ypres
After dinner Wilson, Guthrie & I go to Kroonstraat where I leave them & go on to 139th Bde HQ for the 6th Div attack. They were in Maple Cross in dugouts.

9.8.15

Maple Cross

Bombardment began at 2.45am, a great noise. Then the attack took place at 3.15am. It was very successful but the 18th Bde lost heavily from shellfire after capturing the trenches. The Durham Light Infantry did splendidly, they had to withdraw from some of the trenches which remained empty.[105]

10.8.15

Basselboom

Fairly quiet some shelling at Hooge I return to Div. HQ in afternoon.

13.8.15

Russians will have plenty of arms & ammunition in the spring. He thinks we may get conscription soon. If we don't there is danger the allies may get tired of us and make terms.

Saturday 14.8.15

Went to St Omer for dinner, some little trouble as I had forgotten my forms & was taken before Protheroe Smith the APM.[106] Had dinner with Henry, Tim Holland, Charlie Deedes, Hutch, Montgomery & General Huguet. A cheery party after dinner Tim, Charles & I had a talk with Henry. He thinks we are sure to win if we all hang together but seems to think war may go on for another year.

18.8.15

Went with Philip to see 8th Bde. They are a great crowd, very keen & aggressive. We lunched & walked round their trenches, they have done a lot of good work, had some shells very close to his HQ. Papers very depressing on Russian situation.

19.8.15

In office all day but after tea got out & went to Abele & Bailleul saw Bill Furse not very hopeful of the situation.

20.8.15

Lunch with Uncle Harper he seems to run a good show, then to trenches & back about 9pm General Gosling came to dinner so I missed him.[107]

Sunday 22.8.15

General & General Gosling & I went over to Armentieres & had lunch with 50th Div (General Williamson & Horden & others). Then on to 4th Bn saw Tim, Ponsonby, & Charles. Then on to 12th Bn saw Albert Payne & also Buller.[108]

23.8.15
Stayed in till 4pm then to trenches with 137th Bde went round with Gethin MG Officer for North Midland Div.

24.8.15
A long day in 139th Bde trenches which they took last night, an interesting line. Saw one of our A.A. guns shelled & its lorry on fire. Tea at 138th Be HQ, General Kemp in command.[109] Home about 6pm about midnight Philip came in to say there was a mining scare & he was going to investigate.

25.8.15
Eventually a cammoflat was fired which appears to have made a crater 40 ft across behind out trenches. Must have caught a partially charged German mine.

26.8.15
Nice day rode to Bridge 14 & then went up to Maple Cross which 3rd Div now have. Went to the trenches of 4th Lincoln's, motored home got back about 8.30pm.

Sunday 29.8.15
Nice weather, lunch with de Brett, Haywood, General Haldane.[110] 3rd Div at Reisin in Holst

30.8.15
Very cold, lunch with Abadie & go to trenches with him after, see Germans focusing their periscopes.

31.8.15
A good deal of trouble with Corps over working parties but hope it will settle down alright. Went to trenches with Tim Humphrey's & Bannister who we lost & did not find again but he got back alright.

Sunday 5.9.15
A fine day, trenches are in an awful state in parts. Fear one of our aeroplanes brought down. Went round trenches of 139th.

6.9.15
Promoted Major – dated 1st September over 740 promoted, 29 Captains in Regiment promoted Major!

9.9.15
Took Roberts up to the trenches saw Colonel Raymer & had tea with Colonel Waterhouse.[111] Had to wait ¾ of hour for motor so got back about 9.30pm. Hillchild was driving he is acting CRA now.

10.9.15

In office all morning out in afternoon with Philip. Tea with Colonel Heathcote who has just come to command 4th Lincs.[112]

17.9.15

Basselboom

Went out with Halton to look at some defences, then to trenches of 5th North Staffs who had been shelled so went to see them as I came home a terrific bombardment began again. 384 HE shells fell in ¾ hour. After it was over went back to see how they were. The men were in excellent spirits, casualties were heavy 9 killed 26 wounded.

Saturday 18.9.15

Hoograaf

Move HQ to Hoograaf Cottage only about a mile from old place, much hammering.

19.9.15

Some shelling most of the day culminating in heavy bombardment of the trench held by the 5th North Staffs just under Hill 60 I went round trenches after & found everyone in good spirits but trenches were damaged.

21.9.15

Hoograaf

Took Commandant of Trench Mortar School round trenches. Lovely weather still, glorious sunny days, cold at night. Russian news very depressing.

24.9.15

Near Kroonstraat

In office all day, after dinner to dugouts near Kroonstraat I find I have no feeling of great expectation. It is hard now to even consider the possibility of a move forward & certainly not of a rapid or sudden one. Our dugouts quite good.

Saturday 25.9.15

Hoograaf

Bombardment started at 3.50am & continued till 4.20am. Trenches appear to have been captured easily by 1st & 9th, 8th Bdes however lost again as they were bombed out. Very sorry for the 14th Div should have failed again. News from the South is however most cheering & hope for great things from them. Go back to HQ 4pm. Tea at 5th Corps.

26.9.15

Philip & I go out together to 138th Bde trenches & got back at dinner time. Parts of the trench are very dilapidated they have been shelled a lot lately.

27.9.15

Rode out to HQ to see working party & then on to 14th Div, got an interesting account of their action which only just missed being a success.

28.9.15

Bad news T. Capper died of wounds & Thesiger killed I have lost a real friend & a very good soldier.[113]

30.9.15

With Tim Humphrey's & CRA 17th Div to see some works & hand them over.[114] Much strafing by Bosch they let off several mines & damaged our parapets & caused some casualties.

Saturday 2.10.15

Hoograaf

Take a trip to XI Corps beyond Bethune & return via VI Corps where I see captured guns, a good sight & then tea with tea with Gough's II Corps. Tim Holland came to stay the night & the CRE.[115]

Sunday 3.10.15

Bethune

HQ moves to Bethune, we had one HQ at 50 Rue Sade Carnot. Very nice being with French people again instead of Belgium's.

4.10.15

139 Company go up to dig beyond Vermeils I go to see they get the right place. Tea with General Makins.

5.10.15

Bethune

Go to Army HQ for a Conference at 2.30pm Rode over & got back for tea. Go with General to Conference at Corps HQ. Then help Philip to write orders for march, as we change one billeting area for another. Gas attack by General that's why order's are so late!

8.10.15

Gosmay

To trenches with General Feetham. Germans attacked the Guards & French & got a knock.[116]

12.10.15

Sally la Beire

We move out to our reporting centre in morning. Busy giving out stores in evening as the troops went forward to relieve. Much delay partly due to enemy crumbing Vermelles.

13.10.15

Went into trenches in morning things seem in pretty good order. Attack came off on left to a certain extent but on the right the men got mowed down with rifle & machine gun fire. Very disappointing & we feel so sorry for losses & little gained.[117]

14.10.15

Sally la Beire

Went round trenches with General Feetham. There were some ghastly sights bombing goes on all day. The men must have done very well but the task was really beyond them.

15.10.15

Gosmay

139 Bde came out at night & marched to billets, 137 & 138 Bde also get to billets We are back for dinner, have a tremendous sleep.

Sunday 17.10.15

Go with General to see 1st Bn & then to see Rawly. Colonels Jones & Heathcote come to dinner.[118]

18.10.15

Go with Philip to see some Bn's, then rode off to see Hugh who I find near Bethune but owing to be giving wrong directions I ride 17 miles![119]

19.10.15

Gosmay

Lunch with Tavish then ride to Guards & then I go to HQ 85 Bde but find Hugh is in the trenches.[120] Colonels Raymer & Ratcliffe come to dinner. Hugh's Division is off to Egypt.[121] Decided I am to go on leave.

20.10.15

10 Upper Cheyne Row, Chelsea

Rothesay drives us down in Rolls Royce. Colonel Lewis & Major Lewis (Signals Company) & Henry on board too. Very calm passage & very comfortable in Henry's cabin.

Wednesday 27.10.15

Leave at an end. Leave Victoria Station at 5.40pm cross over with Dick Crichton.

28.10.15

Prevea St Pay

Arrived back at 3pm.

29.10.15
Everything in unsettled state. Conference at Corps HQ I attend with the General.

Sunday 31.10.15
A day of rest, do some office work & take a short walk in evening with
Colonel Heathcote. Corps Commander arrives to dinner.[122]

3.11.15
Still making arrangements for move, ride in morning to starting point in
Bethune.

4.11.15
                                                                Prevea St Pay
Gerald & George Armytage came to dinner.[123]

5.11.15
                                                                    Westrem
We moved about 10am & Philip & I had a long afternoon in our new trenches
which are very bad & we got very wet well over our knees.

Sunday 7.11.15
                                                                      Locon
Went to the trenches of the 7th & 8th Sherwood Foresters & rode to Windy
Corner & rode back.

15.11.15
                                                        92 Rue St Bertox, St Omer
Went over to St Omer with ADMS & Guthrie and saw a new invention for
firing mills bombs invented by Foulkes.[124] Then I went to see Henry, Charles
Deedes etc & dine in their mess.

16.11.15
Go off to Wisquex for the course on machine guns & Davidson (RE), Lewis,
Dumberey in the car with me.

17.11.15
                                                                      St Omer
Lunched with Baker Carr we talked about old times.[125] Henry did not come
back only Hutch, Charles & I went in for dinner.

18.11.15
                                                                    Westrem
I am to command 113th Bde. A wonderful rise for me from Captain to
General in under 3 months I wonder if I shall be able to retain my command
I can but try.[126]

20.11.15

Locon

Went into GHQ taking Evill who is off to Cadet School to see about starting our Divisional School.[127] Saw Henry & had tea with him & got back in time dinner. Orders came in for me to go home.

Sunday 21.11.15

10 Upper Cheyne Row

Went over to St Omer and saw Sir John French who 'remembered the talks we used to have', and was very kind. Lunch with Sweeny, Bailey, General Lowther & Pageter.[128] Then to Boulogne crossed over with General Douglas Haig & Tavish. Got home for dinner.

Monday 22.11.15

10 Upper Cheyne Row

Go to see about getting some clothes to be a General in!

Wednesday 24.11.15

George Hotel, Winchester

Go to Winchester by 4.50pm train saw General Graham from whom I am to take over & Captain Bently, Bde Major.[129] It is very strange arriving as a Brigadier. I find I have an early start tomorrow. Hotel very full & Winchester making all it can out of the war.

25.11.15

Winchester

Breakfast at Winnall Down Camp, ride out with brigade for a route march. Have dinner and return, the Divisional General (Philipps) comes round.[130] Get back about 8.30pm to the Hotel.

26.11.15

Winchester

Practice review for the Queen at Crawley Down, the weather is cold but bright.

Saturday 27.11.15

49 Parchment St, Winchester

Went to see some bombers at work, get back in time for tea.

Sunday 28.11.15

Winchester

Walked up to office got home for lunch. Went to Rifle Brigade depot & saw Colour Sergeant Jones & to see the Addingtons, then to tea with the Beatty's & to cathedral for service.

29.11.15

Winchester

Bad weather. Inspected by the queen, this went off very well. Brigadiers were presented to the Queen. Drove back with Eileen & Audrey (who had come down) in Fords car. Then up to Camp again & home about 8.15pm.

Wednesday 1.12.15

City of Chester

Rode down to Southampton, a horrid day men get very wet. Sail at 5pm, the steward on board looks after us very well.

2.12.15

Havre

Disembark at 8am. Bently & I walk to camp, then Gus Mayne fetches us & we go to have hair cut. Then to lunch with Gus at the Club, Charles & TC were there. Then we go round the battalions. The 15th were delayed by bad weather. Colonel Burton & Major Evans of the rest camp very kind to us.

3.12.15

on train

Start in pouring rain about 5.30am having got up at 3.30am. Train starts at 8.25am. & we go through Rouen & Abbeyville.

4.12.15

Chateau Clarques near Therouanne

Arrive at 4am to be met by Campbell, go out to my new Bde HQ but return to arrange buses for 2 small parties. Have long Conference. Lunch with Henry & others. Rode to see 14th & 13th Bn's.

Sunday 5.12.15

Claques

Visited billets of 13, 14, 15 & 16 Bn's, going round battalions takes a long time. Dinner with Charles Deedes in OB mess, saw Stoppy.

6.12.15

Went to divisional HQ in morning, visited 15th Bn in afternoon. Jordan arrives with my horses.

9.12.15

Very wet all day culminating in a storm at night. Rode in morning to see 15th Bn. Corps Commander came to my HQ about 2.30pm.[131] After lunch Bently & I walked to see Machine Gun's shooting & our bombing parties. Also tea with 13th Bn.

10.12.15
Watched 14th Bn doing wood fighting in afternoon, not so much rain today.

11.12.15
Engineering class assembled. A lot of rain today. Mills. Edwards, & Howell
(RE) came to lunch. Rode over to 15th Bn in afternoon. Wilson & Guthrie
came to tea.

Sunday 12.12.15
Stoppy took me in to St Omer to lunch with him. Had a chat with Henry he
is resigning, I approve.[132]

14.12.15
                                                              Claques
Watched training, Bently gave a lecture to 14th RWF. Dined in St Omer with
General Macdonagh & Kyrke, Cox & Farmer Davies. Howlett there saw
Charles Deedes & Henry Cavendish with him.

16.12.15
About at 6.45am, breakfast Guards division go to trenches with Smith GSO 3,
& see 13, 14, & 15th Bn's attached to Guards. Trenches in very good order. Tea
with 46th Division.

17.12.15
Usual rounds, Farmer Davies to tea, lecture 14th Bn.

18.12.15
Had a gas demonstration, which was very interesting. Rode over to see 15th
Bn in afternoon.

20.12.15
                              Les Lauriers on Hazebruck to Merville Rd
Marched at 7.30am to new area North West of Merville.

21.12.15
                                                          Les Lauriers
Rained most of the day. Rode about looking for the training ground &
making arrangements for starting a bombing school & rifle range. Lectured
13th RWF.

22.12.15
Rode round billets in morning & called on XI Corps. Gave lecture in evening
to 16th Bn.

23.12.15

Rode in forest in morning looking at training. Went to look at 16th Bn in afternoon.

25.12.15

Church at 16th Bn rained. Walked in wood with Bently after tea. Quite good Xmas dinner.

28.12.15

Went to see some evening work, Hodson & Campbell's brother to tea.

29.12.15

Watched training. Lt Hardwick[133] & Naphtali to lunch. Bombing Officer to tea. Went out after & saw Flower[134] & Lamontry.

30.12.15

Les Lauriers

Got my rifle range going. Training continues.

NOTES

1 Deputy Director of Medical Services.

2 Henry refers to Major General Henry H. Wilson as 'MGGS'; 'Uncle' is the nickname of Brigadier General George Montague Harper 'BGGS' (O a). Both men were at GHQ, BEF at this time.

3 Lieutenant Colonel Edward Northey (1868–1953). 1st Bn KRRC, later GOC 15th Inf. Bde, wounded in the Second Battle of Ypres. Later fought in East Africa Campaign. Retired Major General Sir E. Northey.

4 Captain Frank Geoffrey Willan. 1st KRRC, awarded DSO 1915, temporary Brigadier General 1917.

5 Lieutenant A.L. Bonham Carter and Major Geoffrey Charles Shakerley DSO, both 1st KRRC, and Major Ernest Alfred Shakerley, Duke of Cornwall's Light Infantry.

6 Captain Arthur Percivale Evans, 1 KRRC.

7 The 2nd KRRC counter-attacked at 10 p.m. on 1 January but failed to dislodge the Germans. *See Military Operations 1915 France and Belgium* (HMSO), Vol. 1, pp. 29–30.

8 Lieutenant General Sir Henry Seymour Rawlinson, GOC IV Corps (1864–1925).

9 Lieutenant General Archibald 'Old Archie' James Murray CIGS, GHQ, BEF (1860–1945). Was replaced by Sir William Robertson as CIGS.

10 20th Bde was part of 7th Div.; 23rd and 24th Bde of 8th Div., both IV Corps, First Army BEF.

11 Captain (later Major General Sir) Hereward Wake DSO, CB, CMG, 1st KRRC (1876–1963).

12 Major (later Lieutenant Colonel) Bernard John Majendie, 4th KRRC.

13 Brigadier General Lionel Arthur Montague Stopford (1860–1942). GOC 80th Bde, 27th Div. Went sick 9 January 1915. Commandant of RMC Sandhurst 1916–19 where he had been commandant between 1911–14.

14 Captain (later Lieutenant Colonel) Wilfred Wykeham Jelf RHA (1880–1933). Played cricket for Leicestershire 1911.

15 Brigadier General (later Major General) Hon. Sir Cecil Edward Bingham, 1st Cavalry Div.
    (1861–1934).

16 Major General Henry de Beauvoir de Lisle, 1st Cavalry Div. (1864–1955); Major General the
    Hon. Julian Hedworth George Byng, 3rd Cavalry Div. (1862–1935); Major General Hubert
    de la Poer Gough, 2nd Cavalry Div. (1870–1963).

17 Major Arthur Blair (1869–1947). KOSB, DAA & QMG 27th Div. Later BGGS V Corps.

18 Lieutenant Colonel Webb Gillman (1870–1933). Appointed GSO 1, 13th Div., 11 January
    1915. Later Brigadier General, Gallipoli, Major General Sir Webb Gillman, British Salonika
    Force 17 Div. and Chief of Staff Mesopotamia; General Baron Victor D'Urbal, GOC French
    Eighth Army (1858–1943).

19 Major Francis Lyon DSO, RFA, GSO 2; Major Charles John Cecil Grant, Coldstream
    Guards, GSO 2; Major Alexander George Stuart, Royal Scots (serving with 40th Pathans)
    GSO 2.

20 Captain Edward Louis Spears. He was the liaison officer between Sir John French and
    General Lanrezac, GOC French Fifth Army. He was later a major general and published
    several books about his experiences during the First World War; General Louis Ernest
    Maud'huys, later Governor of Metz 19918 (1857–1921); Major Christopher Birdwood
    Thomson RE (1875–1930). GSO 2 at War Office 1914. He was Sir John French's chief
    interpreter with General Joffre. Later Baron Thomson Secretary of State for Air 1924. Killed
    in R101 crash, October 1930.

21 Brigadier General David Graham Muschet Campbell, GOC 6 Cavalry Bde, 3rd Cavalry
    Div.

22 Captain Henry Boyd Rockfort, 21st (Empress of India's) Lancers.

23 Brigadier General Richard 'Goppy Chops' Lucas Mullens, GOC 2nd Cavalry Bde,
    1st Cavalry Div.

24 Brigadier General Hon. Sir Charles 'Tit Willow' John Sackville-West (1870–1962). KRRC,
    GOC 21st Bde, 7th Div. He was wounded twice during the war and served on the Supreme
    War Council 1919.

25 Major Robert Harvey Kearsley, Brigade Major. BGGS VI Corps 21 July 1917.

26 Brigadier General Bernard Francis Drake RHA, BGA 1st Cavalry Div.

27 Lieutenant Colonel George de Symons Barrow, GSO 1, 1st Cavalry Div. (1864–1959).

28 Brigadier General Charles Bulkeley-Johnson (1867–11 April 1917), GOC 8th Cavalry Bde,
    killed while carrying out a personal reconnaissance of the enemy near Monchy-le-Preux;
    Brigadier General Charles James Biggs (1865–1941), GOC 1st Cavalry Bde 1914–15, GOC
    3rd Cavalry Div. May 1915, Major General 28th Div., Salonika and later GOC XVI Corps.

29 Lieutenant Colonel James Bruce Jardine DSO (1870–1955). GOC 5th Lancers, 1st Cavalry
    Div. Later Brigadier General 97th Bde, 32nd Div.

30 Major (later Brigadier General) Charles John Cecil Grant DSO, Coldstream Guards, GSO
    2, was at the War Office 1914 (1877–1950); Frederick Edwin Smith (1872–1930). GCS I, PC,
    KC, 1st Earl of Birkenhead (1919). In 1914, on the outbreak of the war, he was in charge of
    censorship. In 1914–15 he was also a major on the staff of Indian Corps,

31 Lord Edmund Bernard Talbot DSO, MVO, MP (1855–1947). Former Lieutenant Colonel
    11th Hussars. Later Lord Lieutenant of Ireland 1921–22.

32 Major Lord Dudley Churchill Tweedmouth MVO, DSO (1874–1935). Royal Horse Guards.
    Lord in waiting to George V and Edward VII.

33 'TC' refers to Major General Thompson Capper, GOC 7th Div.

34 General Horace Lockwood Smith Dorrien (1858–1930). GOC Second Army, did not have a
    good relationship with Sir John French GOC, BEF and was relieved of his command 6 May
    1915 for lack of trust in chain of command.

35 Lieutenant Colonel Frederick William Lawrence Hart Cavendish (1877–1931). 9th Lancers,
    Staff 3rd Cavalry Div., later attached to French GHQ, Hon. Brigadier General; Lieutenant

Colonel William Albany Featherstonehaugh (Indian Army), later Brigadier General 8th Indian Cavalry (1868–1947).

36 Lieutenant Colonel P. Howell (1862–1930). 4th Hussars, 1st Cavalry Div. Later Lieutenant General XXI Corps.

37 Major General Edward Stanislaus Bulfin, GOC 28th Div.; Lieutenant Colonel Edward Douglas Loch, GSO 1 28th Div. (1873–1942).

38 Brigadier General Francis Alexander Fortesque, Temporary GOC 1st Inf. Bde.

39 Lady Ada Edwina Stewart Lewin was the daughter of Field Marshal Earl Roberts of Kandahar, she married Major (later Brigadier General) F.A.A. Lewin. Their only son, Frederick Roberts Alexander Lewin, was killed in action, Norway, May 1940.

40 Major (later Brigadier General) Philip Howell (1877–1916). GOC 4th Queen's Own Hussars. Killed in action as BGGS II Corps, Authille, France.

41 Brigadier General Alister Grant Dallas (1866–1931). BGGS IV Corps. Brigadier General 32nd Bde and Major General 53rd (Welsh) Div. Egypt and Palestine; Lieutenant Colonel William Forbes Lumsden RGA, later served in Mesopotamia Campaign.

42 Brigadier General John Vaughan DSO (1871–1956). GOC 3rd Cavalry Bde. DSO 1915.

43 Captain (later Major General) Charles Parker Deedes DSO (1879–1969). He served as a GSO at GHQ, BEF at this time.

44 Brigadier General Sir Philip Walhouse Chetwode Bt (1869–1950). GOC 5th Cavalry Bde 1915, later Commander XX Corps Palestine. He became C in C India and was promoted to field marshall 1933.

45 SMS *Blucher* was sunk during a naval battle near Dogger Bank, North Sea 24 January 1915.

46 Lieutenant General Sir William 'Wully' Robert Robertson (1860–1933).

47 Brigadier General Edward Maxwell Perceval (1861–1955). He became Deputy GIGS at GHQ, 26 January 1915. Later Major General GOC 49th (West Riding) Div. on the Somme and the Third Battle of Ypres.

48 Lieutenant Colonel Charles Herbert Rankin CMG, DSO, 7th Hussars.

49 Brigadier General Archibald John Chapman CB, GOC 85th Inf. Bde, 28th Div.

50 Lieutenant Colonel C. Evans appointed GSO 1, 3rd Div.

51 Lieutenant General Sir George Montague Harper (1865–1922). 17th Inf. Bde and later that year GOC 51st Highland Div. After the war he had various postings before being was killed in a car crash.

52 Captain Raymond Sheffield Hamilton Grace, 13th Hussars, Brigade Major 2nd Cavalry Bde. Killed in a motor accident, 4 August 1915.

53 Brigadier General Sir John Gough VC was Chief of Staff to General Douglas Haig. He had been selected to command a division and was visiting his old 2nd Bn RB at Fauquissart when he was mortally wounded by a sniper. His brother was General Hubert Gough. He was the son of a VC and the nephew of a VC.

54 Captain Charles Vernon Leslie Poe KRRC. Killed in action, 2 March 1915 aged 34 years. Commemorated Menin Gate, Ypres, France; Lieutenant Hon. William Alfred Morton Eden KRRC. Killed in action, aged 22 years. Commemorated Menin Gate, Ypres, France; Lieutenant Colonel Humphrey Francis William Bircham, GOC 4th Bn. Killed in action commanding 2nd KRRC on the Somme, 23 July 1916 aged 41 years.

55 Brigadier General Julian Hasler, GOC 11th Bde, 4th Div. Killed by a shell, 26 April 1915 aged 46 years. Buried White House Cemetery, St Jean-les-Ypres, France.

56 Major General Francis John Davies (1864–1948). GOC 8th Div. Military Secretary 1916–19.

57 The Battle of Neuve Chapelle opened 10 March 1915.

58 46th Div. was the first territorial division to serve on the Western Front and was made up of units from the North Midlands.

59 Brigadier General Charles Tyrell Shipley RF, GOC 139th Bde, 46th Div.

60 Captain Francis Henry Dansey, DAA & QMG North Midland Div.

61 Major (later General) Charles Harington Harington (1870–1940). GSO 2, III Corps.

62 Nottingham & Derby Brigades.

63 Major General Hon. Edward James Montague Stuart-Wortley (1857–1934). GOC
46th (North Midland) Div. Incurred Haig's dislike by writing to King George V (with
permission from Sir John French). Disagreed with his corps commander, General Richard
Haking, over the attack on the Hohenzollern Redoubt during the Battle of Loos. Was
controversially sacked for the failure of his attack on Gommecourt, 1 July 1916.

64 Brigadier General Edward 'Inky Bill' 'Pipe Clay Willy' Charles Ingoville Williams CB, DSO,
GOC 16th Bde, 6th Div. Later Major General GOC 34th Div. Killed near Mametz Wood,
22 July 1916; Major General John Emerson Wharton Headlam DSO (1864–1946), was CRA
Second Army. He was wounded four times during the war and was promoted to major general.

65 Lieutenant Colonel Gerald Hamilton Martin KRRC, AA & QMG 4th Div. 1916.

66 Lieutenant Colonel Aylmer Richard Sancton Martin. GOC 1st Bn King's Own Lancaster
Regt, 12th Bde, 4th Div. Killed, 9 May 1915.

67 Arthur Foley Winnington-Ingram (1858–1946). He was Bishop of London 1901–39. He
wholeheartedly supported the First World War effort and visited troops on the Western
Front and Salonica.

68 Major Richard Neville Abadie DSO, KRRC, Brigade Major, 137th Bde, 46th (North
Midland) Div. Killed commanding 2nd KRRC at the Battle of Nieuport, 10 July 1917 aged
35 years.

69 Brigadier General Edward Feetham. GOC 137th Inf. Bde, 46th Div. Appointed Major
General 39th Div. August 1917. Killed, 29 March 1918 aged 57 years. Buried Picquighy
Cemetery, Somme, France.

70 Major General R.C.B. Haking (1862–1945). GOC 1st Div., later XI Corps Commander
4 September 1915.

71 George Nathaniel Curzon (later Lord Curzon of Kedleston) (1859–1925). Viceroy and
Governor of India (1899–1905), and Secretary of State for Foreign Affairs (1919–1924).
On 12 April [1915?] he dined at GHQ and sat next to Sir Douglas Haig. *See* Sheffield and
Borne, *Douglas Haig, War Diaries and Letters 1914–1918* (London, 2005), p. 115; Lieutenant
Colonel Brinsley Fitzgerald (1859–1931), Sir John French's private secretary. Somerset
Yeomanry, served in South African War as ADC to General French.

72 Lieutenant Colonel Geoffrey Davenport Goodman VD. GOC 1/6th the Sherwood
Foresters (Nottingham & Derbyshire Regt). Later GOC 56th and 21st Inf. Bdes; Lieutenant
Colonel Charles Wilfred Birkin TD (1865–1932). GOC 1/7th the Sherwood Foresters.

73 Lieutenant (later Major) Colonel Charles Cameron Leveson Gower (1866–1951). GOC
3rd North Midland Bde, RFA 1915. Retired Indian Army.

74 Trench Mortars.

75 Lieutenant Colonel Charles Herbert Jones, GOC 1/5 Leicester TF; Lieutenant Colonel J.W.
Jessop, 1/4 Lincolnshire Regt; Lieutenant Colonel T.E. Sandall, TD 1/5 Lincs.

76 Hill 60 was recaptured by the Germans on 5 May 1915 as a result of repeated gas attacks –
see Military Operations, Vol. 1 (1915), pp. 166–70.

77 Lieutenant H.E.F. Wyncoll, Sherwood Foresters.

78 Brigadier General William Thomas Furse DSO, RA (1865–1953). BGGS II Corps, later Major
General 9th (Scottish) Div. at Delville Wood. Master General Ordnance 1916–19. Oversaw the
introduction of the Lewis Gun; The Right Reverend Michael Bolton Furse KCMG, DD was
Bishop of Pretoria 1909–1920 (1870–1955). Both were educated at Eton College.

79 Colonel (later Major General) Charles Clarkson Martin Maynard, staff officer and involved
with expeditions to Murmanks.

80 Lieutenant Colonel John Hall Knight, 1/5th North Staffordshire Regt. Killed in action
during the final attacks at the Battle of Loos, 13 October 1915 aged 50 years. His battalion
was practically destroyed. Commemorated Loos Memorial, France.

81 Captain Cyril Benson Johnson, Adjutant 6th Bn (Sherwood Foresters), Notts & Derby Regt. Wounded by shrapnel on the attack at Gommecourt by 46th Div., 1 July 1917. Returned to the battalion October 1916 and in March 1917 became lieutenant colonel, the following month he was MID. Killed by shell fire near Hill 70, Loos, 21 September 1917. Buried Sailley-Labourse Communal Cemetery Extension, Pas de Calais, France.

82 Lieutenant Colonel R. Richmond Rayner; Major (later Lieutenant Colonel) William Burnett, 1/5 South Staffs, awarded DSO (LG 3 June 1916). Died of his wounds, 3 July 1916 aged 36 years. Buried Warlincourt Halte British Cemetery, Salty, France.

83 Lieutenant Colonel Albermarle Cator Annesley DSO (1874–1916). 8th Royal Fusiliers. He was trying to invent a machine to dry men's socks. Died of his wounds, 7 July 1916. Buried III.B.1 Warloy-Baillon Communal Cemetery Extension, Somme, France.

84 Captain Herbert Selwyn Scorer. Killed during the final attacks at the Battle of Loos, 13 October 1915 aged 29 years. Commemorated Loos Memorial, France.

85 Brigadier General Herbert Montgomery Campbell (1861–1937). CRA 46th Div. Wounded three times during the war.

86 Brigadier General Henry Frederick Hugh Clifford DSO. GOC 149th Bde, 50th Div. He was the second son of Hon. Sir Henry Clifford VC. Killed by a sniper at High Wood, the Somme, 11 September 1916 aged 49 years. Buried Albert Communal Cemetery Extension.

87 Brigadier General Edward Feetham (1863–1918). GOC 137th Bde, 46th (North Midland) Div. Later Major General GOC 39th Div. Killed by shrapnel while walking down the main street of Demuin, 29 March 1918 aged 57 years. Buried Picquign Cemetery, France.

88 Lieutenant Colonel Reginald Burge Shipley, 9th (Queen Victoria Rifles) Royal Fusiliers.

89 Captain Walter Tyrwhitt Bromfield, Adjutant 5th Leicester Regt.

90 Lieutenant (later Major General) Sir Thomas 'Snowball' 'Slush' D'oyly Snow (1858–1940). GOC 4th Div. 1914, then 27th Div. 1915. A VII Corps Commander, he was educated at Eton College.

91 Lieutenant Colonel (later Brigadier General) Charles Gosling. Killed in action, 12 April 1917 aged 48 years. Buried Hervin Farm British Cemetery, St Laurent-Blangy, France; Major (later Hon. Brigadier General) Gwyn Venables Hordern (1870–1945), 3 KRRC.

92 Lieutenant General Sir William Pulteney (1861–1941). III Corps Commander from 1914 to early 1918. Educated Eton College.

93 Major General Henry Newport Charles Heath. GOC 48th (South Midland) Div. He relinquished command of the division due to illness. Died, 27 July 1915 aged 54 years. Buried Brookwood Cemetery, Surrey, UK.

94 Millicent Levenson Gower, Duchess of Sutherland (née Lady Fanny St Clair-Erskine) (1867–1955). She was awarded the Croix de Guerre for her work with the Red Cross during the First World War.

95 Captain Henry Newton DSO. 5th Notts & Derby Regt 1912–15. This territorial officer was the director of an electrical engineering company in Derby before the war. From 1915–17 he was Officer Commanding Eleventh Army RE Workshops, Hazebrouck. From 1917–19 he was Chief of Design, Mechanical Transport Department. He designed various fuses and the Newton Trench Mortar, as well as bombs, grenades and the Newton Pippin Rifle. He was a member of the Trench Warfare Committee and Deputy Controller Trench Warfare Department.

96 Lieutenant Colonel J. W. Allen, 4 King's Regt, was in Sirhind Bde, Lahore Div.

97 Brigadier General Ernest Makins (1869–1959).

98 Brigadier General Anthony Holbeche Short BGRA, II Corps.

99 Major General Sir Walter Fullerton Ludovic Lindsay, GOC 50th Div.

100 Brigadier General Henry George Sandilands, BGRA 3rd Div.

101 Brigadier General Francis Lyon, BGGS V Corps 14 July 1915.

102 Lieutenant Colonel Thomas Roe Christopher Hudson, GSO 1, 17th (Northern) Div.

103 Lieutenant (later Field Marshal) General Edmund Henry Hindman Allenby (1861–1936). GOC V Corps. Left the Western Front and became a very successful GOC Egyptian Expeditionary Force. He later became Viscount Allenby of Megiddo.

104 Major General Victor Arthur Couper RB (1859–1938), GOC 14th (Light) Div.; Lieutenant Colonel Hubert Isacke (1872–1943), GSO 1. He was mentioned six times in despatches.

105 The Battle of Hooge opens, VI Corps, Second Army.

106 Major Hugh Bateman Prothero-Smith (1879–1961). Reserve of Officer 21st Lancers. Appointed APM 15 January 1915. Formerly Chief Constable of Cornwall 1909. He took part in charge at the Battle of Omdurman.

107 Brigadier General Charles Gosling KRRC, GOC 7th Bde, 3rd Div. Killed while in Command of 4th Bde, 12 April 1917 aged 48 years. Buried Hervin Farm British Cemetery, St Laurent-Blangy, France.

108 Lieutenant (later Major) M.L. Buller MC.

109 Brigadier General Geoffrey Chicheley Kemp, GOC 138th Bde, 46th Div.

110 Major General James Aylmer Lowthorpe Haldane (1862–1950). GOC 3rd Div., later VI Corps Commander 8 August 1916 to end of the war.

111 Lieutenant Colonel Robert Richmond Raymer, GOC 1/5th South Staffs.

112 Lieutenant Colonel Charles Edensor Heathcote, 1/4th Lincolnshire.

113 Major General Sir Thompson Capper KCMG, CB, DSO (1863–1915). GOC 7th Div. Killed by a sniper while reconnoitring the front line during the Battle of Loos, 27 September 1915. Buried Lilliers Communal Cemetery, France; Major General George Handcock Thesiger CB, CMG (1868–1915). GOC 9th (Scottish) Div. Killed by German shellfire at Fosse 8 during the Battle of Loos, 27 September 1915. Commemorated Loos Memorial, France.

114 17th (Northern) Div. CRA was Brigadier General Herbert Kendall Jackson DSO at this time.

115 Major General Arthur Edward Aveline Holland CB, DSO, MVO (1862–1927). GOC 1st Div. He was later I Corps Commander, 19 February 1917. His CRE at this time was Lieutenant Colonel Claude Russell Brown.

116 This was the German counter attack to try to recover Loos and the Lone Tree position.

117 The 46th Div. attacked in an attempt to recapture the Hohenzollern Redoubt. The Official history records that the division lost 180 officers and 3,583 other ranks; *see Military operations, France and Belgian 1915*, Vol. 2, pp. 378–88.

118 Lieutenant Colonel Charles Herbert Jones, GOC 1/5th Leicestershire Regt, 138th Bde, 46th (North Midland) Div.

119 The 28th Div. was ordered to Egypt on 19 October 1915. It was then moved to Salonika and disembarked there 4 January 1916. Price-Davies refers to his brother Captain H.A.L. Price-Davies who was nominally 1st (Garrison) King's Liverpool Regt but was attached 1/6 Middlesex Regt, 95th Inf. Bde.

120 Brigadier General John Humphrey Davidson MGGS, GHQ, BEF.

121 Lieutenant Colonel Robert Frederick Ratcliff MP (1867–1943). Burton Div., Staffs 1900–18. GOC 1/6th North Staffordshire.

122 Lieutenant General Richard Cyril Byrne Haking.

123 Lieutenant Colonel G.A. Armytage, GOC 1st KRRC; Captain E.G.H. Armytage, 8th (S) Bn KRRC.

124 Major General Charles Howard Foulkes RE (1875–1969). He was appointed 'Gas Advisor' 1915 and was Director of Gas Services 1917. By 1918 he was President Chemical Warfare Committee. In the 1908 Olympics he won a bronze medal for hockey.

125 Major Christopher D'Arcy Bloomfield Saltern Baker Carr RB (1878–1949). Commandant of the Machine Gun School at Wisques near St Omer. Lieutenant Colonel Tank Corps 1917, brigadier general 1918–19.

126 113th Inf. Bde, 38th (Welsh) Div.

127 Major (later Lieutenant Colonel acting Brigadier General) Charles Ariel Evill,
    1st Monmouthshire Regt, Pioneers 46th Div.

128 Brigadier General Sir Henry Cecil Lowther MP (1869–1940). Scots Guards. Military
    secretary at GHQ.

129 Captain H.R. Bently, Cheshire Regt.

130 Major General Sir Ivor Philipps MP, DSO (1861–1940). GOC 38th (Welsh) Div.

131 Lieutenant General R.C.B. Haking.

132 In December Sir John French was superseded by Sir Douglas Haig as Commander of the
    British Force in France as Wilson was seen by him as a malevolent intriguer he had no wish
    to employ him. There was a suggestion that he take over as the new CIGS but this post
    went to Sir William Robertson as the Prime Minister Herbert Asquith did not like him
    either. Wilson was eventually given command of IV Corps on 22 December but his time
    with that did not last very long.

133 Second Lieutenant H.W. Hardwick, 13th Bn. Relinquished commission due to ill health,
    13 October 1916; Second Lieutenant Joseph Sydney Napthtali, 13th RWF. Was later MID.

134 Lieutenant Colonel Oswald Swift Flower, GOC 13th RWF.

Three

1916

The brigade he now commands was made up of all Royal Welch Fusilier battalions, which have to learn how to adapt to the conditions of trench warfare. Once again he finds himself in Haking's Corps, a commander who believes in taking the initiative and dominating no-man's-land. The earlier part of the year was taking up with improving the fighting spirit of the New Army division. Constant inspections of forward areas of the trenches and the keeping of the defence lines in good order become part of almost every day of his duty in the spring of 1916.

By mid-June the division moves south to the training areas where they made preparations for what was to be the largest assault on Germans defences on the Somme. Although the opening of the battle was not the great success expected, there was progress in the southern part of the attack which would lead to the Battle for Mametz Wood. The Welsh Division makes two attacks on this wood; the first on 7 July was not a success and leads to the replacement of General Philipps as its commander. The division attacks again on 10 July and they take two days to capture the wood, but at enormous cost in casualties. Brigadier General Price-Davies VC was at the very heart of this second successful attack and his correspondence reflects very much the part he and his troops played in the battle, and the appalling costs.

After the battle, the division moved north and settled back to life once again in the trenches, now under new corps and divisional commander. Price-Davies' brigade also has to absorb new officers and men, and much of his time is taken up in the rebuilding process. By the autumn, they are north of Ypres on the Canal Line where they will spend the winter.

5.1.16

Les Lauriers

Move to Cense du Roux near La Contuse with Campbell to stay with 56th B January de.[1] Go round trenches, never saw such a bad spot, the right nothing but a series of islands.

6.1.16

Cense du Raux

Went round left sector with Major Butterworth (RE) started about noon, then met Flower & walked with him.[2]

7.1.16

My other 2 Bn's & Bde HQ arrive. Go round trenches from 1.45pm to 10.30pm, first with Carden & then with Flower & afterwards joined by Bently & Humphreys.[3]

Friday 14.1.16

Vielle Chapelle

Busy all day going round to see what work has been done, fairly well pleased as a whole. Dinner with McKenzie Stuart & his staff. After we move to our new Bde HQ. Nice little white house by the bridge.

Ride round new billets & inspect 13th RWF. Dine with Bently at 19th Div HQ I see in paper I am a Brevet Lt Colonel.[4]

18.1.16

Tactical exercises under General Bridges then go to see Butterworth & then out to see 13th RWF.[5]

19.1.16

Go round 16th with Carden then to 14th RWF. Day (S.M.O.) & Bell to dinner.[6] All the bombing officers & Colonel Pryce & Major Rees came to tea, a great crowd (14th).[7]

Saturday 22.1.16

Round the trenches with General Jeffrey's[8] saw Long[9] & Burners.[10] Home to lunch General Philipps,[11] Bridges & Marden came in afternoon.[12]

27.1.16

Out with Roberts, got shelled at Carden's HQ. Some German shelling but we gave it them back heavily, remained in trenches all day getting back at 9pm. Kaiser's birthday.

28.1.16

Visited transport in morning met David Davies 2.30pm & walked with him & then met Hodgeson round trenches.[13] Then out with Kirkwood (R.E.Corps) & D. Davies.

29.1.16

Cense du Raux

Round trenches with Anderson, Col Pryce, Col Arthurson & Kirkwood & Lamonby. Out with Pryce at 6.45am to look at communication trench.

1.2.16

Out at 5.30am with Redfern, Humphrey's & Colonel Flower.[14] Clear day got sniped coming back. Round trenches with Carden in afternoon & evening & into 13th RWF line too.

5.2.16

Up at 5am go round with Redfern & Marden & Crawshay come in after breakfast. I go round trenches with Marden & get back for tea.[15]

7.2.16

Ici du Passe

Out early with Miriel. Feel tired get about 4–5 hours sleep these days. Rees & Lamonby to lunch & go round in afternoon we are nearly caught by a shell. Out at night with Philips the Machine Gun Officer of 13th RWF.[16]

8.2.16

Vielle Chapelle

Get a shell close to my HQ meant for the artillery. In office all morning, walking round from 2–7pm. Dine with Marden & Crawshay & staff get back about 11pm.

10.2.16

Round 14th RWF in morning Colonels Bell & Davies to lunch T Rees, Cotterill (14th)[17] R.G. Rees (15th)[18] Tanner (16th)[19] to tea. Major Rees (GSO.2) Capts Evans & Howells (15th)[20] & Owens Secretary Welsh A.C. Committee[21] to dinner, Oysters from Bapaume!

2.2.16

Labussient

Inspect 13th Bn, in by 1pm. off to stay with Henry get there in time for dinner, Bridges & Ma Johnson there for dinner.

Sunday 13.2.16

Vielle Chapelle

Spend day with Henry & visit some schools of instruction, lecture at 1st Division at Lille, very good.

14.2.16

Start at 6am & go over to 99th Bde on canal near Goure & look at Givenchy trenches, General Kellett takes me round.[22] Lunch with Colonel Barker RF, saw George Armitage, Vernon & Ferrand.[23]

16.2.16

near Grovre

Go with Major Belgrave 2nd Div to some French exercise near Abbeville, a vile day gale blowing. French XXIst Corps General de Maltre also met Colonel de Vallieres, General Hygnet's successor at GHQ, Wavell,[24] & Tom Holland. General Petre who commanded the French II Army in Campagne fighting summed up at Conference. Got to 99th Bde, Vernon also there & he took me round the trenches.

19.2.16

Out with Major Richards (1 Bn) Ox & Bucks to 3pm. Sir R. Haking comes to tea & Fred Beaumont Nesbitt.[25] Then at 7pm I have to go out with Carden to see some saps & places where some large minenwerfer has fallen. Dine with Carden, bed 3am, rifles grenades flying about.

22.2.16

Up at 3.30am & into trenches with Hodgeson, nearly get hit by sniper. I met the Divisional General and with him till I go to Conference at 10am. Snow.

24.2.16

Up at 2am & go to trenches with Hodgeson. Conference at 10am Taffy arrives & go round trenches with him & Pringle.[26]

25.2.16

Up at 4am to trenches with Hayes, back to breakfast.[27] Taffy goes off in the Kings car. Bently & I go round the trenches in evening, more snow.

2.3.16

near Gorre

Can you send me some bull's eyes everyone seems to get sweets so I think I ought to get some to pay back I am getting on alright getting things going a bit better I think I was disappointed going round last night I can't get things done but everyone suffers the same.

3.3.16

Went out with David Davies, then to a conference & after that to the trenches again with Marden & Crawshay. We gave the Germans a good doing with our trench mortars today & also with howitzers. Rain tonight I was amused yesterday one of the officers was so excited because he had seen 3 Bosche I thought at first he had shot them!

3.3.16

near Gorre

After tea I go to see 19th Bde, General Robertson.[28]

4.3.16

Such vile weather I got up at 5 & had breakfast & was surprised to see it was snowing after raining all night. I found much damage to the trenches & a fearful lot of water had collected, in fact the trenches are worst than they were the last time we had snow. We have struggled all day with the water it is all rather distressing. I got in about 3pm & went out again at 6.30pm returning at 9pm after a walk with Bell. It was fine then but very slushy & inclined to freeze. Our transport was very clean at a recent inspection I had been very hard at them, so that is satisfactory. Did I tell you about the bantams? There was a mine the Germans fired. There was some excitement & a bantam was seen wearing his gas helmet with the eyepiece at the back of his head. Further on more bantams were found firing from a support trench. They were asked what they were doing & said they were firing high to help the artillery.

7.3.16

I think we loosed a mine off last night & so I had to be up in the trenches by 10pm & went round after it was over & got back at 3am I was very weary the last mile home. I hear there is great optimism at home over the Balkans & Russia etc, one of those phases we go through but we must knock the Germans before we have time for jubilation. News from Verdun seems good. Carden continues to be hard working, cheery & neat as usual. David Davies always full of wonderful ideas. Will you get Bairnsfeathers pictures & keep them they are so good.[29]

8.3.16

We have had much difficulty to contend in the way of weather. Such a lot of water in some of the trenches I think the men have worked well I might have organised better but I was short of RE. Flower goes on some urgent private affairs, some legal business I believe. Brown Clayton has been in, he commands a battalion of bantams![30]

Last night we were talking of war, Muriel, Marden & Pringle. Muriel spoke with much feeling, these French people are much more serious about it than we are. He says if ever they get to Germany they will destroy everything. He spoke feelingly of their losses & with enthusiasm of the 'splendid men' at the depots, his face quite lighting up. He was not very optimistic he thought the Germans would fight to the bitter end. Marden said it would go on for 18 months only Pringle was cheerful he gave it till November.

I must tell you a funny story I came back one night & they all said, 'Did you see the Zeppelin, what Zeppelin, oh didn't you see it, we thought you would know all about it'. Then they described how they had seen a Zeppelin brought down in the wind & the guns were shelling it, all were positive. However no other brigade reported it & next thing another Zeppelin was seen. It was a flight of birds.[31]

11.3.16

Miriel says Portugal has declared War on Germany rather vice versa I thought we were already at War! I am annoyed at Division they ordered me to send 800 men for work 6 miles off, I told them it was essential that the arrangements should be good & that it was no good hurrying into the thing. Well they were bad arrangements & the material did not arrive till late & I was angry, now they find they can only use half the number. When this Verdun thing is over I expect leave will reopen.

12.3.16
Bently & I rode over this afternoon to see the Bde we take over from, the Brigade Major is a noodle I think & maddening knows very little about what is going on. General Philipps came in & talked about the working parties. He said he was sorry about it but didn't think the RE were to blame. I felt inclined to say it was his own staff that muddled it but I just said that I know these muddles occur if one does not take the time to make the arrangements & that was why I had suggested a reduction in numbers. He then owned up that they had hoped everything was alright & that the Corps were anxious to get the work done. I hope the shot went home but Colonel Pryce is very unsatisfactory as he only grunts & shows no sign of shame, sorrow or sympathy. He is a clever but a queer man. However, they are all very helpful as a rule & it is a pity they don't realise their limitations. Anyway I think I frightened them a little as they have cancelled tomorrow's party.

14.3.16
The Divisional commander took me in his car to a conference today, he really is a very nice man & has good manners. The Bde band is now playing for my benefit I sometimes am suspicious whether they all play the same tune, perhaps they have not sufficient copies to go round! I am to see old Munro I wonder will he be changed much.

15.3.16
I saw old Munro yesterday, he met Div Staffs & Brigadiers etc.[32] He could not have been nicer & we had great talks. He looks very well & very young but he is very unsteady on his feet, especially going down stairs! He was in great form. I had dinner with Colonel Rudkin my new gunner.[33] He gave me a good dinner & we had some business to transact. He had a lovely gramophone, which played all through dinner.

See 15th RWF on march, go with Atkinson to support trenches, start at 4.30pm & got back at 11pm.[34]

Thursday 16.3.16
near Soisne

Go to Soisne with Atkinson & gunners, lunch at 115th Bde & Redfern & I go round posts & have teas with Mills[35] near Festubert & met D Davies & Lamonby & go round some proposed work. General Evans & Hinton relief about 9.45pm.[36] Feeling tired, but the spring weather is enervating.

19.3.16

The night before last I got up & went with Pryce & had a good look round I was fairly satisfied with the work, which was good in parts. We got in & had breakfast & was off again & had a long round, missed my lunch but had a good tea with 13th RWF & got in about 6pm. Get up at 2am this morning I went with David Davies & found his men working well but what I complain about is the lack of intelligent control. Haking commands Corps & Munro commands Army.

23.3.16

Yesterday Campbell & I were doing our posts & we took a short cut of a few hundred yards to save a long detour.[37] Campbell got caught up by an overhead wire & in his struggles to get disentangled he strained a muscle in his stomach or chest. He had a good deal of pain & is now in hospital I am afraid he will be away sometime. With Bently on leave & the head clerk & another clerk just back after being sick (sounds nasty) we have great struggles to keep things going. Redfern is excellent & I have got a good man in Davies who has been a secretary to an MP so he has a head on him. Colonel Flower is back & looking better, he is rather a trying man I find, he is very nice but never responds at all to any pleasantries, too solemn for me. The night before last I dined with the 13th RWF & fell into a hole where there was a jump on the way back not much damage but breeches torn.

24.3.16

Yesterday I went round some posts with a sapper & Humphrey's from 10am to 5pm when I got back to see the Corps commander. He did not come in till late, he was very cheery & had a chat. I went to bed at 10 & got up at 1 & went round with Carden I had no nails in my boots & everything was slimy & I kept falling. Carden laughed at me & about 4am it began to snow & the ground got quite white. I had a conference at 10am for my day's work I had to wait for the morning report to see what had been going on. Things run quite smoothly in spite of both staff officers being away & chief clerk. After my conference it was snowing & weather thick & I went to places it would have risky to go to on a bright day & had a great time till I got into a trench with a dead dog! On my way back with Davies we came across a whole lot of Germans. Bare skulls & nothing but bones inside their clothes!

26.3.16

A tragedy has occurred Davies (the man I had in Bentley's place) Carden, Rudkin & I were choosing a place to work on suddenly we were spotted & a few well directed shells came over. Poor Davies was killed I am rather miserable apart from the fact of his death as we left him for a few minutes thinking that movement would draw fire & I feel perhaps I did not do all I could to save him.[38] The Doctor says there was no real chance anyway as he was hit in the groin & the femoral artery was cut.

27.3.16

I believe nothing we could have done could have saved Davies but I feel very guilty in not having tried to staunch the wound. When he fell I thought he was hit in the leg but did not think it was so bad. My first instinct was to go to him & help carry him away but he was in the open, where a shell has just fallen & I thought my presence would bring more fire on him & on us also I never like moving a wounded man without a stretcher until I know what is the matter. It never occurred to me at the time that he might bleed to death so we lay down in a ditch & after a bit Carden went off for stretcher bearers. Then I realised I should have done something & went to Davies to put a dressing on his wound. He had a big hole in his groin & evidently the artery was cut I found great difficulty in putting a bandage on as the wound was so high up the leg that as soon as I tried to tighten the bandage it slipped below the wound. However in any case it was too late I now hear that Davies married shortly before coming out here I must write to Mrs Davies.

27.3.16

near Soisne

After lunch went to Davies funeral, his brother there & came to tea. Had a practice with Bangalore torpedo by night. Then to trenches with Rudkin, ground wet & going very heavy.

28.3.16

Round Le Tournai billets with Flower, then round Festubert & O.B.L. back at 6pm, after dinner we have a practical demonstration with live Bangalore torpedo.

29.3.16

Yesterday I had a tramp round billets with Colonel Flower (13th RWF) & then went to see Colonel Bell (15th RWF) & David Davies MP (14th RWF). The improvement in Bells battalion is very marked. They are much more willing now & don't look at me with suspicion as if I was getting at them. As far as work is concerned Carden's (16th RWF) is the worst they don't organise their work well, and yet they do things so well.

31.3.16

Yesterday I spent time in the trenches & then I came home & after dinner went to see a demonstration with explosives & went with Miriel after & got home at 1.30am. I can see my commanding officers & support troops by day. The weather is right for work, no moon but clear starlit nights. The ground has dried up a lot & I think we are making progress but it is slow. Anyway many things I used to be always at CO's about are now a matter of routine & no one can think of doing them wrong so that is an advance. My bad battalion has quite turned a new leaf & is working well, so I patted them on the back (CO's old enough to be my father very nearly – anyway he looks it). Flower much more friendly today I am afraid he is very seedy at times I am told a lot of his good workers have gone away, so I suppose they staff the best ones for him. Today I had a conference & Flower & I went up to reconnoitre with periscopes, it was a lovely day. Rudkin & his satellites are coming for dinner then I am going out to meet Carden at 2. I have heard nothing of Henry for some time. I fear I may have to take General Marden round my trenches tomorrow at 10am!

3.4.16

Locon

Inspection of transport in morning very good. Lunch with Anderson 11th Corps, then see 13th RWF, Thomas, Barrett, Everingham[39] & Lunt[40] to tea

4.4.16

Rode in morning & Corps Commander inspects 14th & 16th & transport of all 4 battalions. Bell & Bently to dine with Corps commander, Holman,[41] Anderson,[42] Carey,[43] Blackworth & Nesbitt.

6.4.16

Rode with Williams to see 14th & 16th catch a company on the march saw Charles Hickie. Swan, Hodson & Roberts to tea. Nesbitt, Hodson & Tanner to dinner.[44]

Saturday 15.4.16

near Locon

Took General Hornby round trenches.[45] 116th relieve us, get to new HQ by 5pm

16.4.16

Estaires

Go to new trenches north of Neuve Chapelle. Got back for tea rather tired. Have dinner in a little house where the women cook for us. Hutchinson, Australian Transport Coy, cousin of Prialux comes to dinner.

17.4.16

Laventie

Go round trenches with General Twyford at 3pm we relieve 57th Bde & move to Rue du Paradis, Laventie.[46]

25.4.16

54 Elm Park Road, London

Start at 11am & motor to Boulogne with Mainwaring, Thynne & Dadis.[47] Two tyres go on the way. Lunch at restaurant at Mony, lovely gossip met Sir P. Chetwode,[48] Ruthven, Eddie Wortley,[49] Claycroft, Hugo Montgomery & Stockwell.[50]

27.4.16

London

Go to Thompson in morning to get new summer jacket, Mr T introduces me to his son who is now an officer. We dine with John Brough & he take us to 'A Kiss for Tinderella' Gerald Du Maurier.[51]

28.4.16

Johnny arrives about 9pm from Dublin, he looks very worn. He says there have been 200 casualties amongst the troops in Dublin, see Henry after tea.

Tuesday 2.5.16

The Irish question has been settled by prompt action.[52]

8.5.16

Raiding party gets into German trenches about 1.30am & inflicts much loss on the Germans. They unfortunately lose 2 Officers. Osborne Jones[53] & Taggart otherwise the casualties were slight.[54]

10.5.16

Went round some OP's with Pattison, then into trenches. After dinner go out with Freeth round working parties back 12, bed 2am. Raiding party had another try night was bright & still & Germans on alert so they could not go in.

Friday 12.5.16

Laventie

Out with Lloyd George 5am to 8am, with Redfern 12.30pm to 6pm with Miriel 9pm to 11pm.[55]

15.5.16

Went out at 6.45 to site some work. Back at 9 bombarded the Bosche with Artillery, trench mortars & rifle grenades, very successful. Saw an ingenious mining device.

16.5.16

Up at 1.30 & went round line with Hodson a lovely day.[56] Enemy's parapets a good deal damaged by our bombardment. We get bombarded in afternoon but have few casualties & not much damage to parapets. Divisional commander comes in after lunch. Paterson to dinner.

19.5.16

Went round 13th billets, Lunt & Morgan Jones came to lunch.[57] Badham & MG Company arrived. Thomas & Morris came to tea, lectured young officers after dinner.

20.5.16

Our engagement day anniversary <u>10 happy years.</u>

Sunday 21.5.16

Battalions are digging these days making trenches for practising the attack. 130 Field Ambulance to dinner, conference of young officers after.

23.5.16

La Gorgene

Busy day gas demonstration, young officer's course. Inspection of billets by Div Commander. Round line with Badham, dinner in Div. HQ.

25.5.16

Welsby House, Laventie

Go back to the trenches & relieve the 115th Bde General Evans & I went round the trenches. Went to see the battalion commanders in support in evening.

Thursday 1.6.16

Up at 8am office & round Carden's trenches on Dick Bill crater in afternoon, conference at Rudkin's HQ 5.30pm which I just arrive on time. Up at midnight & out with Hodson.

Saturday 3.6.16

Laventie

Up at 4.45am & out to trenches with Bell, Thompson[58] killed last night & W.E. Jones wounded, very sad.[59]

4.6.16

Breakfast at 6.30am then off to trenches & met Gwyther, get back for tea at 4.45pm. Rudkin & Balfour (Commanding 2/5th Gloucester's) came to dinner. Attempted a raid but not a success. Later more of a success than we thought as many as 3 were killed.

7.6.16

A long day up at 5am made plans for digging a new trench & I went up with Miriel to see it. Some men were jumpy & I had to hit them with my stick to make them go on digging! Owing to an officer hurting himself there was a delay & we only got about an hour's work done.

Saturday 10.6.16

Up at 5am & study training pamphlets & General Cosmo Stuart comes over (180 Bde) to go round line at 5pm. Rudkin & Boyd Rookfelt came to dinner.

13.6.16
Breakfast & off with Bell & Carden to training area near St Pol. Saw Generals Gough, Allenby, Bainbridge (25th Div), Birch his GSO,[60] Tim Hollond, George Armitage 74th Bde, Heathcote 7th Bde.[61] Went to see Henry but he was on leave. Excellent concert by 13th RWF.

14.6.16

Raimbert

Go with Evans & Marden to 17th Corps who are taking over the ground behind the labyrinth (part of St Eloi) Got back & see some battalions march in. Have to alter our watches putting them on 1 hour.

Sunday 17.6.16
Visited billets of the 16th RWF, then into conference with the Divisional General, then to see training & back 5pm. Tim Hollond took me over to dinner with Henry. Had a cheery evening & interesting talks. Redfern leaving me on appointment as Staff Capt 114th Bde.

18.6.16
Henry took me to lunch with Uncle very nice chateaux got back 4pm & band played at tea.

20.6.16
Went to 13th RWF billets at 6.30am then to training ground. Great event Henry & Charles Deedes came over they stayed for dinner & we had the band.

23.6.16
Up at 5.30am see training area & back at noon saw Bde billets. Flower, Williams (Ham) & I go to Henry's & concert party also. They are late & most of the party also, but they gave us a concert & sang all dinner.

24.6.16
Brigade exercise goes off pretty well.

Sunday 25.6.16

Bailleuls aux Cornailles

Divisional exercise, we had not very much to do but I was pleased with the way the brigade worked.

26.6.16

Varquenes le Borcq

March at 5am, roads good but we had to make a detour, as one set of non-metalled road was quite impossible. Everyone very wet when we arrive in billets (Good billets) about 1pm. I have very good quarters.

27.6.16

Bernaville

Rode round billets with Williams in the afternoon, hilly country this. Marched at 8.30pm fine night & good going but for the hills. Got in at 1am good billets again.

28.6.16

Bernaville

Were to have marched on but got orders not to move which is a blessing.

30.6.16

Haissant

Dined with Philip Game last night. Reconnaissance with Marden & Evans. Tea 6.45pm join column on the march.

Saturday 1.7.16

Lealvillers

Good news of attacks, lovely day. Several orders & counter orders but everything got off & we finally settle down at 4am.[62]

1.7.16

Such a glorious day. Quite different from the weather we have been having, we had good news of the attack but of course without details & without knowing exactly what the programme is (though they were good to us & explained it all beforehand). It is hard to judge very well I'm told the bombardment was terrific we could hear it all from here.

Yesterday I spent with General Evans & Marden reconnoitring we had a long day. Starting at 8.30am & finally got an omelette & cup of coffee at the village where Douglas Haig is I believe.[63] Then I went & found my brigade on the march, they are pretty hard now, as we have had a lot of training & marching. I didn't like to say much about it before, we have normally marched at night.

2.7.16

We had it pretty warm yesterday & marched at night a little confusion but we all settled in, in the end. All of us at HQ put into a hut & slept on the floor. It's a boiling hot day again. We have got no news now & are wandering what is happening. The French appear to have done very well but one cannot tell. Philipps says that the people who give the most trouble to the staff are his own men.

Just been up to see what there is of the battle it is a very long way away but you can see smoke of bursting shells & the air looks very thick.

Letter to Lieutenant General Sir Henry Hughes Wilson, IV Corps, 1st Army

2.7.16

My dear Henry

It was awfully nice to see so much of you & I am glad you heard my concerts. Carden says his choir are better than Flowers I have never heard them but must do so some time. They have taken Carden to put in cotton wool which is of course alright.

D. Davies has leave till the 11th. The Divisional Commander has backed me strongly & I should think he will not come back to the battalion I suppose Lloyd George thinks the battle will be over by the 11th I expect they didn't like such a source of their party funds going into danger! The fighting must be desperate, there is a terrific amount of shelling going on just now & has been all day. What do you think of things?

I don't think my late division are in very good order I wonder how long their Commander will last but I think they are afraid of him, but heaven knows why they should be.[64]

3.7.16

Treux

In afternoon motor over with Evans & Marden to XV Corps.[65] And on to 54th Bde (Shoubridge) & then over our old front line & German front line & support & walk to Mametz. Everything very quiet on these fronts & we have got the upper hand but not so in the north I feel we are back in our old front line trenches a great disappointment. We got back about 10.30pm to Div. HQ & I saw my people on the march & got to Treux about 3.30am heavy shower before we came.

4.7.16

I met Shoubridge his brigade has done awfully well & he was of course pleased as anything with them.[66] Then I went on & found my people on the march just before getting in at 3.30, the rain came down in torrents & so suddenly we got quite wet before we could get our waterproofs on. I met so many friends yesterday when motoring with the other brigadiers & they did not meet any. I met father Vaughan[67] & Horne[68] who I know slightly.

Such a wet day & rather heavy rain for a short time it came down in torrents & the whole country was swimming. Camps were under water & mud roads were so slippery that the horses could hardly stand. Bell fell & so did Gwyther & we had to walk most of the way home I went off with Chamberlain & Flower & we met Carden & others at a certain HQ & we had look again at the battle. This time we saw Minshull-Ford's brigade.[69] He was very delighted to see us & asked after you. His spirit is fine & he has been very successful.

4.7.16

I had a great day yesterday we motored across the old front line & the Bosche old front line & support then we walked to Mametz. Everything was perfectly quiet & though the Bosche should have been able to overlook everything, there was a great deal of traffic all over the country.

I saw Shoubridge his brigade did splendidly & their tails are up & so are those of other troops near I don't think the Bosche defences from what I saw of them were organised with anything like the thoroughness they must have been at Theipval for instance I think there is something wrong with the method of disseminating information. A few Officers & NCO's from the troops sent to lecture & converse with troops in reserve would be an excellent tonic. Instead they are fed the railhead memories & alarming reports of the medical services who always dwell on the fearful losses & catastrophes which must occur in every battle, rather than the glorious deeds of those who fought well & often successfully. Shoubridge says he does not think there are Bosche within 800x of him now & his people were out wiring in full daylight. Then again to return to the subject, troops that succeeded are quiet ignorant of the task which confronted them. Those that are successful are apt to enquire why if they themselves can get through, others cannot do the same. This leads to ill feeling Shoubridge says some of the Bosche fought very well, but I fancy the Bosche has been turning his attention more to the north than the south. However some of the prisoners had had enough of it as they ran down the hill shouting 'which way have the prisoners gone'.

Great downing those sausages.[70] Philip told me some days ago that between us and the French we have downed 14. I saw Father yesterday in great form we go to his Corps & take over trenches tomorrow I fancy.

Those new handcarts for the Lewis guns are no use. They are fitted for issue to Belgium refugees for their dogs to pull.[71]

5.7.16

dugout near Mametz

Sudden orders to march to take over the line from Ford, do it somehow but have casualties in the night. Didn't get much sleep, fine dugouts we are in.[72]

6.7.16

I had a little sleep last night & I was walking from 4.14am to about 12, then had to see some orders & at 3 I had a wash & shave & lunch & more to do after 1½ hour sleep at 4pm I am living in a beautiful dugout very deep & very safe but of course we are not too comfortable. Arrangements have not gone too well. Partly my fault but partly my staff too but we are getting it straight-ened out now I had Carden at Corps HQ & he looks none the worse for it.[73]

6.7.16

Go out at 4.45am with Smith, Kirkwood & Renton, go round all trenches & rearrange garrisons, back at 12 noon.

?.7.16 [letter undated, but clearly posted after the battle]

I am very well but a little shaky from lack of sleep, food & drink. You will know by this time of our capture of Mametz Wood I think it was a fine piece of work on the 8/9th I was to have carried out an attack on a small scale. It was miscarried owing to a battalion taking too long to reach the starting point.[74] The Divisional Commander has been degummed.[75] I am sorry, as I fear I contributed but the plan I thought a bad one & I was entirely borne out at a conference by the success of the present plan, which was what I advocated. Well I hadn't much sleep that night & then moved to an advanced HQ for our attack which began at 4am but was out most of the night seeing that things were alright I saw Carden for the last time at 4.30am, a fine gallant soldier I feel his loss very much.[76]

At 4.15am I felt fearfully hungry & had a cup of tea & a sandwich. About 7am we were told that we had captured the whole wood & prisoners I went off to see the captured wood. There was a great number of dead Germans & we took some machine guns too. After that it became clear that we had not captured even half of the wood, also things were not going well that's how I got tangled up in it. I thank God I have come through. Well I stayed & tried to do my level best as a commander. I think I inspired them, Harry Williams who blows my horn so violently says the men say I saved the situation!! So nice of them. What I lack is power of organisation & I don't suppose I will ever overcome it & I think I shall put it to our HQ so as to give them the chance of getting rid of me if they want. Well we remained in the fighting in the thickest undergrowth all day. Machine guns bothered us a great deal & snipers. Well tired as we were the Bosche was more tired & kept surrendering but it was a job to get hold of such a great wood with tired men. Well-trained fresh regulars would have found it hard on manoeuvres even!! We had no water up there & I got so dry I had nothing to eat but an officer gave me some jam sandwiches & about 11pm Marden gave me chocolate & biscuits but still no drink accept two tiny sips from a water bottle.

Practically no sleep at night as we were very busy with a number of arrangements, we took two or 3 biggish guns in the wood & a lot of machine guns. Some alterations were made to the dispositions in the morning & General Evans took over command & I came out. Everyone is delighted at the success as ones reputation was at low ebb. It was not only my brigade but Marden was there also. About 4am my servant appeared with coffee & sandwiches I got back about 7 but all my kit is scattered in different places & has to be collected so I cannot wash or shave but I had a good breakfast & feel fine I forgot to say I thought I was wounded I felt a very violent bang in the left corner of my tummy & felt a warm feeling like blood I was sure I was badly hit (it was a piece of shell) that I was done for I thought I ought to be down & be carried out & so looked to see where I should lie down. Then I thought I didn't want to lie down!! My coat was all in shreds at the pocket of my breeches so I was not cut at all only burned I suffered no inconveniences after minute or two. I must sleep only a bit as I must watch my battalions coming in I don't know the numbers of prisoners probably about 200 I am in a Bosche dugout now quite comfy little place & comfy chair. The weather has been fine but there was a fearful wind in the wood.

12.7.16

My staff are so good I came in yesterday they fussed about & got me breakfast as our HQ was being shelled. Did I tell you we took 3 siege guns in our attack our losses are not heavy but we lost Carden & Flower both killed. Flower did most awfully well I never saw a man with so much go he was beaten to the world & actually fainted right off once & fell flat down so many times it made me laugh. The fighting took place on the 10th & 11th I came away as General Evans took over command.[77] It was late in the day when Flower was killed I fancy I forgot I told you I was sent all the way back to the wood yesterday afternoon I was not required as the message had been wrongly addressed I was rather annoyed as it took 2 hours & there was a lot of shelling going on I told you about our prisoners I hear the total for the Division is about 300. Some of them were delighted to be taken. After dinner I went to see another Division I had been working with. They were very pleased with results. When I got back we had to move again I had time for breakfast & a wash & shave & then went off to the station I slept well in the train.

Diary entry dated 13.7.16, on page Friday 7.7.16

It is difficult to write an account of the next few days.

We had several wires along the line. We had orders to undertake several enterprises but in almost all cases the orders were too late to admit to being carried out & troops got tired to no purpose.

On the night of the 8/9th for instance the 14th were to have carried an enterprise but were delayed reaching the place from which they were to start. After this General Philipps was relieved of his command I felt very guilty about it. On the morning of the 11 July at 4.15am we attacked Mametz Wood. The fight went pretty well but the wood was fearfully thick and communication difficult. Hearing we had captured it I went forward about 7am but found we had only reached our first objective. The men were very tired & moral at a low ebb. Subsequently we made a considerable advance, took some more prisoners & machine guns. In the operation the Division took about 300 prisoners, 3 siege guns & several machine guns.[78]

The night was very noisy & men inclined to panic but the enemy made no attack. General Evans took over command of the wood (then General Marden and myself had each commanded a portion).

On the morning of July 11th I left 3 battalions behind however in the afternoon I received orders to go back to the wood & did so only to find I wasn't required there when I arrived. We were supposed to be relieved in the evening of the 11th but Bently & I waited in vain & thinking they had found another way.

Moved to our new HQ at Ribemont on arrival at 6.15am we found we were to entrain at 7.30am we then went to Ailly near Abbeville taking 15th with us but the others did not come along until midnight 12/13th & the 14th RWF put in an appearance on the 13th. One does not get much sleep on these occasions. Since arriving in the forward area the total must be small. Up to the night 8/9th probably about 4½ to 5 hours I had a few fragments of hours during the night at the advanced report centre. 9/10th 1½ hours before dinner, night 10/11th in the wood & hardly any sleep night 11/12th none at all.

13.7.16

The remainder of the Brigade arrived during the night they have had a hard time & look very worn but a bit of sleep will put them right. Perhaps I might give you a little information of the fight. We started from the top of the ridge at 4.14am & got as far as the ride we suffered casualties but not very heavy. We heard that the whole wood had been taken but this was not so I went down to the wood at 7am & remained there all day & night during which time we advanced slowly & took some prisoners I believe they are well pleased with us but I hope we shall do better next time profiting from our experience there is lots to correct. One thing I was pleased about I had thought I was losing my nerve but I found that it is not so but I lack power of inspiration I fear.

13.7.16

Ailly

My host is a great old man. The fine French gentleman of fiction Norman du Rousseu. Battalions will be sleeping today. William & I go round brigade on a bicycle in the afternoon.

15.7.16

Really I think they have moved us about unnecessarily I came along in the car with Marden, Chamberlain & Miriel & I had lunch with Solly-Flood.[79] Tomorrow the new Corps Commander Hunter-Weston inspects us. Tomorrow I hope to see Tavish & Hesseltine I thought the latter might make a Brigade Major or battalion commander[80] I should like to have someone in the regiment with me I shall hope to get Campbell back tomorrow I shall be glad to see him he is a first class man.

16.7.16

Authie

Corps Commander was to have inspected us but he cannot come as the Army commander wished to see him I inspected the 14th & 15th & dismissed the remainder. Some rain in the afternoon, which lays the dust. Good news from the front 19 guns captured which is good.[81] Douglas Haig came in & congratulated me on our success at Mametz. Dined at GHQ with Heseltine, Tavish was there.

17.7.16

The Corps commander inspected us today & spoke to each battalion I think he spoke very well. He was in a frantic hurry & there was trouble at first because he was mounted & the parade was on foot.

17.7.16

St Leger les Authie

Moved to St Leger in the afternoon. Have to send off 780 men to assist miners. A bother as it interferes with training.

18.7.16

The Dell near Courcelles

Fearful rain early, better later. Move to a new Camp a few miles off I go to see 16th RWF at Mailly-Maillet. Jones from 11th Middx comes to command 16th RWF, Hodson to command 14th RWF.

19.7.16

I took Westbrooke out today & up to the trenches it was very hot up there & we felt tired.[82] I had a conference with all my new Co's only one of the old ones left now. I was in the wood how did you guess I was there. No Darling it was not so terrible there at all, I had no food or drink because when I went out in the morning I thought I was only going for an hour or so and somehow it never occurred to anyone to send food till next morning I think my people did better than I thought at first, many gallant actions have come to light I wish I could think my people are marvels I think perhaps I don't advertise them enough but I do hate people who brag on the other hand if you back people up & tell them they are fine fellows they sometimes turn out to be so because they feel they have made a name for themselves.

My new CO Jones (Jacob's Horse) seems a nice man I have had several changes & I hope things will go on all right the new divisional commander is very nice.[83]

My HQ is in the funniest little hole in the ground in a sort of chalk pit. Very tiny & everything jammed together of course we moved yesterday. Price told us to look for German balloons in a certain direction so I was up early & had a look round & spied it I went round to arrange my company's out of view. When I got back I counted 9. This made me suspicious as the Bosche has not more than 2 up for a long time so we went to the gunners & found out they were ours!

Hodson who was Bells 2nd in command goes to the 14th re-David Davies, Campbell is a great wonder.[84]

20.7.16

What I wrote was that Flower was only wounded but he has since died I have not of course been in desperate danger but I have been in a certain amount. Carden was killed on the 10th our casualties have not been very heavy about a 1000 of course we lost some good officers. I think they did very well getting into the wood I went up the trenches with Bell today. My new CO's now are 13th Campbell, 14th Hodson, 15th Bell, 16th Jones.[85]

21.7.16

I was out before breakfast seeing my people doing physical training I then went & watched a practice with our trench mortars. First of all one fellow got lost through inability to read a map & so getting to the wrong windmill, eventually things went right. Then I told them to have dinner & try in the afternoon with live bombs I told them which trench they were to shell but they thought better & chose one close to some telephone lines I had to stop them. Then endless delays because they could not hit it because it was to near them & they tried them further off. In the end they got going but ended by making a violent switch to the right which brought them bang under both sets of lines I had been trying to avoid.

We were further worried because we had been for such large working parties we really cannot find them. The working parties go off & no one meets them & their labour is lost I expect the new divisional commander will keep all more up to the mark than before but it will do us good.

21.7.16

The Dell

Busy with stokes mortars all day no success except that we cut about 30 VIII Corps telephone line!!

22.7.16

Hull came in tonight to see us.[86] He is not far from here, it was awfully nice his coming in, he looks very well but a bit older. Great artillery fire going on all day & still going on now 10pm.

Today I went with Major Campbell to the trenches, he is a white man & we get on well together. Very friendly he is & we had long walks rambling round the trenches, telling a good deal about Flower. He is a fine man & in many ways a wonderful man. We were inconvenienced by corpses, which are unpleasant otherwise it was a very pleasant afternoon.

I don't know what Douglas Haig had heard, he merely said, 'I hear you did great things' or something of that kind.

23.7.16

We go to the trenches tomorrow I was out today looking for ground to work a scheme out when who should turn up but Frank Lym so he took me off in a car for lunch. He told me about the 46th Division attack I am afraid poor Denis Wilson was killed & one or two others I knew.[87]

After lunch I had to go off to see the brigade I take over from. Yes Jones is a regular I like the look of him. No I was not alone when I thought I was hit, there was quiet a crowd. Corps commander appealed to the men's patriotism & he said they must prove their worth & then he would be glad to have them as comrades, meanwhile he said 'Welcome to the Corps'.

Not much news of the fighting, which I don't like. We are to take over the trenches from 36th Bde. General Boyd Moss[88] & Anderson (Late 5th Corps) so I went for a rummage.

25.7.16

My trenches are good in part but part has been knocked about a good deal but we are working away. Evan Williams is next to us in the line so I went to see him whilst there a couple of shells burst outside & 3 men came in & claimed they had been hit in the back but on examination it proved nothing but bruises.

Russian news seems to continue good there the Germans seem to be hard put to it to get reinforcements which is good & will anyway help Russia.

26.7.16

The interview with the divisional commander went off all right. He never asked any difficult questions after all. Then I went back & started out with the commander of my brigade machine gun company & was about the line from 11am & got back at 8.30pm. Somehow my feet fell very tired today. The Germans have been shooting at my trenches a lot & they make holes in them one has to move across for fear of snipers. If only I had my arrangements as good as they were at Givenchy I would give them stuff!! Campbell (my Campbell's brother) commands in Flowers place. A good energetic man I like him. Bently has gone off & feel very sad & lonesome as I have no regular officer on my staff. The new man Capt. Dr Stewart is a new army man, he seems very nice & is probably capable but I am afraid he can't help me much over the training. Bently goes off to man a Divisional school.

27.7.16

I went to see the next brigade & whom should I find but General Pratt, so funny after hearing so much of him from you.[89]

Colonel Flower was not married, he had a mother & two sisters I had a letter from one (Mrs Sanford) they were devoted to him & are broken hearted. I think Major Campbell will do well & his second in command will be a good combination. Bell is always a trouble a fine fighting soldier but things in the trenches do not get done somehow.

27.7.16

Mailly-Mallet

61st Bde is to relieve us & we are off to Ypres.[90] Take acting Brigadier, Colonel Ballock through communication trench in afternoon. Very hot & it gets very close. Got in for tea, then out with Stewart to recon roads on a bicycle.

We had our fight & have come away. It was rather fun at times but the men were tired before they got there. They did so splendidly until they got into the wood. Then we had great difficulty in getting them on as the wood was fearfully thick & they kept on losing direction & cohesion & by that time a good many officers & Co's had been hit, one battalion for instance lost 14 out of 17 officers who went into action.

The old plan of advancing in small parallel lines does not work when you have no one to lead the columns & your men are not trained for such fighting. The only plan seems to be to have regular horde of men so thick they can't lose touch.

28.7.16

The Divisional commander came round my camps & complained of one or two things I am afraid I have got slack. Probably because no one even came near the show before & because I thought I had got things in order but it is the old story & I must get busy again I saw Albert Paine today he looked very well I also saw his bandmaster who was bandmaster of the 2nd Bn when I joined.

Letter to Lieutenant General Sir Henry Wilson [from?] Major George Cecil Westbrooke

28.7.16

We are off North again YPRES Salient Ugh!! The 29th Division go to so I may be near my brother as he commands DAC. I do think it is scandalous we cannot stick to the truth in our communiqués I never know what to believe now & news is so scarce. Why not say we made a gallant attack & failed if it is so? No one knows anything except what the Angres do & that appears quick enough in the papers I hear that my late Corps Commander made a bit of a miscalculation. Has he gone? However he captured 140 prisoners. It has been rather pathetic here we are in one of the sectors where we attacked & failed & the whole place is knocked to pieces & there are copses about & any amount of derelict equipment.

I lunched with Frank Lym the other day a nice chateau they have. Any chance of Rex getting a brigade I have got a new brigade Major a new Army man I doubt I can carry on without a regular to help in training & discipline & what can he about it I feel very sad at going north because I shall lose my interpreter when I go into Belgium. He will be quite 'irreplaceable' & I shall be 'desulte' not sure of the first accent.

DH rode into my HQ a week back & said 'I hear you did great things' I don't know what he had heard but it was very nice of him I am afraid my people are tired not my fault altogether I think as the other brigades are the same.

I have a great fellow I think to command Carden's battalion from Jacobs Horse. Bell is a brother (28 years in Central Indian Horse). He did splendidly in Mametz Wood. His clothes were pierced 4 times by bullets & he was hit pretty hard by a bit of shell.

But in the trenches nothing seems to get done & I am distracted I had a row some time back & told him off & he could have gone for two pence. He asked me if I had confidence in him & I told him tactfully I was perfectly satisfied. It turned out I was right so Eddie Wortley has gone. It would have saved some lives if he had gone long ago.

I like the new Divisional Commander (Blackader). He commands.

Things seem to be going well now don't you think so I wonder what further advance we shall have. If only we had not wasted men on side shows. We have been living in cellars they get a bit damp sometimes & I hate doing office work by candle light by day not that the office work worries me much when we are in the line I do not know what happened to all the songsters but the leader of the choir L/Cpl (now Sergeant) Roberts was not sent into the battle (he is a signaller) & is all right.[91]

29.7.16

My staff is Capt Stewart (I find he was in the Army for 1½ years & was at Sandhurst). Capt Campbell, Staff Captain, Lt Macdonald assistant Staff Capt & as before. The men got bathing today, which they enjoyed.

30.7.16

Russian news excellent, we have received a wire about it. Of course our deeds read small beside the Russian achievements but I think the fighting can't be the same there.

The old principles hold good after all, in the end it is the men that tell the course you must have other things & to a certain extent you can hold a position with machine guns & artillery but it is the men who take the position & what is more the Germans cannot counter attack without men. If only the dearth of reinforcements is accentuated by these Russian successes, as it must be there may come a time when the line will breach under the pressure if only we can keep on pushing, as push he must.

Progress is of course a great gain. It is high ground & the Bosche always fights hard for high ground he has lost. You bet he did not give it up without a great struggle. And we have more troops still. How many more I don't know but still I think a great deal more.

31.7.16

A great trouble arriving in the dark & we found most of the billets full of gunners. It is beautiful & hot like August 1914. Last night we had great relish knocking up the Marie at midnight at least Miriel & Campbell did that as they came on motors & I rode & found them engaged pouring over a large scale map asking the old boy. He was a little shaky sometimes as to whether a house was occupied or not but his little slip of a daughter came to the rescue several times. However he was a nice good-natured old thing & did not appear to mind being rousted out.

Miriel the old blackguard introduced me as 'Le General a peit du bois du Mametz', it did not make much impression. This afternoon Humphries & I rode round the billets some very comfortable quarters but on the whole it is the men who have good accommodation as usual. We seem to press forward gradually the fighting is desperate.

1.8.16

The little office is like an oven & we are sitting in shirtsleeves I was at a conference at Div HQ today, nothing new. They have lovely chateaux like a medieval castle I am told they have mixed bathing in the moat but the drains go into it.

I have been trying hard to find out if the Division is badly thought of or not. Yes I go to the trenches a lot when there are new ones but the other day the man who took over from me how much I knew in 4 days.

2.8.16

I went to a demonstration today, it was rotten but you never saw such a gathering.[92] People from all parts Bungo,[93] called it Ascot, I spoke to General Plumer,[94] Billy Lampton,[95] Mullens[96] who I know as a Cavalry Brigadier, Tim Harrington[97] (very well) Wilding,[98] Shoubridge, Braithwaite RWF (he knew us in Dublin),[99] Boyd (an old friend), P de Radcliffe, Colonels Bartholomew (Berty) Liveney, Fuller, Edmonds (Archimedes),[100] Place. Majors Knowles (Nancy's husband) Wavell, Turner and I dare say one or two others. I had great chats with all I got back to my HQ about 6pm & had tea & then the Div commander came in & I got off again with Stewart & we rode round the battalions as we have moved.

4.8.16

Missed breakfast had coffee & butter & went off with Stewart to see people training & went straight from there to Corps HQ for a conference. The 3 Divisional commanders & 9 Brigadiers were there. A great bag for a bomb. That lasted till 12 & then I went back & worked on a lecture I was giving. Then started out at 3 & went back to the camp to see more of the training. Had tea with 16th & gave lecture to the officers of the 15th & 16th for nearly an hour!! Then back in time for dinner, Tim Harrington paid me a visit. My guard turned out with great éclat, he begged them to turn in but I told him he had to go through with it.

We don't know what the Russians can do, what if their offensive is finished for this year? I don't think it is myself but you see we don't know. Very glad the German helmet arrived alright I was afraid it had been stolen, as it is not a bad one at all. They have round caps too but they seem to stick to the helmet. They have wonderful kit always & everything they have always looks clean & new. I hope to have lunch with Bungo on Sunday.

4.8.16

Proven

Saw 16th training today then to Corps HQ, 3 Divisional commanders, 4th Lampton, 29th & 38th Blackader[101] & 9 brigadiers. Lovre Chateaux is a very pretty place.

5.8.16

Good news capture of the mill at Pozieres I only hope we keep it as I think it is important I do hope we shall be able to keep gradually & kill & capture Bosche. Of course it cannot lead to anything decisive but it keeps them here and helps the Russians.

Sunday 6.8.16

Proven

I have a nice Belgium interpreter, which is a good thing I gave all my men a rest today, which I am sure they enjoyed. Campbell & some others were inoculated & are very sorry for themselves. We are going round the trenches tomorrow so I hope this nice weather will continue.

7.8.16

We had a great day. Up at 6, breakfast then we rode over to the camp & inspected some drafts. To my surprise I found a lot of men with black buttons! They came from a South Wales battalion & seem good men. Plumer commands 2nd Army & Tim is Major General Staff. A lot of men wounded at Mametz are already back with me.

10.8.16

It was piping hot yesterday, out to look at training met Intelligence Officer in village. It was scorching & the steel helmets didn't help matters. However, we stuck to it walking till about 6pm then we got back to the village. All the inoculations are going on all night I am to be done Saturday night. Beatty is in charge of the Divisional school for training Officers & NCO's of course, not such a bad billet but he is not fit for an active job, oh yes he knows it.

11.8.16

Quite a misty morning I got a note saying that the Corps commander was going round camps so I just had to turn round & go back & meet him, He was pleased at first & I was rather mad as we had always prided ourselves in the cleanliness of our billets.

Great news of the Italian victory, the Austrians must be in a bad way 15,000 prisoners is a lot.

I find this training period very tiring, the Corps commander said to me 'you know you brigadiers must go round more than you would in peace time!' I said with emphasis 'I think we do.'

12.8.16

I had a long sleep & was lazy this morning when suddenly I was told a car would pick me up at 10.15am & take me off I knew not what for. It was to see the King, General Evans & I stood in the wood and the King came with the Prince of Wales. He asked me where I had got my VC & said, 'You are in the 60th Rifles are you not?' I got back at 1.45pm & then at 2.15pm a car came & took me to Corps HQ for a conference, the Corps commander is a terrible man for talking.

Sunday 13.8.16

Proven

Not feeling up to much, go to Wormhoult & see the King who shakes my hand & talks to us, also see Clive Wigram & Lord Stamfordham.[102] After lunch go to Corps HQ the usual stuff about sanitation most unreasonable after the complimentary remarks he made when he came round the camp.

14.8.16

The Corps commander is an unreasonable man I was with him yesterday, he said only one battalion in the Corps had good arrangements in his camps & he generalised the remainder as being higgardly & piggardly pigsty's. But only a few days before he had been around mine & complimented me on them I can't understand the man unless he has not recovered from the sun-stroke I believe he had! I got to bed early but had to get up early because the Divisional commander has a new plan for physical training. & I had to round & arrange it. Physical training now all the rage, all the whole brigade in classes.

17.8.16

I can't understand how the Turks can have been so foolish as to attack the Suez Canal at the bidding of the Bosche. The French papers say the total prisoners the Russian have taken since this offensive 350,000, 7,000 Officers & 400 guns, a big total.

Letter to Lieutenant General Sir Henry Wilson

August 17 [1916]

My dear Henry

I am awfully miserable at the way you have been treated & I am afraid the present regime can do little good. A poor return for all the work you did with the Expeditionary Force & the Military Entente I wonder where England would be today if it were not for you.

We have been very worried. We have not been moved since I last wrote but we have had unreasonable straffings from the Corps about training, sanitation etc & the like. The unusual thing only we are expected to make more bricks now & have less straw to make them with. The fever is at such a height that I have to get up at 5.15am everyday & ride up to Camp which is 3½ miles from here & then I have to arrange for breakfast & lunch at a farm to be on the spot. However a change is taking place as all the men are being taken away to dig so that will simplify matters.

We have had a dose of inoculations I was done on Saturday night & was reading the paper in bed on Sunday morning when I was sent for to see the King & in the afternoon I had to attend a Corps Conference. However I felt perfectly fit the next day & had a long day at a little tactical problems I wish I could say something wise at the tactical problems but it is not in me to do so & I am afraid all my instructions rotten & that I work very hard for minimum results. Two days ago my groom was laid up with a bad leg, my servant had gone to have some teeth out, the mess man had gone away because the bombing officer whose servant he is has got tonsillitis. So there I was – but today my servant returned without teeth & things are better. [103]

Saturday 19.8.16
We ride to Brieton & into the trenches to see Wilding & arrange to take over from the 10th Brigade.

20.8.16
I am afraid Henry is done I am very miserable about it I didn't want him to be a big man I know he will take it well as he always does but I feel so angry with those who won't do anything for him.

22.8.16
Yesterday afternoon the Divisional commander held a conference here I think the CRA will be degummed soon it all shades that way.

23.8.16
I went round with the Divisional commander yesterday, if we did all he wants doing it would take a million men, the Corps commander will come round soon no doubt. Then about 3pm Miriel & I went to see the French. We had a long tramp & if I had known it was so far I would have arranged a horse. Their sanitation is not as good as ours. Salonika does not look very encouraging however, that is only a sideshow. We have very good gunners in this Division.

23.8.16

Canal Bank
Up at 4am & out with General Evans to see the junction point between brigades. He is going soon having fallen out with the Corps commander I part with him & come back alone.

24.8.16
I went out with Colonel Jones & a sapper, all my arrangements have been upset, as the supplies seem to do everything but help me! We had to look at

the trenches & I got back at 6am I was out again with the Divisional commander & got back at 1.15pm. One learns a bit going round with him but he
makes me feel ones deficiencies very much. After lunch I had a conference on
the points the Divisional commander had noticed.

26.8.16

I never could work out why the Germans did not get through at Ypres, it's
one of the finest things we have done. I am getting a man called Hull as
Intelligence officer.[104] He is not a gentleman but he is a good fellow.

Henry thinks under the present regime he is lucky to retain his Corps.

27.8.16

It is Sunday today I went out yesterday round the trenches with Bell. I had a conference at 10am, now I am off again. General Evans is off glad to get away.[105] Carlos
Hickie is coming in his place, won't that be lovely I do so want a pal here.[106]

So Rumania has come in that's good I wonder what she can do with
Germany & what will she do when she comes up against the German troops.

29.8.16

Marden is on my right temporarily. I have had no more trouble with Bell I am
afraid the long sojourn in India has not fitted him for such work as this I am
afraid he will have to go. At present his battalion takes up too much of my time.

We have heard rumours of a great naval battle that Ferdinand had abdicated
& that Bulgaria would change sides & Greece would come in. also that the
Russians had had a enormous victory, a pretty good crop for one day.

30.8.16

I got up at 4.15am & went out with Hull my intelligence officer. Such rain the
trenches are awful. Trenches pulling in, dugouts pulling down, water getting in
everywhere. Of course I have waterproof boots now two pairs. We had a good
tramp & I am awfully stiff after it I suppose it's the damp. We got in about 9am
& had breakfast then I over to see Hudson.

31.8.16

It was a fine day after all & everyone worked away digging the place up &
carrying away all the stuff that had fallen down. We did a little reconnaissance
with a periscope then came back at 4.45pm to meet the Co's at 5pm. Carlos
was there, very well I wonder how well he will do as a Brigadier. A new Major
has turned up Major Norman an acquisition I think, he will do for the 15th
RWF if Bell leaves.[107] I lost an officer today who used to be my MG Officer
I felt very sad when I heard it I am afraid it was carelessness on his part the
poor fellow he has paid the penalty.

More pieces of my dugout have fallen but it has iron inside so that the rain can
only get in at the joints. There was a great crash this morning when an ancient
sandbag fell into the stream outside my door. One of my bombing officers who

was wounded has come back, a nice little fellow quiet as a mouse but a regular tiger I am told his language is awful at times. Time in trenches simply flies.

2.9.16

I went out with Miriel yesterday to look at some billets then back for tea & after that with Stewart round trenches. We got delayed with one thing or another & got back at 10.30 I go out with Campbell this morning to look at drainage. Good news from Rumania capturing 15,000 men I think Rumania coming in will have an enormous effect. Surely Austrian is in no shape to with stand this further offensive, anyway we shall see.

4.9.16

I have just written a letter to Div. HQ asking if I could be informed of anything, which has met with approval. We get nothing but fault finding & I am sure a little praise helps us all I don't want him to think I am disrespectful but I told him I think we all need praise & blame to keep us up to the mark, but one without the other is no good I told him too that the feeling from all these letters that I have failed in my duty & I thought the regimental officers & men were working well I wonder what will come of it but I really think it was time someone stuck up for the battalions who always seem to get it I notice a tendency of Div HQ not to blame me or my staff but to blame the poor battalion commanders who have a great deal of work to see too.

5.9.16

Meet Corps & Divisional commanders 5am & go round trenches. The Corps commander most genial.

I had a conference at 10 & then off with Pringle & Norman to have a look at the country & got back to lunch at 1.30pm I am having tea with Campbell & am going round his line at 4.30pm so that's my day. Rained most of the day. Carlos Hickie & I go round trenches after tea, more rain. We have been some time in the trenches 18 days today but I missed a day.

6.9.16

I am wondering how much time the men's health will stand or mine either! I think it can't be sound to give them hardly a nights rest. Now we shall get little rest when not in the trenches. The weather has been bad again, yesterday was vile from 11am onwards it was very wet & I had to put on gumboots I hope my Harrods will hurry up with my boots it is so inconvenient getting all my boots & putties wet. My lamp is now going well what a blessing to have it. Did I tell you about the rat? She apparently has a hole in the corner of my dugout & she makes queer noises I had a look in with my electric light & could see her peeping out.

The divisional commander is to interview me tomorrow I wonder what line he will take, he may be angry I don't know. Things are getting better they have eased off a bit over work in answer to my protest.

7.9.16

I went round my 2 camps yesterday & then in for tea at Div. HQ. Billy was there I like him he is always friendly.[108] He was very nice & I felt on more friendly terms after all. Before I felt as if I was being treated as a little boy. He could not have been nicer. He was upset because I written instead of speaking to him but I told him I did not feel I knew him well enough & also that if he held the opinion that I was not trying I thought writing was better I told him I realised my own deficiencies very keenly. He said he thought me a conscientious & hardworking man. They all say that! So I said then that didn't necessarily mean that I was fitted for command of a brigade. However he said he was perfectly satisfied with me, so now I am happier.

7.9.16

A.30 Camp near Vlamertinge, Camp D

Stewart & I arrive about 6am, breakfast 9.15! I go round 13th Camp in morning & 16th in afternoon.

9.9.16

I rode over to Div. HQ for dinner, it was a lovely evening General Thompson was there too. We talked over South African times, Blackader was at Wynberg with our 2nd battalion but his battalion had left by the time I had joined. We had a great dinner, Pringle went home on urgent private affairs! Chicken, apple tart & some form of poached egg I had white wine, port & excellent brandy! They sent me home in a car (sounds as if I was drunk). No news these days but I take it the Rumanians made dash for the mountains.

10.9.16

I have sent Stewart off to a school of instruction I don't know how he will like it but it will do him good. General Blackader came in looking very hot. Had dinner at 7.25pm & rode up to the line & went round working parties with Carlos. He is very slow going round the trenches but such a nice old thing. I got back at 2am, Harvey of course was waiting very patiently for me with the horses, it was a lovely moonlight night.

I think we have learnt a bit about fighting & the Bosche has to think a bit of how to deal with us as we see from captured documents. Rumania cannot be expected to do things at once. What splendid fighters the Germans are, each evening finds them ready & they attack & attack I expect they long for winter to get a breathing space.

Norman the new RWF Major came to dinner he seems nice & a good type of regular officer quite the old school I am having a little trouble with the staff until the wrench of Stewart's departure is over, nothing serious.

Monday 11.9.16

Camp D

Walker (Gas Officer) & Ross to tea. Dinner with 13th RWF & concert, the old glee singers broken up by the fighting.

Letter to Lieutenant General Henry Wilson

11.9.16

I have just come back from a concert Sgt Roberts was there in great form but his choir has ceased to exist for the time being. He hopes to get another but it is rather sad. The RAMC Corporal with the good tenor voice was there but out of practice. QMS Davies there in good form with several new skits, not so good as his old ones.

We are working here like the deuce we have never worked so hard before. We work even at rest!! I think the last of my old Co's is off soon. The new commander is a topper & is awfully nice to me. Corps Commander!!?

I have to be President of a General Court Martial on the 14th rather a bore. How do you think things are going? We seem to continue on the Somme I expect the Bosche is rather looking forward to the winter. Don't you think. How I wish I had some pals up here. Bungo going was a blow.[109]

12.9.16

I was up early today & saw some physical exercise at 7am, spent a wasteful morning & had a conference at noon. Hudson & Jones stayed for lunch & then I went with Macdonald to the transport lines. Then back for tea but on the way Macdonald's horse, that fat beast I rode at Winchester fell into a ditch instead of jumping it. It was deep & she was almost hidden in it, no harm done. We had two boys in for tea, one a gent, called Griffiths. He was very chatty & a nice boy, other boy spent some time in the ranks & was rather tired of the life – Knight. I have some nice boys on the whole I think.

Tomorrow I go with Pringle to stay at Cassel for a Court Martial, the following day. The only thing that worries me is that Tim Harrington who I think is there somewhere I don't want to upset my plan & yet Tim may feel annoyed at not staying with him. Gwyther is a Major & was to have commanded in David Davies place.[110]

I dined with the 13 RWF & went to the concert, rather too much recitation but I like the music. I suppose Eric Bourdain is still the Prince? A rotten life, what did you do in the Great War Daddy!!!

13.9.16

Great news today but I think there must be something wrong the French captured Bunchavesnes & they say captured 1,200 prisoners I think they must mean a total of 12,000 they had 8,000 before, anyway it's good.

Pringle arrived in the car & came along here for the Court martial. We had dinner & a bottle of champagne I am afraid this trip will cost money but it is such a change. I read up military law until 12, when the paper round the candle caught fire, then I went to sleep. This morning a lovely morning, I looked out on an old cobbled square with a quaint old archway.

We had breakfast at 8.45am then to the court martial, a nasty case, we got away for lunch at 2pm & then out again at 3pm & went on until 6pm. Then we went round to see Tim, he told me some very interesting things, which may be in the papers in a day, or two. Very lucky finding him, he is well & full of optimism.

The view from the hotel is glorious I must bring you here when the war is over.[III] Pringle rather surprised me last night saying my conferences had been so well run! Those of another brigadier had not been which surprised me very much.

14.9.16

Cassell

Court martial all day, saw Tim he showed me plans for tomorrows offensive, very interesting & exciting.

15.9.16

I am writing this in a fearful hubbub, a lot of officers are singing & playing the piano, one boy has a good voice & sang a song or two but of course nothing like my people. We have not yet finished the court martial but I hope so tomorrow. Campbell tells me leave has been reopened but of course generals Thompson & Marden will go before me & probably the Divisional commander will want to go to, so I don't think too much about it. Bell goes back to his old regiment. I saw Tim today, he is a big man, as nice as ever, we went off with him & got the news, it is splendid we have got Flers, Martinpuch & Courcellette. A backslap for the Brigade.

We saw a wire saying we had counted 22 Bosche aeroplanes. It is enormous the success today has been due to a new device. Probably you know all about it but I won't mention it in case you don't. The Bosche may have something to say about it. It is very refreshing that we have at last thought of something. John Brough was with this new device but I was sorry to hear he has been sent home.

Good news but the French attack hangs fine however.

16.9.16

Still doing this wretched court martial. No news of the fighting yet today. We are both dining with Tim tonight & I presume the Army commander. No news sitting in a court martial does not give me much to chat about I think the brigade must be glad to be having a rest from me.

My brigade goes into the trenches tomorrow. We dine at Army HQ with General Plumer, Chichester, Tim & Knowles & Heywood (ADC).

17.9.16

Today we went to the court martial I feel so sorry for the wretched man, he is getting tired of it. As my court does not assemble before 2pm tomorrow we asked Tim for a car. The dear old thing is giving us one & we are running out to Kemmel to see the view but it is raining now so perhaps we won't go.

18.9.16
We never got to Kemmel the weather was hopeless. Tim says the French captured 700 prisoners yesterday. Things go well I think the wearing down process goes on on all fronts. Italy captured 3,000 prisoners in the last few days. A letter from Henry, he went down to see the French offensive & was delighted. Bumper wrote a glorious account to Tim of the attack, which seems to have been fine.

18.9.16
                                                                    Cassell
The Court assembles 2pm & finishes at 7pm. Tonight we shall be in the trenches.

20.9.16
Back to work & so much rain & mud I was up in the line yesterday, today busy with office work & conferences, one with my Co's, one with Div commander & all the Brigadiers & battalion commanders. The car that was bringing Carlos broke down & they sent another for him & the wheel came off that! We did not get away till 5 so I had tea with Rudkin at whose HQ we were. Bell has gone & I have Major Norman in his place, the new RWF man. The hotel bill was moderate, my room only 3F, lunch 2.50F, and dinner 3.50F. No Pringle is not married.

   13th try a raid unsuccessful. Trouble with the divisional commander.

21.9.16
Went out with Colonel Jones & had a good look round at various things, then in at 8.45am for breakfast & the Divisional commander arrived at 10.30am & I went off with him getting back at 1.15pm. Then lunch & interviews with various people & out with Miriel at 3.30pm to see something & then tea with Pringle. My trip cost 120.Fr which was not much as it included champagne & tips.

22.9.16
I know my feelings about the war, Colonel Campbell is very optimistic but losses his optimism on the Turks giving in. But I don't see how they can give in because the Russians want Constantinople, they will fight to the last for that. However, it is a good sign the Germans sending a division over to the east & bringing it back when it got half way & then it got here & got a deuce of a knock.

   Pringle is younger than me I think he was at Staff College after me. Poor old John Brough he was OC tanks but something went wrong & he had to go I am awfully sorry for him poor old thing.[112]

23.9.16

Up at 2.30am & went out with Major Norman round trenches getting back at 6.45am, slept till 8am & got up & had breakfast. Then at 10.30am I had a conference of Co's which lasted till 12.30 & at 12.45 I went off & had lunch with Huw Williams 14th RWF where he is the adjutant now. He is devoted to them & thinks no end of me, and thinks he knows me well, a cut above the others you see. Then I was busy with some parties that were training & made some arrangements with Campbell & Pringle. Then back at 5.30pm to see some scout training Norman I am very lucky to get him.

25.9.16

I believe the Somme pictures are good so you say I am fixed here for the duration of the war unless I get degummed I expect Stewart back about the 10th of course I cannot leave while he is away. My battalion commanders are working awfully well for me & they heave a heavy sigh at each new thing I have asked them to do.

26.9.16

I was over at Hickie's camp yesterday Colonel Campbell was with me & we called in on Pringle on the way back & he came down in his PJ's & a leather waistcoat. I got back to find Campbell & Davies chasing rats!

Up at 7.15am spend morning with trench mortars. Divisional commander came in to see the 13th party & was very pleased.

27.9.16

Great excitement as the news of the capture of Thiepval, Combles & Friedcourt came in. The moral effect of Theipval will be good. Certainly we don't seem to lose what we captured like we did. The weather is grand for us we are all working like beavers here & preparing for winter.

28.9.16

In the trenches yesterday afternoon looking at drains, started at 2.45am back at 7.15am Macdonald fell over once or twice & went in over his long gun boots. The divisional commander has been round he is very genial but has a training ache! Marden also came round this morning & I gave evidence about a man I had found asleep.

Then afternoon with the CRE, 2.30pm to 6.15pm arranging work. Raid at 11.30pm quite a success men determined to get in but unfortunately no I.D. was secured. Glover & Hill did well but Jack missing.

29.9.16

We carried out a raid last night, which was rather pleasing though a little disappointing. They got into the German trenches all right & killed 2 Bosche that we know of & possibly others. They all behaved in the most gallant way & gave me a straightforward account of the proceedings on their return. As bad luck would have it an officer is missing he seems to have gone astray on the return journey & must have been stranded.

I quite understand your feelings about the war & it is just that feeling which prevents England getting excited over the present successes. We want something bigger, some real advance, some wholesale success. I read a communiqué from the RFC (Flying Corps) today, it is wonderful reading & what these fellows have done is marvellous.

I feel so happy my people done well I do hope the Divisional commander is pleased, as it will buck up the men a lot. I have been very lucky about the raid because of course the men all think that the first would have been a success had I been there, which is absurd as the conditions were quite difficult but it is just as well they think so.

1.10.16
Tim & Warner came over for tea, it was nice seeing them, and it does make things so different to see Tim a bit occasionally. Unfortunately Pryce was here but I got a chat with him later. Davies works with Tim now, he seems pretty well but a bit lame. Yes the tanks are well thought of. The young Lloyd George is here still but Gwilym, the late Generals ADC is not here now. I hope you will get a chat with Henry but you know what he is.

4.10.16
Beastly weather this morning, it was misty about 6am when I started out & it cleared later & I thought we were in for clear weather, now it is belting down & looks a real wet day. It is hard work the Somme fighting. We gave the Bosche a trench mortar bombardment yesterday, which astonished him I think in return for what was done to us anyway we had a quiet night last night. It is dark at 6pm & light before 6am I find it a great bore as before it remained light until dinnertime. I am off to see the Corps commander this morning he is presenting medal ribbons. Marden's leave has not been approved yet but I expect there will be no difficulty.

6.10.16
More wind today which is good for drying, but I fear the wind will bring more rain. Yesterday everything dried up wonderfully. Good news from Rumania we get the wireless on the breakfast table.

7.10.16
The evening began firing some very big trench mortar stuff, it is very terrifying & makes a terrible noise & you see it coming & wonder if it will hit you or not. It makes a crater the size of a large part of the drawing room. We had to remain where we were.

9.10.16

I think I am really tired this morning & will take a rest but General Blackader is coming & I hate his going round my line without me I am getting to like him very much, he is awfully nice to me I never saw Taffy it was too bad. When I got to where he had been I found he had left that morning. There was nothing for it but to go & dine at Div. HQ. We had a very good dinner, soup, fish, pheasant & excellent soufflé. White wine, port, & brandy!! I got back at 11.30pm up at 2.30am & out with Major

Mclellan I wanted to see a place at dusk.[113] When I was on the way I heard a very young officer had been killed.

10.10.16

After breakfast with Campbell & I went off to see our transport lines I can never make it out whenever I go round I nearly always find everything in excellent order but when the Divisional commander goes round there is always something wrong. We got back at lunchtime then I presented some medal ribbon to a man & then did some office work. I then took Carpenter RFC out at 3.30pm he is an instructor at 2nd Army school & has come here for a few days to be attached. Stewart is back which is a blessing as he is more thorough than these other people.

11.10.16

I am waiting for the Corps commander he said he would be here at 3pm & it is now 3.45pm, a great nuisance, as I wanted to go out with Jones.

Well done Hereward & Lady H of course. I am sorry to hear of Billy Ragsdale, such a fine little soldier.

Corps commander came at 4.45pm, 1½ hours late, he had a cup of tea & was very interested in our pictures & was very affable, he took me off for a walk & nearly made me late for a show I was going to see.

12.10.16

Canal Bank

Tea at Corps Commanders HQ for conference of Co's. 13th pull off another raid capture one & take a machine gun, very successful.

13.10.16

Another successful raid, aren't we lucky the same battalion & in the same place as before, so they knew the way. We were rather worried about the moon but luckily it was cloudy, we had some wounded but all came back all right. We killed some Bosche & brought back some prisoners & an MG & a lot of odds & ends of papers, rifles, helmets etc. I didn't get much done yesterday, there were various points to settle in connection with the raid & then I went off with Stewart to the trenches. At 4pm I started in a car with Carlos & went to Corps HQ for a conference, when we had tea then the Corps commander addressed us.

001 – The Cloth Hall, Ypres.

002 – Field Marshal Sir John French.

003 – Field Marshal
Sir Douglas Haig.

004 – Field Marshal
Sir Henry Wilson.

005 – The Italian Front.

006 – The Battle of Mametz Wood. (John Christopher)

007 – Major General Price Davies medal collection 1. (The Royal Green Jackets (Rifles) Museum)

008 – Major General Price Davies medal collection 2. (The Royal Green Jackets (Rifles) Museum)

009 – Major General Price Davies medal collection 3. (The Royal Green Jackets (Rifles) Museum)

010 – Damage to Rheims Cathedral.

011 – Dead artillery horses and men on a road. The Battle of the Aisne, 1914.

012 – British Troops in the trenches at the Battle of the Aisne, 1914.

Stockwell is a Brigadier now. We got back at 7.30 pm the men were delighted with themselves after the raid & all gathered round me to tell their stories. Then the mess room was full of people who wanted to hear the news & those who wanted to tell it.

14.10.16

We brought off another raid last night & took 4 prisoners, Norman's brigade this time. I am so thankful that is 3 successes in a fortnight I felt I could not go on leave at a better time I think we do not leave Boulogne till after 2pm.

Letter to Lieutenant General Sir Henry Wilson

14.10.16

I have had great luck lately three successful raids in a fortnight.

Entered under an artillery barrage with stokes in Salient to a flank (900 rounds).

Very successful men went with determination about 6 Bosche killed but unfortunately the identifications was handed to an officer who is missing.

2. By the same battalion at the same place but penetrating to the second trench about 15x behind the first scheme, much the same stokes fired 1080 rounds, captured one machine gun and a prisoner.

3. A preparation of 15 minutes by stokes & 2 inch – fired 1,500 stokes fired during which the raiders moved forward. Artillery chipped in at 0017 & fired 4 minutes before raiders entered – all opposition from the machine guns etc was knocked out.

I wonder if there has been a fight today on the Somme I am anxiously waiting news.[114]

26.10.16

Here I am again in my old dugout, as far as I know the things I wanted done have been tackled well. Tim was here today thinking I was back. We had a glorious passage & I got the account finished for Conan Doyle.[115] Lunch at a restaurant Morney, Boulogne, and Mears joined us there the roads were good & the news splendid.[116]

27.10.16

The rain has done damage but everything is quite hopeful I expect I shall see Carlos today. Blackader is going on leave & Marden is commanding the Division. Stewart is going on leave too, Macdonald has just gone on leave, also the cook Morris, very pleased with the cigarettes.

28.10.16

Settling down a bit now I was so wet yesterday evening that we cancelled part of the programme & I came back with Pringle & Jones in the motor. I saw

Lawford aboard the train, he was a great mounted infantryman, he was one of TC's brigadiers in the early days & now has a Division. [117]

30.10.16

29.10.16

After breakfast I went to see the French & had a chat & got back for lunch. Pringle came & we did some work together & watched a shoot & then I went off for a walk to the trenches & now I feel better but still a bit heady. The stove has been lit but the damper was left in & the whole room is full of smoke & the wind blows in at the door, there is no prospect of the smoke going away.

30.10.16

Last night we brought off another raid, we got 3 prisoners 7 as they showed a relief has taken place opposite us & everyone has been highly delighted. We only had three slight wounds & all went off very well I am thankful it is over.

After breakfast I was doing a bit of work when Marden came in & asked if I was going round with him. He thought I had been told he was coming round, so I put on my gumboots & off we went. It rained most of the time but that suited our purpose I think he was very impressed by the work we are doing, as my fellows were very busy & I was pleased with them. I picked up another Luger like the one we have but Marden asked for it so I did not like to say no. The CRE carried it but put it down at lunchtime & forgot it. [118]

1.11.16

Pringle & I went out together but we didn't get much done as we should have as the Bosche stared shelling. Came back for lunch & then out with Campbell (Capt) round dugouts, kitchens & had the Doctor to tea & we discussed gumboots, trench feet & massage. Then Jones & Norman came about important business & so that's the story of the day.

2.11.16

I went out with Hull at 7 had a good walk round the front line looking at work etc. After breakfast I interviewed two or three people & then had a terribly long conference with Co's & Pringle & Engineer officer & Doctor. We discussed countless subjects & it lasted till 10.30!

3.11.16

I had a long day yesterday 22 hours but felt quite fresh at the end & got a good sleep 7 hours. Good Italian news this morning, the old Austrian must be a bit worried having an odd 5,000 taken from him every now & then probably means having to withdraw at least a division from Transylvania.

5.11.16

Queer weather a gale & bright sunshine just what we want so may it continue it dries the ground up I saw the Divisional commander yesterday I always feel after seeing him everything is bad & that we are not doing any good at all I know it is stupid to do so because he never says anything nasty but he expects so much that it makes me feel my deficiencies. He's coming round my trenches tomorrow. I went out with Colonel Jones & Norman two hard-working fellows, at 5pm we had a nice moonlight & saw what we wanted.

I read in the Times that Russian prisoners enjoy a great deal of liberty so I expect it is not difficult to escape.

6.11.16

Colonel Price did not come till 5pm & then went to his HQ I met the Divisional commander & CRE & went along with them. They did not go to my show places unfortunately but were very pleased with the work.

10.11.16

General Blackader came round for a chat when I was waiting for Pringle. Then we went to see Carlos who was heavily engaged aligning a new French broad path leading to his HQ. Pringle & I left them & we went on to some observation posts to see the country. We got a fine view I ate sandwiches & then got in about 2pm & had a cup of coffee. These nights have lovely moonlight.

Nice letter from Rifleman Smith. You must be careful of the censor when answering I expect about people being wounded I am afraid several from that battalion have been killed. Trout of course, Foogle, Foljambe, Upton all killed. Both Jacksons killed. Heseltine with Haig as ADC.

11.11.16

We had a trench mortar show last night just to give the Bosche some work to do in the winter or he might feel cold I went out about 6pm with Hull my intelligence officer. A nice fellow & a good hand writer but he gets terribly confused sometimes I can't make out what he says. Back at 9pm dinner 9.45pm & I Miriel out to see the trench mortar people before their strafe & got back at 11pm. Up at 6.30am breakfast at 7am then off to line with RE fellow (Barber) returning at 10am & had a conference. Then Heywood came in followed by Carlos & Gaussen, it was nearly 12 when I left & rode over to out transport picking up Miriel & Campbell en route I also saw Marden & had a chat with him & the Divisional commander. Transport lines progress slowly but they are much better.

I don't know what I want for. A box of cigarettes would be a treat & a pair of stockings. As for the mess those puddings you sent last year in bowls were excellent, some almonds & a bottle of sloe gin. If you can get some crystallised apple we should like that. Morris liked those Gold Flake cigarettes & Harvey of course his tobacco, then some writing things. Perhaps if I had 500 Gold Flake it would be nice for me to give to HQ for their dinner. Possible some cheap literature for them too.

12.11.16

Still fine here which is grand & the ground is drying wonderfully. The Army staff are so nice it is always refreshing to see them I see much more of them now than I do of the Corps staff who I hardly ever see at all though they do something besides write. We really have been doing good work lately but I don't suppose anyone will ever tell us so I am not going to tell them. Oysters were good last night & as Davies & Pearson did not take any we had a feast. I saw the Duke of Connaught the other day he is looking well but walks like an old man, which of course he is. Now I shall take a little walk before lunch & go to the trenches afterwards. Bosche very quiet.

13.11.16

Just heard of the capture of Beaumont Hamel & 2.000 prisoners, that is rather good & should make the Bosche careful of how he withdraws troops, I hope it means we get the whole of Beaumont Hamel.

This morning was misty so I went off with some officers & gave a little tactical exercise from 9.30am to 12.30 pm, we were all very interested in the little problems. Then a short conference about Christmas turkeys,

Campbell stayed for dinner & told us of a queer house he lived in Samoa where everyone seemed to sleep in any room they pleased & when you woke up in the morning you probably found the Lady of the house in the next bed. It was all quite proper & not quite what you would imagine because these women apparently wore nothing but a native smock. No undies I suppose & no shoes or stockings.

14.11.16

Last night I went out & had dinner with Hodson & went round the trenches & working parties. Then at 1am my stokes mortar did a good shot, it made a terrific noise & I hope it was a success, anyway it made the Bosche very angry & I had to give him a dose of artillery to quiet him.

The Divisional commander came round my trenches this morning & I really think he is pleased with what I showed him I was glad that he came because the last time he went round was rather depressing. Isn't the Somme news grand quite a haul of prisoners?

Letter to Lieutenant General Sir Henry Wilson

13.11.16

My dear Henry

I am wondering where you are & what you are doing. We have just heard the good news of Beaumont Hamel & the haul of prisoners. We are enjoying the drying weather here I expect with you the wind is very bad I expect I told you of our last raid. That makes 4 successful ones we were lucky last time in obtaining a new identification which gives us much kudos. The Bosche here is very quiet unless you stir him up which we do frequently.

It is a cheerful sign of the times that he does not throw much ammunition about.

Tom Harrington is a blessing here. In part all the Army staff are gents & I am always pleased to see them I am to give some tactical exercises on the lessons of the Somme (only for my brigade). I find it very difficult to do much of the time is just a question of sticking at it & determination & morale.

14.11.16

Just in the middle of a stokes straff. It's making a topping noise. The Bosche were naughty last night so we are giving him a dose. The stokes is rather our speciality & they are firing like mad tonight because I got them two Military Medals.

Jolly good business about Beaumont Hamel.[119]

17.11.16

I am so glad to get my watch back, the other stopped regularly every day. It is so miserably cold, the huts are not warm & there is not enough fuel but we manage to get a little wood from fallen trees. Bed at 11pm up at 3.30am it was bitterly cold but I soon got warm by riding. I had some cocoa at 3pm & when I got back to Campbell's HQ at 5.15am I had some tea. Then we went round the trenches it was a glorious morning. We got back at 7.45am & they gave me a great breakfast omelette & bacon. I saw the Corps commander on my way back he seemed surprised at my getting up so early. After lunch I slept in the chair for 20 minutes, then I went out & watched a football match.

I am handicapped without Stewart & have to do a lot of my own staff work & redo things that have been done. The dinner with the Corps commander went off very well I was there a half hour too soon because the car came too early. There were gunner & sapper generals & administrative generals. All very nice, a man called Carr who is the Duke of Westminster's agent is ADC he seems a nice man. Dunmore was there too. The Corps commander goes into dinner in just the same way as he goes down the trenches – 1,000 miles an hour along the passages.

So glad Henry is home & I hope you see him.

Go to see 13th who are in the line in sight of the Rifle Brigade, very cold still. Very successful raid by 14th Welsh Regiment (Swansea Bn) (Colonel Hayes) 20 prisoners & a MG.

18.11.16

Such a change in the weather this morning it was bitter & there was a little snow & then cold rain. Now it is quite warm & my hut is impressive, no medium I went out this morning & looked at cold men drilling. After lunch I went over to the 14th who are a little way from here & spent the afternoon there & had tea & walked back & got quite lost I am to have a new French interpreter I wonder what he will be like. One of my brigades (Marden's) carried out a very good raid last night & got some 20 prisoners & a machine gun. The men belonged to Colonel Hayes battalion, he is a nice man I crossed with him when I went on leave.

18.11.16

I arrived this morning about 11.30am I know Hasty Andrew a real good sort I have known most of the war, he was GSO 1, 8th Division.[120]

I hope they don't send Henry off I should hate it.

19.11.16

I feel as if I have got to the end of my repertoire as I have taught the brigade all I know & they had got beyond me. A year ago was different all were ignorant & looked to me for instruction & there was so much to get right. A year ago we were content with trying to put our trenches in order but now we have raids & all sorts of tactical things to think of.

The Corps commander is coming to see my battalions & is going round the trenches I have to go to Divisional HQ for a conference tomorrow I went to church today not a very cheerful sermon. Norman & Jones came to dinner. Stewart & I went for a walk this afternoon, very glad to have him back I had to send him off tonight to a working party.

20.11.16

I feel better tonight & we had a conference with the Divisional commander & I let off some steam I didn't get much change out of it but I had my say.

Elias the adjutant of the 15th is getting up a good magazine for Xmas, he is getting good artists & writers at home to do things.[121]

22.11.16

I went over to see the 14th today & had lunch there, on the way back I went to the MG Company, I'm not very pleased with my new commander. He may be a great fighter but he is not a nice man to deal with, he thinks it quite unnecessary to have things clean & tidy. After tea we all went off to a concert, quite good but I miss the old glee singers so.

Stewart, Campbell, Davies & the interpreter & Hull all went off to dinner with the 13th, you never saw such a gathering we had great laughs after dinner.

I have a court martial tomorrow of which I am President & most of my Co's are members.

23.11.16

I inspected camps 9–10.30am, they were very good I thought. Then a long court martial till tea time & even then I was not done as I had proceedings to get into order, as the judge advocate knew nothing of it.

Divisional competitions came off alright, I was not present but the Divisional commander was there & seemed pleased with things. He has no doubt a sort of contempt for the New Army & can't help showing it at times though he says he doesn't of course it has the worse effect on the Officers. Bad business the Britannic[122].

Davies has gone to the MG Corps at Grantham I am sorry to lose him.

23.11.16

Camp D

A very busy time as reserves & yet we don't get much <u>done</u>. Tactical exercises with each battalion. I have a Court Martial. Then there is the scheme to give Brigadiers & Co's a month's leave. Div Commander told me to send someone & no sooner had I done so he said I was to go of course I don't like to disappoint Jones. It was such a pity he did not think it out before he said anything about it. Working parties are very troublesome, some men go out digging 3 nights in a row which is rather hard & I have also to do a bit in the line when we are out.

25.11.16

A very wet day but the wind is getting up now I am glad to say. Off to transport lines with Campbell, my waterproof boots very good but Campbell's feet got wet before we got to the transport lines. Transport was a sea of mud but conditions better than they were. At 12.15pm I walked over to the Divisional School & had lunch with Bently. At 3pm Stewart & I go to the trenches, we had tea & dinner with Carlos & his people I am told they have a caricature of me on the Xmas Magazine.

Sorry you missed Henry.

I wonder what the King said to Henry, or Henry to the King? These damned submarines are bad I think don't you I expect the Navy will find some way out of it. Finch Halton is near here & Stockwell.[123]

27.11.16

I was just off after breakfast when the Divisional commander sent word he was coming over & we went round together. He could not be nicer to me but his manner with the New Army officers is bad & the result is they don't like it & the manner extends to the Co's too & puts their backs up.

Henry seems to have had a good leave.

Fancy I have been a General for over a year. The little mans letter is interesting. Gough seems to be one of your pets & you one of his! Very glad he is nice to you. I don't suppose any change will be made to the government we shall muddle along & provided the submarines don't beat us. We shall cease to have any standing as a nation because anyone who can build submarines can knock us out.

I don't know what will happen to Henry?

28.11.16

Captain Campbell is leaving me, he is going to 19th Division I shall miss him very much he is so reliable. Up early round the trenches, rather disappointed about the work but it will settle down soon I hope. Back at 10.30am, Pringle is off on leave tomorrow, after lunch Stewart & I went for a good walk.

Letter to Major General Price-Davies

28.11.16

Dear General

Thanks very much for your letter I was very glad to hear news of you & your brigade & congrats to you on your successful raid I heard about from some of the 15th I sympathise with you on losing Miriel. I am afraid you are not likely to get as good a man again.

I am having a peaceful time at present training reinforcements for my division I am going north today I am afraid you must have been having a very unpleasant time of it with all the bad weather there has been of late.

I was very glad to hear that Morgan had got the Military Cross I'm sure he thoroughly earned it I should hardly recognise the line now I expect I suppose 'Fargate' is finished long ago & the dugout in the front line.

There are a lot of things I should like to ask about but fear of the censor prevents me. You will be soon coming out into Corps reserve I suppose. In asking of Morgan's MC reminds me that there are other officers here who have never been a hundred miles of the front who have received the same decorations, it seems a pity.

R.C. Bell[124]

30.11.16

I am delighted to hear your news about Henry, he will get a decoration. I have been out all day, this morning I went round with Norman & Colonel Llewelyn who is attached to me for instruction. It was much warmer but one gets chilly when you start pottering in the trenches. Things are getting on pretty well, back for lunch & conference with the gunner, a nice man & capable but not Pringle.

2.12.16

Went out with Humphrey's at 6.45am, got back at 11.30am. Had to go off with Marden to Divisional HQ, we picked up Carlos & Halton, the latter looks very tired. We had lunch at HQ & we all went off to Corps. The Corps commander had a conference mostly the old things washed up again I saw Stockwell, Freen Wilkinson & Godfrey Gillson. We had tea at Divisional HQ on the way back & I got in at 7pm a wasted day. At 9pm Hull & I went to see some men at work & back at 12 midnight I was going to have a cup of cocoa when the Bosche began to bombard.

Saturday 2.12.16

Bosche raided us & unluckily Roberts (16th) taken prisoner as he was going round the line otherwise not much of a raid.[125] Went with the CRE to arrange working parties Hull & I go out after dinner to see the working parties.

3.12.16

Went round the lines to see the damage of last night's bombardment & settled some work I wanted done. Back at 11.15am & rush off to conference, lunched at Divisional HQ & then got permission to come straight back to see about the work & brought the CRE with me.

We had a great dinner turkey with sausage & chestnuts, after Hull & I went round the line to see the work I am pleased with the work done & we got in at 1am. It is milder however & I fear a change. Harrods never sent my boots, awkward without them I am tired tonight & have a sore heel & got a medical orderly to dress it. Finch Hatten is a brigadier I hear.[126] Messing at Divisional HQ is 16F a day! Could you give me a pair of thick socks for wearing with the ski-boot's.

4.12.16

2 lovely cakes & Swiss rolls & also sausages (an extravagance) Hallwick is running the mess quiet well but I think the cost will rise I had a good sleep last night. This morning the Army commander came along at 10am I had a conference with Co's at 11am. After lunch at 2.15pm Stewart & I started out & went round trenches getting back at 5pm. Tattler arrived thank you Baby.

At last I see Lloyd George is moving which is good I hope he gets Squiff out of course, Balfour might go.[127] The Times leading articles are very strong just now. I have a letter from Lord Erskine, Flowers brother-in-law to try to get Flower a DSO for which he was recommended but of course it is impossible. From all accounts this brigade does more work than others I wonder will we ever get credit for it.

5.12.16

Go to meet the Divisional commander who was 1½ hour late. He had had some boots & the boot maker had made him pay before delivery & then they were too tight & he can't wear them & struggling made him late.

Finished with the divisional commander at 12.30pm, afternoon at work with Paterson, the gunner to look at his new dugouts & at 5.20pm off again to look at the working parties & got in for dinner at 9.30pm not a bad day I think!

General Blackader is badly off for staff now, Pryce sick with trench fever, Smith (GSO 2) away on a course & now he has lost one of his Q staff who goes to India.

6.12.16

Office work all day I took Anthony* out & round the trenches for 2 hours in the pm I have arranged for the battery commanders to come to stay here in turns, the first arrived tonight I had some chats over old times he came out with the 1st Division originally. Woods is still a captain! I was out with 2 sappers & an infantry officer this morning I have a good deal to arrange these days but the results have been good I am taking Woods out so as to make the most of his knowledge of the country I wonder when the Corps commander will come round I am sure he will come soon he has not been for a long time. The prisoners got lost in the fog & our new men rounded them up.

7.12.16

Breakfast & out with Woods (Gunner) for a walk, back for lunch, went & saw Carlos he has a temperature & has gone to hospital. Tea time another gunner arrived Marsden by name he & I have been chatting a bit, but Anthony took him off my hands, he is not as good as Campbell.

Queer of Tavish, Henry will put him in his place now I expect I think Bill Furse will do the job well.[128]

Marsden the gunner is a cheery soul, he was one of the first 'incurables' the Bosche exchange & is now quite well again & commanding a battery. Patterson came to lunch & talk afterwards. After tea a Co's conference, the chief clerk gone sick with a temperature, Stewart has a cold too I think the paper is very distressing today except for Lloyd George becoming PM as I suppose he does I think that is very good.

9.12.16

You seem low over politics but I thought it was clear that Lloyd George must be PM anyway it's all settled now. Glad Henry told Tavish what he thought of him.

Flowers people could only have got his DSO if he had been awarded one, all that are recommended don't get it.

10.12.16

Breakfast & went off with Norman, Hudson & Anthony. The Polish chauffeur had no breakfast & had not filled up with petrol, so we had to go to Divisional HQ & on the way there we had a puncture. We had a bad driver. Eventually at 11am we reached the end of the journey it was discovered that the steering gear had broken, so we had a lucky escape. We had a good walk round some training ground.

11.12.16

The gunner visits have been quite a success socially as they like coming here it is a great change for them. Unfortunately I have been too busy to look after

---

* Captain David Brynmor Anthony MC & Bar, Italian Soldier Medal for Valour, Capt RWF served with 38th Division in Calais. Was a fluent French speaker and schoolmaster by profession.

them, tonight we had Captain Pryce, Colonel Pryce's brother I know him from South Africa.

Very good Henry is cheerful I don't feel very cheerful myself. Where is Barber off? Macdonald was assistant staff captain. The bill is for the steel helmet. (£1.1s op W Cater & Co, 56 Pall Mall, London SW1, dated 5th May 16. Cap helmet & Accoutrements Manufacturers.)

13.12.16

Stewart & I went round the trenches this afternoon there was a little shelling on our way back. We found a shell had hit the trench boards just where we had passed over a short time before.

I forgot if I told you of how Carlos brother went to present a VC to a man near Waterford. Everyone was there & all was ready but the man had got drunk on the way & the decoration had to be given to his sister. Carlos said his brother spoke his mind over Ireland but it did not get in the papers, as there were only nationalist reporters. He told them Irelands time was coming when they would have something else to think of other than horse racing. He also said America's time would come.

I think Lloyd George should do well anyway he has a handy sized Cabinet. Can't make out why Henry does not start. Balfour remaining but I suppose there was some difficult about it. Yes I wonder what will be done in Ireland I hope they will settle that question.

13.12.16

Poperinghe

General Oldham 117th Brigade relieved us & I slept in his dugout, then we had some soup & got off with Stewart in a car getting to Poperinghe after 11pm.[129]

14.12.16

Your box has arrived full of lovely things for Christmas I feel all muggy in the head & deaf!! I am better tonight & all the parcels have bucked me up no end. What does Henry think of the German peace proposals?

16.12.16

Isn't the Verdun news magnificent a good answer to the peace proposals? Today I went out with Stewart to watch training I rode one of Colonel Campbell's, a nice little beast & a regular old-fashioned groom.

I hear the Divisional commander has flu, there seems to be a lot of it about. The chief clerk has not come back yet, which is a loss. Hull & the intelligence officer have gone on leave now, lucky fellows who go & get away for Christmas.

17.12.16

I took about 1 to 1½ hours to get to Corps HQ. The funny thing is we got to within 3 miles of the place when we ran into fog I think I was only at the conference because General Blackader is not well enough yet, Smith (GSO 2) & General Thompson were with me.

Sunday today I am better now but so deaf in my left ear I must get syringed I went to a service today of the Church Mission. We had to say a prayer after I forget it but it was to the effect that we must do our duty because of our dead pals & that we hate with all the hatred we can these deeds which brought about their deaths. Church is a blessing.

The conference was interesting but lasted a long time I thought the Corps commander looking old & rather subdued I got back at 8.30pm so my dinner party was in full swing. Then we had the gramophone.

General Watt is a very nice man it was under his orders that we attacked Mametz Wood.[130] He was one of Tommy's brigadiers I don't think it is time to talk of peace yet, Germany must feel victorious after the Rumanian business & we surely can cause her a lot of harm next year, as we shall be in a position to start earlier than last. The easy captures we made in the last fight in the Somme (Ward told me his battalion 250 strong captured 700 Bosches & had to be reinforced by 2 more battalions to be able to deal with the prisoner's). This French bad news at Verdun are significant. We were not doing that a year ago, which shows I think that Germany is pretty well stretched, I dare say I may be a while before Germany is absolutely crushed to her knees but I am sure this is not the time to stop. Also we want to see what a strong Government can do for us.

Sunday 17.12.16

Bolligcele

Parson came to lunch. I went with General Thompson & Freeth to Corps HQ for conference. General Jeudwine & Cuthbert & others were there.[131]

18.12.16

I have been much better today but tonight my nose has started again & I have a little neuralgia nothing much I am going to have my ear syringed tomorrow. I was out with Stewart this morning a glorious day. Then Tim came & we had a chat, they seem to think a lot of this brigade. He laughed like anything when I told him of the letter I wrote when I asked about going home he seemed to think that was great joke. He seemed very well he was discussing my prospects with me I never thought I had any chance to get much higher than I have the right to expect.

Carlos is back. Lucky Henry didn't hurt himself? Would you like to be in a hospital like Lady Diana Manners?[132]

19.12.16

We were inspected today by Sir Douglas Haig, it all went off very well, it was rather a cold day so I let all the men run about & get warm.[133] If the C in C had been ½ hour before time he would have found a queer sight men running in all directions & some very busy against the hedge as it was so cold. Then they all fell in & had not a long wait & all the signals & words of command went like clockwork. DH inspected us & then the men all filed past him, he was very pleased & congratulated me on the improvement in the brigade & the Corps commander was delighted too, so all was well. DH was very affable it appears that Tavish does not go with Henry now?

20.12.16

Just back from Divisional HQ I spent time on the training ground I rode my little horse, he is very well, Harvey says the vet saved him. The Divisional commander came out, he appears to be alright & was in good form I got in at 3.30pm & at 5.15pm a car took me to Divisional HQ & I had about 1½ hours discussion with him, which was interesting.

22.12.16

I don't see why we should not break through the Germans but so much depends on the Russians. We ought to put up a better show than the Somme. The great thing which cheer me are that the Germans put their hands up more regularly & in large numbers than they used to & that Lloyd George means to end the war I feel much more hopeful than I did a month ago.

23.12.16

After lunch Stewart & I went out at 3pm just before we went out the Divisional commander came along. He had been to the training ground & found nothing having read the programme wrong. I went off & saw the 13th & 15th. Colonel Campbell has just come back. After that I had tea with the 16th & gave a lecture. Imagine my dismay when at tea I found I had left my lecture behind. However I set out to write a few notes & it went off without a hitch. Rather absurd having to give the lecture 3 times but otherwise the officers would have to come some way to hear it, as the battalions are so scattered.

25.12.16

We had a little dinner last night with Baron de Vinck, the Belgium interpreter from Divisional HQ, a funny little man but plucky. He has a Military Cross, Medaille Militaire & a Belgium decoration. Pratt Barham one of the Generals ADC's came also. He plays the piano & gave us some tunes. Then we had Elias in & Captain Elias ADC 15th RWF. He is a journalist of some standing in the Daily Chronicle, he married Marchmair's daughter he is very talented & plays the piano beautifully.

In the afternoon I went for a good walk with Colonel Campbell, he is full of London Club gossip. He says there is a strong feeling in some circles that Henry ought to be Chief of Staff but of course he would not take it under the present circumstances nor is there the slightest chance of the present C in C accepting him.

We are having a football match against Divisional HQ & I am playing. Our Divisional magazine has not come through yet I believe it is on sale at the

Bookstalls I hear there are three sketches of me in it!! I hope I shall see Henry before he goes off.

26.12.16

I shall come on the 30th my leave is through I am stiff after the football, however it is good form, we were beat 6 to 2. The Divisional HQ had some good fellows. Today we had a route march. The Divisional commander saw us & seemed pleased. Got in at lunchtime having started at 8.30am then after lunch Hudson & Edwards (15th RWF) went in the car to see the 38th Division play rugby against the Kiwi's, we had a very good team with several internationals & we beat them easily but it was a good match to watch.

After that I had tea with Hudson & lectured his battalion at 6pm for half an hour. Pretty good I hardly looked at my notes at all, then I walked back here in the rain. Tomorrow we have a climax in training I hope it will go alright. The men have been very well behaved & have had great beanos. The 15th put up the most wonderful decorations.
Hope I see Henry I want a chat with him.

27.12.16

Weary tonight neuralgia all day on the right side of my knee. The Divisional commander chugged past in his motor car to the training ground but no one was there! Which he might have known if he had looked at our programme. My leave is signed 30th–14th I have had such a nice Xmas greetings & notes of appreciation from one of the gunners Brysides, not Pringle curiously.

28.12.16

We had a little show today, the Divisional commander was out, it did not go so well. The Divisional commander appeared fairly pleased as he was off to Paris. So Marden commands at present, he came over at 7, had a chat for about an hour before tea & then went off.

Saturday 30.12.16

54 Elm Park Road, London
Brigade moves to D, E & P Camps I go to Calais as Boulogne is closed. Get there at 11.30am & sail 3pm I am OC troops so get a cabin. Eileen after meeting 5 trains finds me & I get home for dinner.

NOTES

1 Major Reginald Francis Amhurst Butterworth. GOC 82nd Field Company, 56th Bde, 19th (Western) Div., XI Corps. This officer was awarded DSO and Bar. MID five times. CMG 1919. Made lieutenant colonel 1918.
2 Lieutenant Colonel Oswald Swift Flower, CO 13th RWF.
3 Lieutenant Colonel Ronald James Walter Carden, 17th Lancers, CO 16th RWF.

4 Captain H.R. Bently, Cheshire Regt, Brigade Major 113th Inf. Bde, 38th (Welsh) Div.

5 Major General George Tom Molesworth Bridges CMG, RA (1871–1939). GOC 19th Div. commander. He lost a leg during the Battle of Passchendaele. He was Governor of South Australia 1922–27.

6 Lieutenant Colonel Richard Carmichael Bell OBE, DSO, MID. Indian Cavalry, CO 15th RWF.

7 Lieutenant Colonel Henry Edward ap Rhys Pryce (1874–1950). GSO 1, 38th (Welsh) Div. Later knighted and promoted to major general after the war. He was an Indian Army officer who was on leave when the war started; Major (later Brigadier General) Hubert Conway Rees DSO (1882–1948). Welsh Regt, GSO 2. He was captured and was summoned to speak to the Kaiser 28 May 1918.

8 Brigadier General George Darell Jeffreys (1878–1960). GOC 58th Bde, 19th Div. Later major general in command of this division from 1917 to the end of the war.

9 Lieutenant Colonel William Long, Acting GOC 57th Bde, 19th Div.

10 Lieutenant Colonel Ralph Abercrombie Berners RWF (1871–1949). Acting GOC 58th Bde, 19th Div. DSO 1917. Retired 1921.

11 Major General Sir Ivor Philipps DSO, MP (1861–1940). He had been commissioned in the Manchester Regt in 1883. He retired as major in 1903 and joined the Pembrokeshire Yeomanry, which he commanded from 1908–12. He became a Liberal MP for Southampton at the outbreak of the First World War and, in the November of that year, he was called to the War Office for staff duties. He was then given command of the 115th Bde, and further promoted to Major General 38th (Welsh) Div. Lloyd George's younger son, Gwilym, was appointed his ADC; his brother was John Wynford Philipps, 1st Viscount St David's (1860–1938). He was a financier and politician; a close supporter of Lloyd George, he helped fund his political independence.

12 Brigadier General Thomas Owen Marden (1866–1951). Welsh Regt, GOC 114th Inf. Bde. Later Major General 6th Div. He was knighted for his role in negotiations during the Chanak Crisis 1922.

13 Lieutenant Colonel David Davies MP (1880–1944). 14th RWF until 17 June 1916 when transferred to Territorial Force Reserve. He was the grandson of David Davies of Llandinam, the industrialist and self-made millionaire. He became the first Baron Davies. He was a great supporter of the Liberal Party and was Parliamentary Secretary to David Lloyd George.

14 Captain Arthur Edward Redfern, 16th RWF.

15 Major Codrington Howard Rees Crawshay RWF (1882–1937). Staff Officer 38th Div. He was severely wounded as Temporary Lieutenant Colonel commanding 2nd RWF. He retired with the rank of lieutenant colonel.

16 Lieutenant Ernest Frank Philips, 13th RWF, later transferred to the Machine Gun Corps.

17 Lieutenant Bertram Broom Cotterill, 14th RWF, Wounded at Mametz Wood and on 25 July 1917.

18 Lieutenant Robert Griffith Rees, 15th RWF. Killed in action, 11 July 1916 aged 25 years. Buried Serre Road Cemetery No. 2, Beaumont Hamel, France.

19 Captain David Thomas Tanner, 16th RWF, Brigade Machine Gun Officer. Killed in action, 31 August 1916 aged 31 years. Buried Essex Farm Cemetery, Boesinghe, Belgium.

20 Captain A.W. Howells, 15th RWF, wounded 6 July 1916 and seconded Special Works School, Kensington.

21 The National Executive Committee had been set up to organise a Welsh Army Corps (WAEC).

22 Brigadier General Richard Orlando Kellett, Royal Irish Rifles, 99th Bde, 2nd Div. Later major general and GOC Machine Gun Training Centre, 1918–19. CMG 1917. CB 1918. Reputedly a 'Big Game Hunter'.

23 Major S.H. Ferrand KRRC. Later commanded 11th (S) Bn, E. Yorks Regt.

24 Lieutenant Colonel Archibald 'Weevil' Percival Wavell MC (1883–1950). Later to become First Earl, he was a staff officer with General Allenby's Third Army at this time. See his most recent biography: Victoria Scholfield, *Soldier & Statesman* (2006).

25 Lieutenant General Richard Cyril Byrne Haking, GOC XI Corps.

26 Lieutenant Jack Archibald Pringle MC, 14th RWF. Wounded in late 1918 and awarded MC for his gallantry.

27 Lieutenant (later Captian) Reginald Gordon Hayes MC, 14th RWF. MC 1918.

28 Brigadier General Philip Rynd Robertson CMG (1866–1936). GOC 19th Bde, 33rd Div. CB 1917. KCB 1919. Major General Lowland Div. (TF) 1919.

29 Charles Bruce Bairnsfather (1888–1959). British cartoonist; inventor of the immortal character 'Old Bill'. 1st Bn Royal Warwickshire Regt.

30 Lieutenant Colonel (later Hon. Brigadier General) Robert Clayton Browne-Clayton (1870–1939). South Irish Horse. GOC 16th (Service) Bn (2nd Birkenhead) the Cheshire Regt. Awarded a DSO for his services at Trones Wood 20 July 1916.

31 *See* Wyn Griffiths, *Up to Mametz* (Faber, 1931; Gliddon, 1988), p. 100.

32 Sir Charles Monro reassumed command of First Army on 4 February after an assessment trip to Gallipoli.

33 Lieutenant Colonel William Charles Eric Rudkin DSO. GOC 122 Bde RA. Later Brigadier General CRA 57th Div.

34 Lieutenant Robert John Atkinson, 16th RWF. Wounded Mametz Wood. Transferred MGC 1 January 1917.

35 Major Robert Henry Mills, 14th RWF. Killed Mametz Wood, 10 July 1916 aged 35 years. Buried Danzig Alley Cemetery, Somme, France.

36 Brigadier General Horatio James Evans, GOC 114th Bde, 38th (Welsh) Div.

37 Lieutenant Colonel Robert Ormus Campbell DSO, 13th RWF. Promoted temporary lieutenant colonel 3 July 1916.

38 Lieutenant John Wesley Davies, 16th RWF. Killed in action, 26 March 1916 aged 31 years. Buried Le Touret Military Cemetery, Richelbourg-l'Avoue, France.

39 Lieutenant Guy Everingham, 13th RWF. Transferred to 16th Squadron RFC and was killed in action over Vimy Ridge, 8 April 1917 aged 22 years. Buried Bois-Gare British Cemetery, Thelius, France.

40 Lieutenant Peter Lunt, 13th RWF, later employed by the Ministry of Labour.

41 Brigadier General Herbert Campbell Holman DSO, CMG, DA & QMG XI Corps.

42 Brigadier General William Henniker Anderson, BGGS XI Corps.

43 Brigadier General George Glas Sandeman Carey (1876–1948). BGRA XI Corps. GOC 20th Div. 1918. Major General 1922.

44 Lieutenant David Thomas Tanner, 16th Bn, Temporary Captain 21 February 1916. Brigade Machine Gun Officer 7 May 1916. Killed, 31 August 1916 aged 31 years. Buried Essex Farm Cemetery, Boesinghe, Belgium.

45 Brigadier General Montagu Leland Hornby (1870–1948). GOC 116th Bde, 39th Div.

46 Brigadier General Lionel Thomas Twyford, GOC 57th Bde, 19th (Western) Div.

47 Major Lord Alexander George Thynne DSO, Croix de Guerre (French), MP. Lieutenant Colonel 6th Wiltshire Yeomanry. Son of the Marchioness of Bath. MP for Bath. Severely wounded 30 July 1916. Killed, 9 September 1918 aged 45 years. Buried Bethune Town Cemetery, France.

48 Sir Philip Walhouse Chetwode, Cavalry Commander (1869–1950).

49 Major General Hon. E.J. Montagu-Stuart-Wortley, 46th Div.

50 Lieutenant Colonel George Clifton Inglis Stockwell DSO, RWF (1879–1953). GOC 154th Bde, 55th Div. September 1916. CMG 1918. Brigade Commander Irish Command 1922. Retired hon. major general but returned to service during Second World War.

51 *A Kiss for Cinderella* was a stage play (later made into a film) by J.M. Barrie. Gerald du

Maurier (1873–1934) was a celebrated actor of the time. His sister's children were the inspiration for Barrie's *Peter Pan*. He was the father of the writer Daphne du Maurier.

52 I believe what he is saying is that all the ring leaders of the Sein Fein who took part in the uprising had been arrested and would be duly processed through the courts.

53 Lieutenant Noel Osbourne-Jones, 15th RWF. This raid was the first by the 38th Div.; they caught a German wiring part and followed them back into their lines, killing and wounding sixty. Killed during the raid, 8 May 1916 aged 21 years. Buried Loos Memorial, France.

54 Lieutenant Herbert Taggart, 15th RWF. Killed returning to his lines in the same raid as Osborne-Jones, 8 May 1916 aged 22 years. Buried Loos Memorial, France.

55 David Lloyd George (1863–1945). He was Minister of Munitions 1916. He had been a central figure in the raising of the 38th (Welsh) Div. In December 1916 he became prime minister. Both his sons Gwilym and Richard were serving officers in this division at this time.

56 Lieutenant Colonel Harry Vivian Robert Hodson, Second in Command 15th RWF. Commanded 14th RWF 17 July 1916–June 1917 when appointed Officer Commanding Brigade School.

57 Lieutenant John Cawrdaf Melville Morgan-Jones, 14th RWF. Relinquished commission 9 August 1916 due to ill health.

58 Second Lieutenant Arthur George Thompson, 14th RWF. Killed by a stray bullet while on patrol, 3 June 1916 aged 20 years. Buried Pont-du-Hem Military Cemetery, La Gorge, France.

59 Captain William Ellis Jones, 14th RWF, later seconded to 52nd Grad. Bn Cheshire Regt.

60 Lieutenant Colonel Edward Massey Birch DSO, RA. GSO 1, 25th Div. GSO 1, Sixth Army January–May 1917. GSO 1, 17th Div. CMG 1917. CB 1919.

61 Brigadier General Charles Edensor Heathcote DSO, KOYLI. GOC 7th Bde, 25th Div. Served in the Egyptian Campaign May 1917. Returned to France late 1917–18. MID seven times. CMG 1918. CB 1919.

62 Essentially, the 38th Div. was going south into GHQ reserve and would in due course be released to Fourth Army and then into XV Corps Reserve.

63 GHQ advanced headquarters was prepared for Douglas Haig at Chateaux in Beauquesne, 15 miles behind the battle line.

64 IWM Correspondence: Field Marshall Sir Henry Hughes Wilson, HHW 2/83/57: Major General Philip Woolcott Game DSO (1876–1961). Attached RFC as staff officer. Later commissioner Metropolitan Police.

65 XV Corps HQ was situated at Heilly.

66 Brigadier General T.H. Shoubridge, 54th Inf. Bde, 18th (Eastern) Div., XIII Corps, attacked on 1 July 1916.

67 Brigadier General Louis Ridley Vaughan (1875–1942). BGGS XV Corps. MGGS Third Army May 1917–18. Made lieutenant general 1926.

68 Lieutenant General Henry Sinclair Horne, XV (France) Corps Commander under which 38th Div. was to serve during the attack on the Somme. *See* Don Farr, *The Silent General* (West Midlands, 2006).

69 Lieutenant Colonel John Randle Minshull-Ford DSO, MC, RWF. Commanding 91st Bde, 7th Div. from 3 February 1916. This brigade was relieved by 113rd Bde, 38th Div.

70 He is referring here to 'sausage-type' German balloons.

71 IWM: Wilson papers: HHW 2/83/61.

72 At 12.45 a.m. 7th and 17th Divs attacked on a line Contalmaison–Mametz Wood unsuccessfully (7th Div. included 1st RWF) 7th Div. was relieved by 38th Div. at 1.00 a.m. on 6 July 1916. They would take over the line from Bottom Wood in the west to Caterpillar Wood in the east.

73 Horne issued his orders at 10 a.m. for the attack on the Mametz Wood; it was to take place the following day at 8 a.m. General Pilcher's 17th Div. would attack the western edge,

while 38th Div. would attack the wood from the east. General Pilcher protested, but he was brushed aside and the attack went on.

74 The 113rd Bde was to have supported the 17th Div. attack on Quadrangle & Wood support trench by the 15th RWF, however in the confusion a patrol was sent forward.

75 Both Major General Pilcher & Philipps were degummed (sacked) as a result of this failure. Philipps was replaced by Major General H.E. Watts (he appears to have been highly regarded by Horne) on 9 July 1916; Major General C.G. Blackader took over the division permanently on 12 July 1916.

76 Zero hour was set at 4.15 a.m. on 10 July 1916.

77 Brigadier General Horatio James Evans, 115th Bde and 38th Div., this would have been about 5–5.30 a.m. on 11 July 1916. The 38th Div. was relieved by the 21st Div. on the night of 11/12 July.

78 The division had 3,993 casualties, 600 missing and 600 killed in the six days during which they saw action. The suggestion that the reason the division had failed in its first attack on the Wood was because, as Haig's remark in his diary puts it, 'total casualties for the 24 hours are under 150', was actually wide of the mark but nevertheless this was sufficient enough to cast a shadow over the division. The true figure is somewhere in the region of at least 400.

79 Brigadier General Arthur Solly-Flood, GOC 35th Bde.

80 Lieutenant Colonel Christopher Heseltine RF (1869–1944).

81 Sir Douglas Haig visited General Horne's XV Corps HQ on 9 July 1916, Horne had recommended that both Pilcher (17th Div.) and Philipps (38th Welsh Div.) be removed. It has to be remembered that XV Corps itself repeatedly interfered with both these divisions. Haig's comments in his diary & his treatment of Price-Davies show the human side of his character.

82 Major George Cecil Westbrooke RWF was awarded a MC for gallantry in Mametz Wood. Later, DA & QMG VIII Corps February 1917 to July 1918. Returned to 38th Welsh Div.

83 Lieutenant Colonel Archibald Nelson Gavin Jones DSO, GOC 16th RWF July 1916.

84 Lieutenant Colonel David Davies was an MP and was wanted by Lloyd George back in England.

85 Lieutenant Colonel Campbell; Lieutenant Colonel H.V.R. Hodson; Lieutenant Colonel J.C. Bell.

86 Major General Charles Patrick Amyatt Hull, Royal Scots Fusiliers, GOC 56th Div.

87 Lieutenant Colonel Denis Daly Wilson MC, 17th Indian Cavalry attached 1/5th Sherwood Foresters. Killed in action, 1 July 1916 aged 38 years.

88 Brigadier General Lionel Boyd-Moss, South Staffs Regt, GOC 36th Bde.

89 Brigadier General Ernest St George Pratt DSO, Durham Light Inf., GOC 75th Bde. Died in London 23 November 1918.

90 61st Bde was part of 20th (Light) Div.

91 IWM: Wilson Papers HHW 2/83/90.

92 The demonstration was at Berthern.

93 Lieutenant General Hon. Sir Julian Hedworth George Byng, GOC Canadian Corps (1862–1935).

94 General Sir Herbert Charles Onslow Plumer, GOC Second Army.

95 Major General Hon. William Lampton, GOC 4th Div.

96 Major General Richard Lucas Mullens, GOC 1st Cavalry Div.

97 Major General Charles Harrington Harrington (1872–1940). MGGS Second Army, formerly BGGS.

98 Brigadier General Charles Arthur Wilding, GOC 10th Bde (1868–1953).

99 Brigadier General William Garnett Braithwaite CB, CMG, RWF (1870–1937).

100 Brigadier General James Edward 'Archimedes' Edmonds RE (1861–1956). After the war he edited the *Official War Histories*.

101 Major General Charles Gunnard Blackader joined the Leicester Regt in 1888. He served in South Africa during the Second Boer War with his battalion. He came to France as a brigadier general with the Gawal Bde, Indian Expeditionary Force. He then served in Dublin before being posted to the 38th Div. on 20 July 1916. He was in the habit of taking a large dog round the trenches with him and it is possible that he contracted rabies in this way. He underwent treatment for this at the Pasteur Institute from May 1918. He died after an operation at Milbank Military Hospital on 2 April 1921 and was given a full military funeral with bearers and firing party at Putney Cemetery on 4 April 1921. For further information see WO.374/6825.

102 Lord Stamfordham was the private secretary to Queen Victoria, Edward VII and George V. He lost his only son, Captain Hon. John Neville Bigge, 1st Bn 60th Rifles (KRRC): he was killed in action, 15 May 1915 aged 27 years. He has no known grave; commemorated Le Touret Memorial, Calais, France.

103 IWM: Wilson Papers HHW 2/83/112.

104 Lieutenant Lyman Sawley Hull (originally served in the ranks) 13th RWF, later awarded MC & Bar for gallantry.

105 Brigadier General Horatio James Evans had led the failed initial attack on Mametz Wood and predicted his replacement as a result.

106 Brigadier General Carlos Joseph Hickie KOYLI.

107 Lieutenant Colonel Compton Cardew Norman CMG, DSO, 15th RWF (1877–1955).

108 Major General Hon. William Lampton, GOC 4th Div.

109 IWM: Wilson Papers HHW 2/84/9.

110 Lieutenant Colonel Graham Howard Gwyther DSO, 14th RWF (1872–1934).

111 Hotel Sauosge, Cassell.

112 Lieutenant Colonel John Brough (1872–1917). Officer commanding the fledgling Tank Corps in France. He fell out with GHQ over the use of tanks during the Battle of the Somme and returned to England.

113 Major F.R.H. Mc Lellan, 16th Bn RWF. This officer was a member of the Field General Court-Martial of Sapper Robert Bell, 123 Field Company, RE, 38th Welsh Div. He was convicted of the murder of Lieutenant Wynell Hastings Lloyd 17 April 1918. He was executed 22 May 1918. He was the last RE to be executed during the war.

114 IWM: Wilson Papers HHW 2/84/55.

115 Sir Arthur Ignatius Conan Doyle (1859–1930). He is remembered as a physician, novelist and short-story writer. He wrote *The Great Boer War* (1900) and *The British Campaign in France and Flanders* (1916–20). Tragically he lost his brother, Brigadier General John Francis Innes Hay Doyle CMG, DSO: he died of pneumonia due to the influenza pandemic, 19 February 1919 aged 45 years. He lost his son Captain Arthur Alleyne Kingsley Conan Doyle, Hampshire Regt, who died from wounds during the fighting on the Somme, 1 November 1918 aged 24 years. He also lost two brother-in-laws: Captain Malcolm Leckie RAMC (married to Selina) on 28 August 1914 aged 34 years; Major Leslie W.S. Oldham RE (married to Caroline) on 28 July 1915 aged 45 years. He also lost two nephews: Second Lieutenant Afred Oscar Hornung, Essex Regt, on 6 July 1915; Captain Alec Forbes, Royal Warwickshire Regt, on 3 September 1916 aged 28 years.

116 The raid was carried out by 16th RWF.

117 Major General (later Lieutenant General) Sydney 'Swanky Sid' Turing Barlow Lawford (1865–1953). GOC 41st Div. Father of the actor Peter Lawford.

118 Lieutenant Colonel Brian Surtees Phillpotts, Commander RE, 38th Div.

119 IWM: Wilson Papers HHW 2/84/100.

120 Lieutenant Colonel William Henniker Anderson, GSO 1 September 1914–October 1915.

121 Captain Thomas Elias, Adjutant 15th RWF. Relinquished his commission 8 March 1918 due to ill-health contracted on active service.

122 The *Britannic* was the sister ship of the *Titanic* and was being used as a hospital ship in the Adriatic. There has been a great deal of speculation whether it was hit by a torpedo or struck a mine.

123 Brigadier General C.I. Stockwell, 164th Inf. Bde, 55th Div.

124 Lieutenant Colonel Richard Carmichael Bell DSO, OBE, GOC 15th RWF.

125 Lieutenant Peter Aubrey Roberts, 16th RWF, embarked with the battalion for France in 1915, was taken prisoner. He was repatriated 7 January 1919.

126 Brigadier General Edward Henry Finch Hatton, GOC 118th Bde, 39th Div.

127 This is a reference to Right Hon. Herbert H. Asquith MP, the prime minister at the time.

128 Major General William Thomas Furse (1865–1953). GOC 9th (Scottish) Div., later Master Gunner. Supported the introduction of the Lewis gun.

129 Brigadier General R.D.F. Oldman, GOC 117th Inf. Bde, 39th Div.

130 Major General Herbert Edward Watts, GOC 7th Div., later XIX Corps Commander (1858–1934).

131 Major General Hugh Sandham Jeudwine (1862–1942). GOC 55th Div. Later Lieutenant General, Director General of Territorial Army; Major General Gerald James Cuthbert Division [?] (1861–1931).

132 Lady Diana Olivia Winifred Maud Manners (1892–1986). She was the legal daughter of the Duke of Rutland; a beautiful socialite who became a nurse during the war. Later she married Duff Cooper.

133 Sir Douglas Haig, C in C British Forces in France.

Four

1917

The early parts of this year were spent rebuilding and reinforcing the trench system they had inherited, and working out various schemes to improve machine-gun posts and trench mortar positions. All this hard work was to be commended by their new corps commander and the in-coming Guards Division, who took over the northern part of their line. Once again he was very aware of the greater war being fought outside the Western Front and what progress was being made. He continues to be engaged in training and attending conferences where best practice of other units is passed on from the early battles of the year. He also is in regular touch with various senior officers, including his brother-in-law Lt General Henry Wilson.

By early summer, the Welsh Division was taking part in substantial training exercises in preparation for the opening of the Third Battle of Ypres. Unlike the previous year, the division is now fully prepared for the ordeal of battle that was Pilckem Ridge. Their attack was highly successful and they fought with great valour, holding the gained positions tenaciously. Price-Davies' letters reflect how difficult this task was, and the frustration that rain had held up their progress and was to do so for the rest of their time in the Salient. The Battle for Langemarck is fought out in the mud of Flanders and was the last action his brigade took part in.

The letters for the latter part of the year reflect a man who has been in command of a brigade for over two years and is growing more and more weary of the stress incurred. As a result, his application for a home command posting saw him return to England for the winter and early spring months of 1918.

January 1917
There is peace talk in the air, Germany having made some effort to get the allies to consider peace but I hope nothing will come of it as I am sure Germany will not consider any proposals at present which we could possibly accept also I hope that this year we will be able to inflict severe losses on Germany. The submarine menace is of course serious but if we are to lose the war for that reason it appear that after we shall have to give in to any power, which can build sufficient submarines.[1]

Saw Henry a little but he was difficult to get at these days being so many visitors to his house. He went to Rome with Lloyd George a historic conference. In the War Office I saw Dick Wortley & Furse who has just been appointed Master Gunner of Ordnance.

My leave ended 12 January & I went back to the line staying on the Canal Bank, north of Ypres till March 10th. During the 5 weeks we had a very severe frost, the trenches pop up & blocks of ice formed at the bottom of the communication trench. The canal was frozen early as the frost was very severe, & the men stood the cold wonderfully. Companies went to Poperinghe for 2 days at a time, which was a great treat. Then they had baths, so everyone got a bath about once in 10 days & some went to the cinema. Conditions on the Canal Bank were not too bad at this time however many of the elephant dugouts had been shut up

The period was uneventful except for an unsuccessful raid by the 14th in which Munsby was killed at the beginning. I took over a long sector with my brigade & 2nd Battalion from the 114th Brigade. The Corps Commander considers 2 machine gun companies, 2 trench mortars, medium trench mortar & other ordnance was too strenuous. We moved nearer Ypres which quieter & into the 114th HQ by the 7th.

I dined the other night with Corps Commander, Minshull-Ford has relieved Carlos Hickie & much of 65th Brigade, also Thompson, Pereman CRA 55th Division & Corps Staff, General Huenson, Strong, Cartwright, Ellington & the ADC's Chaplin & Crichton.

We had concerts as usual in the Camps, Beynon 13th RWF a professional tenor was excellent.[2] The German retirement on the Somme seems to have caused a good deal of nonsense & speculation. Rather curious after looking forward to the day the Bosche would retire to find we don't want it when it comes. The anxiety is of course is how the Bosche will use the pieces he saves by strengthening his line & also how we are going to put up an offensive against if he keeps on going back. How are we going to carry over dumps, railways, roads, trenches etc, over ground that has been cut up by shells in a previous undertaking & one that caught the command out all in a minute? The time for offensive operations may slip by in the meantime.[3]

1.3.17

I inspected some dugouts, I have moved to some other dugouts not far from my old one & felt rather lost tonight, though these dugouts are much nicer. In my present quarters I have a little sitting room but my bedroom gets no daylight which I don't like much. Rudkin comes to dinner tomorrow night for our St David's Day dinner.[4] We shall make him eat a leak.

2.3.17

We had such a dinner Halewych had been off to a certain town by train & brought back all sorts of good things & some champagne, which he did not give us until the sweet. Awfully good pheasants, which Campbell sent us. Rudkin came to dinner, & Redfern is here for a week. There has been a reorganisation of the line I can't tell you about it of course but it gives me an infernal amount of work.

Tim Hollond is BGGS somewhere I quite agree with Alan Paley that Haig won't give Henry anything I said all along.[5]

3.3.17

Humphrey's & I went round the line with battalion commanders & got back for breakfast at 8am I took the most priceless toss I have ever taken. Close to my dugout is a short flight of steps a total drop of about 5 feet I had forgotten their existence & boldly went right on & fell from the top to the bottom, practically clearing the whole of the steps. Humphrey's was in a great state of mind of mind over this & could not believe I was not hurt. The funny thing is I wasn't bruised nor did I feel shaken. In fact I wouldn't have known I had fallen. Humphrey's said he was just going to tell the sentry to get the stretcher-bearers! Then we did not quite get off the right way & in trying to avoid obstacles Humphrey's got separated from me, suddenly I heard great struggling & swearing & blowing. Humphrey's had got into the middle of a barbed wire entanglement. He was in a great state as he thought I had gone off & left him! I had visions of him sinking exhausted & my having to go back for wire cutters to cut him out. However he emerged eventually. In the afternoon I went out again & went round with Elias & Colonel Llewelyn attached to one of my battalions.[6] I was very impressed with the work & cleanliness of the line.

5.3.17

It was a glorious day with good light & we went on to the Artillery OP's & had quite a look at the country. After that I went on to the trenches & got into a very wet one & my boots leaked.

Minshull-Ford comes here I shall be glad to see him he is a fine man.[7] We shall be a very young pair of brigadiers & Marden the other extreme very old!

All my staff working very well for me still we don't appear to get work done I am pleased with the result as a whole & just at present I have the opportunity of seeing what another Brigade do & in something's I find we can compare very favourably with them but these are I am afraid not the soldierly qualities!

7.3.17

Ellington came in & I took him round & got back at 1.30pm.[8] Then Rudkin came & had a chat & Carlos came to tea, nice old thing rode over on a bicycle. Then I had a conference & after that went round trenches with Colonel Kennedy who commands a battalion here. We got back to his HQ at 10pm & I had dinner with him I am awfully glad you saw Campbell, isn't he splendid? Norman is back & very full of life I am glad to have him back he is a good standby.[9]

8.3.17
Colonel De Houghton who is the Machine Gun Officer came round for tea
& I went out with him.[10] His brother was one of the Adjutant's in the 46th
Division & was killed. I think Marden was coming to but we went out with-
out him & he turned up afterwards & ran across us.

Henry & the ladies is priceless, he is an old black guard isn't he? Does he
tell Cecil about it, how does she like the idea of a ballet girl sitting on his
knee? Tell him I want to go & see him if I am out of the line when he comes
back but of course he is a long way from me for all I know.

9.3.17
I don't think Campbell has any real business he is a director of one or two
companies. He passed into Sandhurst & then hurt his eye either before going
there or passing out. He has knocked about town a good lot & knows everyone especially Guardsmen & then he was for a long time (I am not sure when)
on a launch & he's travelled a bit. The story is he took over the launch in a bad
condition & made it a success & made a lot of money. He shot an Italian in
South Africa who tried to knife him, that is all I know of his history.

Great news in the House about Home Rule, what is the next move I suppose Henry is in his element? I presented some medal ribbons & prizes for
sports today & made a speech! Marden not well the cold wind effects his liver.

11.3.17
Breakfast & then a little walk with Stewart & Hallewyck & his dog & after
lunch we went to see a test being carried out. No I didn't over eat on St
David's day, and 'St David' is a toast. On St David's day they always drink &
say 'St David' after every toast. The speeches were bad as we were only told to
make them 5 minutes before dinner.

News of Baghdad has just come in. Two years ago I went to the 46th
Division. Blackader is back I have not seen him.

12.3.17
The Corps commander rang to ask if I should be in & we told him no & then
he dropped in at Fords & found me having tea. He was very effusive 'well my
good fellow nice seeing you', & all sort of things but I never think it's sincere.
He talked a lot of course & he told us (He tells everyone) of how he cut the
railway in South Africa I daresay a fine performance but quite unnecessary to
tell us. Tomorrow I go to dine with him we are getting the Divisional band
& a concert party over also. Bevan who also comes to lunch sings very well.[11]

14.3.17
I have just come back from dinning with the Corps commander, Minshull-
Ford & several other brigadiers. We had a very good little dinner & afterwards
the Corps commander showed us his maps of different points etc & discussed
them all with us, which was interesting. He was very amicable tonight.

I am sorry about Henrys Corps I wonder what they will do about him now, it makes me feel miserable & impatient over it all.

The story Tavish refers to took place in Cairo. The next day but on (I spent the next day in bed) we went to a battalion scheme & I was very angry because Charles John Markham made us move in a sort of box formation irrespective of ground.[12] Whilst I was trying to get possession of the high ground, CJM wheeled the whole show & I had to collect my men & hurry round. I was very angry & told Tavish afterwards & ended by saying 'I was properly had in the hills' so he has pulled my leg ever since I don't quite see why he has the monopoly on feelings!

Just off to a conference, I am feeling rather miserable tonight I have just come back from a good concert given by the 15th. A man called Beynon an Officer sang awfully well, he is a professional. He sang a duet 'Watchman of the Night' with a sergeant who has a good baritone, Bevan sang a tenor. We ended by singing 'Land of my Fathers, Men of Harlech, Goodbless the Prince of Wales, British Grenadiers & God save the King'. Beynon sang, 'Land of my fathers' in Welsh.

15.3.17

The Army commander came round this morning & looked at training. They are going to get up a Regimental dinner (60th) which should be good fun.[13]

16.3.17

Today I had a good day with my trench mortars & hustled them up with their training a bit. After lunch I went out to look at the banking scheme Humphrey's had on. At 6pm we had a Divisional concert party, I said a few words of thanks. They were quite good, a few glee singers & then some good solo's & some indifferent comics.

St Patrick's Day 17.3.17

We have had a least praise from the Divisional commander for the state of the camp it gave me quite a shock! I was out when he came as I had spent the day trying to help Marden with some work. I had lunch with Hodson & it was a glorious day & I had too many clothes on.[14] Wonderful news from Russia.

18.3.17

I went to church today I found they wanted me to get up & sit down before they moved & I got up before the epistle by mistake! The parson gave me a sermon on courage & took Peter as his model, he then landed himself in the difficulty of denial & I didn't think came out of it very well but apart from that there was a lot of good in the sermon.

We had some sports today, military sports with bombs & rifle grenades, they went off very well & I think were a success. The Divisional Band played for us also two fellows came to dinner. One was a Major Partridge, a regular full of chat, which makes a change, so many of these fellows have so little to say.

Good news came of the advance of 3rd & 5th Armies but no prisoners mentioned & I am afraid it is just the Bosche going back to back.

19.3.17
The Divisional commander took me in his car to a conference with other brigadiers. It did not last long & then he & Marden & I went round the defences. Norman & Stockwell came to dinner the latter is rather a brick stick, holds himself up as a strong man who is not afraid of degumming any officer etc & won't stand any nonsense. What a pity Henry didn't come over last week I could have got away quite easily. Great advance seems to have been made on the Somme but no prisoners apparently. The Bosche seem to have done it very well, still it seems he has gone back which is a great thing.

20.3.17
I got a wire from Henry asking me to stay a few nights. Last week I could have done it easily but now it is out of the question. However I have asked permission to go for a night on the 26th but I have no answer yet I hear Henry has been promoted which is good. Jordan knows Foch well & says Foch says Henry is the only general in the British Army worth a damn.

The Bosche seems to be back as far as he will go for the present, he has worked it cunningly.

21.3.17
The man I dined with last night was 2nd in command to Blackader I find I had summed him up exactly. His great fault was apparently that he can't say 'well done' & he knows he can't! It is a great handicap not having commanded a battalion first.

22.3.17
My leave of one day had to be sanctioned by GHQ!!!
Such a horrid day, snow fell in the night & the storm came on about 9am. However it cleared & Humphrey's & I rode over to see the 15th & it was fine & sunny & really nice till about 12.30 & then came on hard driving snow.

The three came to tea, rather nice lads though one was a bit above himself however I think it was mostly high spirits. He is the son of General Sir F. Lloyd's agent & is an agent himself (Williams by name).[15] He loves dogs & shooting & fishing & does not want to be a soldier at all, but I believe he is full of energy. He comes from Oswestry & knows the Lees of Wordmill well but my knowledge of them is 20 years old so they are changed now.

Two fellows who came to dinner were quite cheery so often they are glum but I think they like coming. They can't say I don't try to get to know them anyway & all the old officer's are friendly with me, in fact they all meet me with a cheery smile as a rule.

No sign of leave to go to Henry yet, it is very strange I wonder if it has been sent to the War Office. Great rumour of a revolution in Berlin.

23.3.17

I went to the 114th to give a lecture & after they asked me to dinner I refused but thinking they were disappointed changed my mind & it was well I did as they had laid out a nice place for me & chicken. We pulled the Canadian doctors leg about the Americans, he is great on the Americans says they are slow to go to war but make great splendid soldiers. So we told him we could not afford to wait 5 years & then we agreed about the American War of Secession & the Civil War & 1812 & so on.

Your meeting does seem to have been a success I certainly think the women deserve the vote now it's wonderful what they have done.

25.3.17

My leave had to be approved by GHQ, this morning I got a wire from Henry saying the car would be here at 9am but now it is 10am & no car I have just heard that my leave has been approved so I go off as soon as the car comes & come back tomorrow. It is quite exciting the idea of seeing Henry I wish the car would come.

Yesterday I was on the training ground in the morning & afternoon. Then some boys came to tea, Wynne Edwards a nice boy in the 13th & we were a cheery party.[16]

Here I am with Henry he is in good spirits I had an eventful journey I got to GHQ at 12 & had to go to Army HQ on the way to see some letter about leave. However the letter was not there & they said it did not matter so I came on. We went like the wind 110 km/hr part of the way 68¾ miles an hour. We may have been going faster but the speedometer only showed that much, then something went wrong with the oil pump & the engine knocked badly & we didn't do much more than 6k after that though he inched up again at the end & ran up to 90 again.

This country is lovely & the day glorious I am out with Henry for a walk, his house is a nice square one, inside full of carpets & rather in the nouveau riche.

26.3.17

Great lunch we had & I am going to take Henry off for a walk, to walk the brandy etc off! I went into his office & saw Cavendish[17] & Dillon[18] & had a long chat with them. After tea yesterday he told me the whole story. I think he is on top now & I am much happier now also he has cleared the air with certain people. Very interesting chat we had I hope to call with Tavish on my way back. Henry is busy working he must get a great many letters written.

28.3.17

I spent the morning in the training area & had lunch with Norman & inspected the billets & then back to the training area & got in for tea. Then I went to the concert, one of the best I have been to. All the best talent we have except Bevan & 2 others. Corporal Williams sang 'A Perfect Day' so beautifully he has a fine voice. The Sgt Roberts sang 'The Old Shako' &

other favourites. Corporal Williams is a fine man & has got the MM for a very gallant action.

After the concert Colonel Jones said a few words, he hoped they could keep their singing up & how he liked to hear them & then I thanked them I told them I often stopped work to listen to them in their dugouts as I walked along the trench boards.[19]

I have heard from Pringle to say he is not coming back his lungs are not fit enough after the pneumonia I am awfully sorry I could never hope to live up to the wonderful opinion he has of me. I am quite happy with my relations with the Co's except Campbell I feel they don't think very much of me, it's a horrible feeling. Norman is a fine soldier that is not surprising but I find with him he seems to resent me so to speak interfering with him. Any suggestion I have to make about training he takes it badly & he hates me finding fault with anything his people do. I think the last raid did me a lot of harm, it has depressed me for some time I try & struggle against it but it is hard with a man of that sort to assert oneself without appearing ridiculous.

I left Henry after tea at 5pm. The car came along very quietly & I got to GHQ at 8pm. Tavish was on leave but Tandy & others gave me dinner including a man who was TC's signal officer.[20] Then I went to the office to look at maps & when the door opened I came face to face with Crichton, 'Mary' he says, 'Dick' says I. Then we walked along the passage & straight into the arms of who do you think, Dicky Follett.[21]

31.3.17

The Corps commander called for me in his car & took me to see some training & then round some billets. He was very pleasant & all his criticisms were to the point. He was pleased enough to say he thought the training was going alright but I was not too pleased with it myself. He then took me to his HQ & gave me lunch. On the way he talked about Henry & told me the reason H did not get Chief of Staff was because people said he intrigued to get rid of Murray and that Sir J didn't want him! I was very angry about it & told him that the people who said that H did a thing like that were people who could not understand a man with his opportunities doing otherwise! He agreed with this I shall tell H it is too bad to circulate things like that.

Letters from Henry must be very slow if they are beaten by Robertson I only told Henry that a change might be good for me but I didn't think I would be good as a BGGS I had an idea he was going to write about me as he always says nowadays he can never get anything he wants. We only discussed for 5 minutes while he washed his hands.

April Fool's Day

You would have laughed at the Corps commander today. He tore along the trenches he put Nixon in front of him & made him go as hard as he could & that didn't suit him & he saw them going round a corner neck & neck![22] Marden couldn't be hurried & told the Corps commander they were all rather tired.[23] The Corps commander was quite stuffy about it but afterwards he was alright.

4.4.17

I had to go to Stewarts room to work as it was so cold in here I went out in the morning with Hull, it was blowing a blizzard & a lot of snow fell but it has gone now. Then I met O'Kelly & I went out with him.[24] Then work till dinner, a gunner McClelland came to dinner he seems a good sort.[25]

Glad it is warmer with you, not much spring here yet. Henry has Sydney Clive & Woodroffe & Cavendish & Eric Dillon & Skeffington-Smyth.[26] Wish the weather would warm up. Two of my lads who were wounded in Mametz are back.

5.4.17

The Corps Commander has sent to say how pleased he was with the work the division has done. I haven't seen the Divisional commander for ages, 3 weeks I should think so I expect he will be due soon.

6.4.17

Campbell is back & full of stories, he can tell me how many submarines are caught. Yes I saw the new order & I told Anthony to apply for a replica I don't suppose I shall wear it as I shall be afraid people will think I have got a bar!

The Divisional commander came round today, he was in a lazy mood going round the line but we stopped at the machine gun emplacements & then sent for the MG Officer. Then he went off & said he would go round the trenches another day!

In the afternoon I went round some dugouts, some good some bad. O'Kelly has gone as second in command of a battalion in another brigade I am sorry to lose him, he was a gent & a trier.

7.4.17

I was in all day working at training programmes & had lunch at 2.30pm & conference at 3pm & then I had dinner with Hodson & was to have gone on with him but he had sprained his knee & I went with Wheldon.[27] It is a brilliantly moonlight & a jolly night.

9.4.17

So the push has begun & appears to have gone well though the weather has been awful I bicycled to meet the Divisional commander today & pressed Stewart all the way, as I would have ridden if he had & persuaded me to bicycle. Then I the General & Pryce went to look at some country & I walked back in a snowstorm.

9.4.17

Up & out with Stewart, it was glorious but turned into intermittent snow, which appears to be the normal thing now. At 11am I went round the trenches with Colonel Llewelyn & got back at 1.30pm. Then out again at 2.45pm with a gunner & in for tea. So now I have had enough added to this I have had a row with Hodson & he wants to see the Divisional commander about it I thought him not so keen as he used to be & told him so & he didn't like it, now I wonder what the Divisional commander will say.

11.4.17

I got up at 4.30am & went out with a gunner to look at the country & got in for breakfast & then off to a conference. My horses were late because Harvey was sick & another man took his place & the horse went lame & he had to get another. Then Marden & I stayed on & had lunch with Minshull Ford & rode back here.[28]

12.4.17

I got a long letter from Miriel today he expects another winter campaign! I wonder what is happening at Arras, as today's news was very meagre.[29]

14.4.17

Off with Harvey I went round with the trench mortar officer & then to a observation station, then on to see Colonel MacClellan a gunner where I had tea.[30]

Raid was not near me but I know the place well I was over there with 4th Division long ago. There seems to be the idea that the Bosche is going back in front of our offensive I can't help thinking that will tell against him in the end. You can't go on teaching people it is a good thing to run away & expect them to hang on when you want them too. The Divisional commander has been round 2 days now but I was away both times, Stewart says he was very genial.

15.4.17

Dick Wortley commands his Division now.

The papers don't seem to be very hopeful over the food question I wonder if they exaggerate. On Tuesday I have to go for 5 days to a course at the Corps School.

17.4.17

We had some ferocious arguments at dinner, the row with Hodson has all ended. He wanted to see the divisional commander but when he was told he had to write this out I supposed he realised it was a very poor one I hope all is well. Jones is queer, he is very bitter against higher authority & for that reason will not pull well. I think he has imbibed some of Normans doctrines of independence, which were all right with Norman & give some good results but were not alright with Jones so he is difficult to manage & always will be I fear.

Appallingly wet tonight it really is awful for our offensive I did hope for some fine weather this is supposed to be the driest month of the year.

Another concert tonight such a good one & we had in addition talent from another brigade, some Belgium sisters from a hospital. But two turned out to be Scottish, MacFie, two cousins I sat next to a Countess. The room was packed & the men enjoyed it immensely & the two sisters sang. The Countess had quite a good voice (& very fine eyes!), she sang something from Madame Butterfly & then a 'Broken Doll'. She did it so nicely with a half sly & half saucy look that the men loved, you know how it goes? It simply brought the house down with a crash & then men all sang the chorus. After it was all over & as we filed out the men sang it again I think the music excites them as always. Then I went out & had dinner with the 16th I sat next to the MacFies. Quite a nice girl her brother is a sapper I have met him I think. But she was scotch, they can't help it & they are so touchy about the spelling of their names. She showed me her passport so I said, 'I see they have spelt the name alright', she never saw her leg being pulled & was very solemn & said 'I saw to that!' A great dinner with Champagne!

It rained so hard this morning it gives me a sickening feeling when one thinks of the offensive I think our prisoner numbers are absolutely reliable because they only count what goes into the cages. The French news seems good but we have had very little yet.

I am finding Minshull-Ford such a help he is a good man but a simple creature like me & we discuss our failings together & that is a great help I like him very much he has such nice manners and is so friendly I hear Shoubridge has a Division which I highly approve of, he is good.[31] Today Ford called for me in a car & we went to the Corps school. All the Co's were there of course & the Corps commander gave an opening speech & the Divisional commanders were there (Blackader was not). We had the most interesting lectures & demonstrations on training & had lunch there. Ford & I went for a walk after lunch it was very cold & work began again at 2pm. After the Corps commander came back & Blackader & the others & we had a great conference & everyone gave their views. It is very interesting and goes on for 3 more days. There was desperate fighting on the French front as both sides report it.

20.4.17

This morning we went again to the Corps school. The Corps commander spent a good deal of the day with us. It was such an interesting day as before & we were taught things we all knew very well I found today that I was not the senior Brigadier there was another there much senior! So I had been taking all the salutes etc. I came back in the car with Ford & Marden & got here about 8pm. Ford is in place of Carlos. The Bosche know we are going to attack it is almost impossible to keep a secret but he made a mistake & thought we were going to attack on the 15th.

I found I had to run the conference after the lecture today & I had to call them to order as they all insisted on talking together I think they were really surprised but they were very good after. Campbell & I walked up to Corps HQ after lunch to see what news had come in, it seems to go well. We did not finish at the school till 7.45pm as the Corps commander had a lot to say! Then I went straight off to dinner with Dick Wortley, Morland,[32] Bainbridge,[33] Campbell,[34] Howard (16th Lancs),[35] Buxton (RB) were there.[36] The last three being on Dick's staff.

21.4.17

Today was the last day of the course, Ford arrived when I was still at breakfast. We had a rather dull day at school, as subjects were not very interesting, there was crowd of brigadiers & in the evening after tea the Corps & Divisional commanders came. The Corps commander ended with an impassioned speech on patriotism & character I wonder how he would finish off, as it is not easy after such flights to return to such mundane affairs, he did rather well. There was a door behind him & when he finished he quietly said goodnight & walked away.

22.4.17

We hope for more news tomorrow, surely this fine weather must bring more fighting I have Vernon Jones with me as Staff Captain, it is about a year since he was with me last. He is a great lad & very useful so I am glad to have him back. By a curious coincidence I have 3 now from Campbell's battalion, him, Hull & Humphreys.

St George's Day, 23.4.17

A fine day today & promise of decent weather I had a conference today & we all talked a lot. Then in the afternoon I went to a demonstration, got in & had tea. Vernon has just brought the news, which is good 1,300 more prisoners & they say they have killed a lot of Bosche. Marden says he is getting tired of the trenches & I think we all are.

24.4.17

A letter from Henry tonight & some maps I asked for, as we had nothing of the French front. He seemed to think the Bosche are having a hard time of it but of course very little ground has been gained yet. I went out with Campbell it was a lovely morning but the light was bad & we had an unprofitable walk. He was as cheery as ever. I went out with Ford & took him round my line. He is always so very polite & enjoyed his morning very much.

27.4.17

I feel very low tonight, poor Stewart has been badly hit, it was such bad luck, as he rarely goes to the trenches being kept busy in the office. This afternoon he went out with Vernon Jones. One of our trench mortars bombs was falling short & Vernon saw it & called to Stewart. But Stewart would not move either way because he did not see it or because he misjudged it. Vernon was scratched in the face but Stewart got a piece in his head & arm. When I saw him he was conscious & spoke quiet sensibly but he was quiet blind & the Doctor fears he will remain so as the wound is in a piece of brain that controls the eyes. I have written to his sister Mrs Marshall & told her it is serious but have said nothing about the blindness. We were great pals & it was so nice having a staff officer you could discuss things freely with much more so than I could with Bently. He was very much a cheery companion too & the whole Brigade will miss him.

No, leave doesn't seem to be about much now I have 500 men who have had none since the division came out so I am not very keen on any officer going at present. Bently is at GHQ I hear, Vernon Jones will be my Brigade Major for the present.

30.4.17
A lovely day I presented medal ribbons, then Jones very foolishly invited me to inspect his dugouts. They were not quite what they might have been! Then I went out with Pearson to see a spot he had chosen for a bit of work & got back at 1pm. I had intended to go to see Stewart but they said I wouldn't be allowed to, however I had a very good report of him, he can distinguish between light & dark & was not in pain. I hope to see him soon but his condition is very serious I will write again to Mrs Marshall. After tea I went with Humphreys around the line, it was a glorious evening such good light. We got back to find Marden here, he had dinner with us & has gone off. We certainly don't seem to get on much with the offensive but the Bosche is doing a lot of counter attacking & that may be good, as he may get through his reserves quicker.

Marden had a successful raid last night I so glad as he has been rather fussed over it & looking old. I have a man called Paine in as a learner now.[37] His face is crooked I don't know what caused it, he has a brother here too, they are both very nice but not exactly soldiers.

News of Stewart is good I shall see him the day after tomorrow. I have a little school of instruction starting tomorrow. Norman is manning it for me of course! He is my standby in these matters, it will mean I shall get some riding as I shall go over to see them as much as I can but it will keep me busy. My relations with Jones are not very happy I think I must have a chat with him I hate these things so. Naturally if a man thinks he has a grievance it is impossible to convince him he has not!

1.5.17
Marden had a successful raid last night I did not stop up for it, as it was at 1am, I was awake when our bombardment began & then went fast to sleep. At 4am I woke up because the Bosche was shelling & after it was over went round the trenches. Such a lovely morning we got back at 7am. About 11.30am I went off riding to see some of my people & to attend a conference. There was a great air fight & a Bosche was brought down I lunched with Ford & Marden & after the conference I rode back.

2.5.17

I went & saw Stewart today, he looks wonderful & was so cheery, we chatted away about the brigade & he laughed at different things I told him. He does not appear to be in pain, he said he could see red tabs I think he is in good hands.[38] One of the doctors is a brain specialist & the sister is nice of course I had to be taken round the hospital, which is very well provided & so clean & cheerful. Stewart has small pieces of shell in his head but they won't matter if they are clean. Colonel Davies who commands one of our field ambulances took me over to the motor ambulances & I had tea with him on the way back.[39]

I took the Divisional commander round this morning he seems pleased I think. Yesterday morning we had an alarm & I went along to my OP in my pyjamas with coat & steel helmet. A sentry stopped me & asked who I was when he saw his mistake he said beg your pardon sir I was looking at your trousers! Another sentry yesterday did not present arms to me I asked him what rank he thought I was & he said 'Staff Captain!'

Very upsetting about Charles Dobell I was afraid he might get into trouble, it was foolish not to give him leave.[40]

3.5.17

You don't say if Henry was pleased with things or not? Better tell him to come back via our Army & let me go & see him.

I find Mrs Marshall is not Stewart's sister! The foolish clerk got this information from his servant & never asked Stewart. Telegrams are no use. Mrs Stewart sent a wire & letter on the 30th & the letter won. Stewart was brought down the dressing station which is close to here & so I saw him before he went off.

5.5.17

Today I went up the line for a bit & then rode over & had lunch with George Armytage, after to that I went off to my little school.[41] Norman is running it so I hope for better results. Isn't it awful I have two W.H. Jones in one battalion, one is William Hughes[42] & the other William Hugh.[43]

Very hot & close today I inspected some of Normans dugouts & found them very nice. Then after lunch I went out for a bit & got in at 4.15pm & found the Divisional commander here looking very hot. He & Smith (GSO 2) had tea here & then I went off with Smith to walk the horses.[44]

8.5.17

Another lovely day but a little rain early, the divisional commander came round the work. He really doesn't understand engineering & so does not quite appreciate our efforts or our difficulties I think the men are working splendidly now, however he was very pleasant. The first thing his beastly dog did was to fight Halewych dog & after lunch he discovered Brierley's under a chair & seized it by the ear & there was a great commotion. Brierley was rather annoyed as the Divisional commander just looks on & makes no attempt to call the dog off & others have to struggle & run the risk of being bitten. Brierley seems quite nice and to have his wits about him, he hasn't the character of Stewart.[45]

10.5.17
Another lovely day I went over to see Norman & his school in the morning. Marden was very sleepy today I thought he ought to get a Division, he is tired of this. Minshull-Ford has to go he is not well enough & thinks he must have a rest I am very sad about it.

11.5.17
The leave problem is very difficult, there is a lot of bitterness I fear over junior officers behind the line (very often those that are sent there because there is no use for them at the front) getting leave whilst regimental Officers don't get it. Minshull-Ford is not well (his last wound) & has to have a rest. Hodson is very seedy & must have a bit of leave too, so the hale & hearty ones like myself have to wait.

HQ 115th Inf Bde.

My Dear Price-Davies
Request for leave – my old wound at Bazentin when I was blown up and got bad concussion.[46] I have had headaches lately that I felt fit for nothing & unable to do justice to my command. This is very hard and difficult to know what to do, but I felt that I should breakdown badly if I went on and now seemed the moment when there is nothing pending actually and when my successor can come easily into my shoes.
    Take care of yourself and don't do too much
    Grateful for your letter – I shall never forget.

Yours ever
Minshull-Ford

17.5.17
Did I tell you Brierley is a good horseman, he has two good little horses, one of which has won jumping competitions I think he will be a success, he is very quick too & a gent. I hope to go to Henry shortly & will let you know. Blackader was very silly about it & thought I ought not to go when out training, as the Corps didn't like it. As the place I was going to has hardly any training ground & as I had arranged to be there Sunday & will only miss one days training it was absurd.
    I went to see Norman at his school where things are going well. Then to lunch with George Armytage, the younger William was there he has a DSO &

MC now. I hear Priaulx did very well with the 11th battalion I also saw a letter from Evan Williams describing the work of his battalion when they captured 18 Bosche guns whilst the gunners were serving them, with surprising small casualties.[47] It was a good performance.

14.5.17
Great excitement last night, the Bosche tried to raid us but got scared off & we captured a prisoner. It happened at 3am & after it was over Campbell & I went round. We found men frightfully pleased with themselves.

15.5.17
I get the subalterns in the morning & talk over their patrol work with them I get to know them that way & may possibly teach them something. That was at 9.30am & at 10am I had some men before me who had applied for commissions, one looked a washy student but I remembered him in the front line when his bloodthirsty attitude towards the Bosche & his desire to send rifle grenades at him struck me as contrasting sharply with his mild exterior.

Jones did not come out of the leave allotment & Co's must be given rest they have a very hard time of it & so much depends on them. John Chamberlain who was on my staff on the Somme has been killed he did not belong to the brigade.[48]

The Divisional commander came in he said he did not wish to complain about work & then did! I'm very pleased with it & told him so! Then we went for a walk & talk about some work, meanwhile Marden has been for breakfast & I was not able to go with him as the Divisional commander got in the way. After lunch Anthony & I & Hallewych went to some billets, on arrival it was found that the front spring had broken but the MT people are handy & mended quickly. I shall get away early on the 18th to see Henry, he is sending a car for me.

18.5.17
Henry's car has come & is in town near here & Hallewych has gone off so as to bring it up in the morning so all plans are made. I went to see Normans school which has now closed & in the afternoon Brierley & I went round the trenches. Then George Armytage came to dinner I wrote to the Divisional commander & objected to his complaints about the work that we have done, now he says he did not complain, but if he didn't he has a queer way.

At Henry's

Henry I find is away which is sad but he ought to be back for dinner. After lunch we were all going for a ride so I thought I might as well go too. You never saw such a lovely forest & you can ride for miles on the most beautiful soft tracks & then you come out into the open glades that remind me of Phoenix Park. We had a good gallop I don't think much of Henrys horse. I came in soon after 4pm & the others went to the office, Woodroffe, Eric Dillon & Hunter (new since I was here before, a Cavalry Officer).

19.5.17

Henry got back last night so we had a chat before dinner in the garden. He didn't have much to tell me but I shall get more out of him later. Russia seems bad. Cecil's idea that Henry wants to give up is entirely wrong.

20.5.17

Yesterday afternoon Henry took me to see Huguet at Soissons.[49] He was rather low about things I was so pleased to see him again & he was as nice as ever. It was a lovely drive down there I had not done it since that famous occasion when Baker-Carr took me along a few hundred yards from the Bosche front line. Huguet gave us tea, it was very quaint he wouldn't take any himself & there was no milk. After that he took us to see a French fellow who has invented something & he held forth about it for hour I found I could understand every word of what he said. It was very interesting & we were to have gone to Paris this morning to see the thing but being Sunday the place would be closed. On the way back Henry kept on stopping to pick people up! First a woman & then a French soldier. Henry has a nice suite of rooms on the ground floor in his home. A sitting room leading to a bath room then a wash place & beyond that a WC, but he has electric light.

21.5.17

Henry saw Petain & had a chat with him I think he is a strong man with some sense in his head.[50] I started off & had a good run to Doullens & then on to see Tavish I had a cup of tea there & a short chat & then on to hunt for Taffy I had some trouble but eventually managed to run him down to earth by picking up one of his men who had a South African ribbon and told me I could drive a car 'across the Veldt!'. Got to Taffy, he is very well but it is a rotten line. Having a young adjutant & a doctor with not a thought in common. He lives in a tent & has a sort of mess line we used to rig up in SA. We had quite a good dinner of course, special whisky & port he gets out himself. On the way yesterday I passed an officer plodding up a hill, when I got to the top I found there appeared to be no way for him to go so I waved for him & gave him a lift, he had 14 kilometre to go!

23.5.17

I went over to see Colonel Jones billets & saw his companies today. Things are not satisfactory with him, but that feeling things are not well run & that he is not putting sufficient energy with it but nothing is tangible & I feel if I say anything over small things he will get more bitter & have a grievance I wish the Indian foot would take him away!!

Hunter who is with Henry is the polo player, he stays with the Duke of Westminster & plays for his teams.[51] He is quite nice & I suspect is a friend of Needham's rather in the same way as he might be of Bryan Carlings I wonder is Needham a 'great friend of Hunters?'

24.5.17

The weather is good now, not too hot. The men are happy in their billets but the training ground is not over good. We have a cinema coming today I must go to see it.

25.5.17

We had a little episode today which are unpleasant & cause a lot of worry & loss of time. Norman's guard did not turn out for me so Brierley went and told his Sgt Major. The Sgt Major complained to Norman that Brierley had 'told him off in front of the other NCO's' which he never did & Norman wrote a furious letter to me & B had to go & see N. It is all right now but it is so unnecessary. Brierley I am sure never said anything wrong to the SM as he is a good fellow with good manners & a gentleman.

Yes, Henry was in good form I don't see how anyone could have foreseen all the remarkable changes that have happened during the war. Even the Bosche didn't think it could safely rely on another winter campaign I think Henrys solution is correct. It is a question now that Russia is useless whether the submarines will stop the America coming over or whether we shall down the submarines & then the Americans will be able to send troops over, but of course they won't be ready till next year as the first lot don't come till September! What peace could we make now? Certainly not a satisfactory one. Germany sees the success of her submarines & sees that Russia is done, for the present any rate & that our offensives this side have made no great headway. It is likely she could give us any terms which would be acceptable with honour or under which we could ever be happy, if we didn't mind about honour. That's all I don't think food will end the war unless Germany starves us!!

27.5.17

Brierley, Anthony & I went off to see a new training area today. I saw Tim on the way back & we tried to see Rothwell but he was out.[52] We met some charming New Zealanders today & had tea with them & Brigade Staff. I had asked Fielding for lunch but had to cancel on account of my trip.[53] Unfortunately he never got the wire & turned up, however he had lunch with Hull & Humphreys I wonder if they talked to him at all.

The weather continues to be glorious. Campbell's & Normans battalions are the best at present. Sorry you did not see Smuts,[54] his remark to Henry was very nice I think I suppose Henry told you, 'Well General I'll give you a toast, a Dutchman & an Irishman both agin the government' I was at advanced GHQ & Dick was there, Tavish said Henry was so nice to work with & so rubbed it in that Henry was the straightest man we have.

28.5.17

We had a church parade & I gave the medal ribbons, then after the band was in fine form & marched off to join the other 2 battalions. It was then that I found my orders not attended to & there was trouble about it. Anthony foolishly put the blame on Vernon but it appears that after I left Brierley went into question & found Vernon was not concerned at all. So Brierley told Anthony what he thought of him & that Anthony must tell me the facts. So last night 'A' owned up, an unpleasant incident. You know Colonel Campbell can't stand 'A' & told Stewart 'mark my words he'll let you down'.

About noon Colonel Rudkin, Kennedy & Harvey came along in a motor & we went to see some tanks.[55] The dust on the road was appalling & we were white with it. We were late too though for a variety of reasons & missed part of the show & a good many of the people to thank as they left early. The tanks were delightful I met Hodson,[56] Blacklock (the latter left the regiment as a 2 Lt & is now a Brigadier with a DSO & bar).[57] I also saw Solly-Flood & others you would not know including my original signalling officer who was very well I was quite close to Taffy but having others with me who had further to go I would not get to see him.

29.5.17

I had a lot of schemes to work out this morning but went out to see some training. Hodson is very sad because he has not mentioned in despatches. Funny some fellows round here are mentioned 2 or 3 times & did not want it I hope I do not get anything this honours list it will be much more satisfactory if I don't. The inevitable has happened a man has got two things because they would not give him one. He did well in a raid and they would not give him a Military Cross, so since his name has gone in regularly for a French decoration etc. Now he has got a mentioned in despatches and a Croix de Guerre! You see when you send in a name you never know if anything will come of it or not.

29.5.17

The Brigade has been in and out of the trenches N of Ypres since I came back from leave on 14th January. There have been slight shifts up at one time we had 3 Brigades in the line I being in the centre. Then I was on the left in command of 6 battalions whilst Marden went out with his. Next I found myself out at D Camp commanding 15th RWF of my brigade & 10th Welch of the 114th Brigade.

The 6 Battalion front was found to be too much & a demi-brigade alternating under Colonel Hayes & Colonel Norman was instituted taking the left battalion front of my Brigade with Brigade HQ at my old place on the Canal Bank. On the right of this 113th Bde & 114th were to go in.

This lasted a short time then there was a reshuffle & some of our trenches went over to the 39th Division & we returned to the arrangement of 2 Brigades in & one out & I found myself in my normal front, offensive echelons were put forward & we are starting to work hard on our preparations in April after a troubled March & in May work went on well.

I am now staying with Henry at his chateaux at Compeigne where he is with the French GQG. The situation is not good & there appears to be no reasonable prospect of the war finishing for several years. Russia is under civil war & quite useless for the present. France just changed Nivelle for Petain in the high command so is temporarily disorganised. America is not yet in a position to help us except with the destroyers. Submarines still very active & there are no signs at present that we have got the better of them in any way.

30.5.17

We marched off at 5 this morning & halted on the way for an hour & came in a great style only about 10 miles but the men went well. The man who runs the mess is sick. Something disagreed with us but I think it was a chill. The chateau is empty, quite a nice little house with wisteria & honeysuckle in it.

31.5.17

This morning we continued our march at 5.30am, we went along as before in 2 columns. One halt was close to my old billet with the Hussets, you can imagine how delighted they were to see me I took Anthony in too. They asked after you. They asked us if we would have something to eat & suggested cold beef. We were not very enthusiastic then an omelette so we jumped at that, the old ladies were delighted & rushed off & we had such a feed. Omelette & good white wine & brown bread (made by themselves) & finally coffee & brandy & all before 10am. However we felt much better for it, then I rejoined the other column. We managed the march very well though it was bitter today & all the arrangements went well.

Of course I see how often Henry has gone wrong but has anyone else been right? The changes were too many for anyone to foresee. If we had good and aggressive statesmen & diplomats they might foresee the results of their actions but as we leave the inniative with the Bosche the whole business becomes bogged down at once.

1.6.17

Did I tell you Follett has now come here & not Kelly (60th) I have not seen him but I have spoken to him on the telephone.[58] Tonight we have a great digging scheme on so we will not have breakfast.

4.6.17

Quite the hottest day we have had, the weather is certainly glorious but the ground is so hard it is no pleasure riding. I went round Campbell's billets & then he & his officers went out to a dinner in a town nearby. Brierley & I went out to see some shooting & we have been busy all day with the shoot, which was rather a success. The trench mortars frightened us as they started sending bombs over close to us, however luckily they were not charged & so did not explode.

Hodson is doing well now & at present there is peace with Jones I had a little row with Norman the first day of march. He got his battalion mixed up with others, he was entirely in the wrong but tried to make out it was my fault

& spoke to me in a way he shouldn't, so I let him have it. All is peace I think he had made a fool of himself.

5.6.17

So Campbell & Norman have got the DSO, the former when I told him looked at me in blank amazement & said 'But why? Oh well'. He said, 'It pleases the women folk' and apparently fought no more of it. Ford has been wounded again I don't know how badly but isn't it bad luck I am going to hear P.de B. Radcliffe[59] lecture today on the Vimy fighting, he is giving it two parts & unfortunately I cannot stay for second part.[60] Rothwell came to dinner last night he is running a musketry school.

6.6.17

Such excitement Brierley has lost his nice dog not long ago & I think I saw it in a RFC lorry. Anthony careered after it but could not stop it. Yesterday I spent watching training & Brierley & I went to such a good lecture by P.de B.Radcliffe on the Vimy attack I met several Generals I had not seen for some time including Sammy Wilson, Biddy, & George Armytage I took him & two fellows with him to dinner. The mess rose well to the occasion. They went back to the second part of the lecture, which I couldn't go to because we had night operation. (The lorry has come back but it is another dog.)

7.6.17

Today I went to work at training as usual I don't think I exercise much effort on it though I continually see things being done wrong. Brierley has got an MC, his brother is in the 21st Lancers & is very sick of life in India I can never think of Follett as married it doesn't seem to fit.[61] We dined last night Brierley & I & Rothwell. A very good dinner with strawberries & cream, Rothwell was full of chat as usual.

Today I was watching training & had lunch in the field with Hodson eventually we rode back for tea I saw Leggett this morning he seems a good sort of K man.[62] The news is so good for Plumer sake & Tim too of course.

8.6.17[63]

I rejoined the Brigade at Houtlinque on the 21 June. The training area was bad there but troops get well rested. Then the Wytschaete Messines offensive took place & was a great success. The summer has been brilliant no rain for ages except thunderstorms on the night of the 6th June.

10.6.17

I am perturbed I wrote a letter to the General in which I could not do certain things under certain conditions. This morning I had an interview with him. He was very nice about it & not a bit angry but told me I was wrong to write the letter. I stuck to my point however & tried to convince him that his standpoint was really the same as mine. What worries me are two things, first whether

I have satisfied him or whether he thinks he cannot rely on me in the future. Secondly, whether I wasn't really entirely in the wrong. Anyway I have written an apology & have asked if he has the slightest doubts about me to remove me I don't think he will but it is the least I can do I am afraid I am hasty in writing sometimes & I got annoyed with his staff which doesn't help matters.

I went round the trenches today, the country is so different since the last time I was here things have grown up so. The dry weather continues I hope it will upset the Bosche harvest. The new Brigadier in Fords place is Cope. He has only 12 years service they say, so he must be by far the youngest Brigadier we have.[64]

12.6.17

I don't agree with you about not attacking, we must attack I don't suppose the Bosche wants us to attack him. Anyway he can't have enjoyed the Messines affair very much I believe there was very few dead Bosche to be seen only bits.

I saw Cope today the new brigadier, he looks about 35 certainly no more, and he has a DSO & Bar to it. I have asked to get rid of Anthony so he will go I think. Poor little man he has lost all confidence in himself so the thing is hopeless I hope to get a good man & not a Welshman! Marden caught 3 Bosche last night who tried to raid him. Surely Henry not really thinking of giving up his job I think it would be a great pity I'm sure he won't do so without very strong reasons.

13.6.17

Possibly some in my position would have expected a decoration but really I have done nothing for it, Marden is lucky to get a Legion. They overlooked the fact he had got a Russian decoration! He is thought a great deal of. Why has Dick Bennett been degummed?

14.6.17

I had a letter from Henry he tried to see me but I had moved I am feeling rather low about him. He tells me Congreve has lost an arm, this is a great loss.[65]

15.6.17

Jones has been unlucky & has a few casualties. He feels this was always very much. Pryce & Pryce-Jones came round this afternoon & actually had tea with one of the battalions I told Follett who lunched with me that he should get about & see the Co's.[66] I went round & went to see what work had been done in the night. Hornby has been in.[67] He is very deaf & the Doctor has been syringing his ears, he has been knocked about by a shell.

I think it is absurd trying to pretend that Redmond dying in an Ulster field ambulance can have any bearing on the settlement of the Irish question.[68] Goodlady is right about Lloyd George trying to please everyone & I am afraid it is a Welsh failing & a bad fault.

17.6.17

The General was round today, he expressed sympathy about my having had no leave & said I could not take any just now. He asked if I would like 2 days but I think it is hardly worth it I may go to Henry or Boulogne or Paris or something like that, let me know what you think. The General was here a long time & we had a talk. He was quite alright with me.

18.6.17

Battle of Waterloo

I suppose they give London all the aircraft they can. They must send out here all the aircraft they can & one could never say they were enough considering all that has been done so London must suffer first. George Armytage came over to see me yesterday & was met by a shell almost at the door & took refuge with Brierley & telephoned to say he was there.

19.6.17

Great news Jones is off so there is an end to my troubles anyway I am much relieved as he was a great bother to me now who shall I get? Yesterday Rudkin came back so I shall lose my nice new gunner I wrote to Follett after I had several worries & rows & suggested I should give up the Brigade, as I do not appear to be commanding with much success. He said that was all rot & I make all the difference.

Midnight 19/20.6.17

I have had a nasty bite from a horse fly in the top of my ear, it is painful at times & all swollen up I got the Doctor in & he has proscribed. Also I had a boil on my neck but I think it will go like the other did. Altogether I am a poor person!

22.6.17

We had a little raid last night & got in all right & bombed a Bosche dugout. My ear is practically finished now & it is not so tender, the Doctor has been at the boil with a knife (under cocaine). It is very comfortable now he says my blood is quite alright because the small boil on my forehead did not get big. It is the microbes in the water & he has given me some cocaine to put on

My new Corps Commander came to see me, he really is nice I have known him since the war began he is always so friendly.[69] We had a chat he said I looked 'bonnie', a curious expression but everyone says how well I am looking.

24.6.17

Henry told me about the offer of a Corps I am glad he was offered it. Brierley doing well from a fighting point of view. He is better than Stewart but I don't think he will ever be as popular, but one can't have everything.

25.6.17

If I get leave I will have to return on the 30th, we are very busy & things are going quite well. Last night I went round the battalions after dinner & then up the trenches with Harri Williams & got in about 1am.[70] George Armytage on leave & Herbert Stepney is commanding & came to see me yesterday.[71]

4.7.17

Russian news appears very good. I got over to Boulogne by 9am & not feeling much like dinner alone. There is a scandal, the divisional commander took a car & went to the theatre. The chauffer didn't approve & gave lip, he said something about 'whose paying for the petrol?'

The Corps commander came around & was pleasant I have not got over the after leave depression. Russian news continues good. Mollett will be a very good staff officer I think. Quite giving & a gentleman.

5.7.17

I hear Cavan is very optimistic about the end of the war, can't say I am I hope the Russians will go & have another push.

7.7.17

A lovely day certainly we were lucky with the weather I had a conference yesterday afternoon being on the training ground all morning & then a car picked me up & Cope & Marden & I all went to tea & a conference at Divisional HQ. I go to Divisional HQ tonight for dinner & tomorrow to Vimy with Marden & Hastings.

8.7.17

Just back from Vimy we had a bad day for seeing but it kept fine. It was very interesting such a wilderness as it all is and such a lot of shell holes. It reminded me of Spion Kop in a way, with the flat plain behind.[72] I had breakfast with Marden & then the car called for. We went to Henrys old HQ looking so pretty now, just a year since I was there before.

9.7.17

One of the new Co's is not very satisfactory & it is difficult because he is so much older than me & he is smug & thinks himself very good I think. There was good news from Russia I am getting quite an optimist.

11.7.17

The Divisional band has come. I took some fellows in a tactical exercise & got in about 3.45pm when a car and took me to the Divisional HQ where we had tea and a conference. Things going smoothly between Pryce, now it is only occasionally he reaches the boil. I hope the Russians will continue to push it should have a splendid setting affect on them having these victories.

16.7.17

There are some officers coming for a tactical problem I quite like the new Co, but I was doubtful about his keenness. Uniacke is 45 but you would not think he is older than me, he looks very young.[73]

The Vimy Ridge is not actually like Spion Kop but behind it you have a plain stretching away & nothing to stop you as it were. Tomorrow I am going for a trip to the trenches, a motor car is calling for me at 10am I shall take Brierley, Jourdain & Uniacke.[74]

18.7.17

I am off to see two battalions march in. The Corps commander came round yesterday, very optimistic. Brierley has fever, speculation about hospital, we had two doctors with him tonight. Vernon Jones will have to be the Brigade Major.

19.7.17

I went round to see the battalions today, they are very comfortable. Then there was a conference with the Divisional commander & after lunch we moved a short distance. You could have laughed, Hull told me to go to a certain cross roads & we all duly arrived there but found no sign of brigade HQ or any guides or tents or anything. What was to be done & how would anyone find us or we them! I was lost & had lost my brigade I was arguing with my staff about it. Luckily we found the camp about a mile away but in this flat country we might have to go miles without finding anyone. Brierley looked awful & had a temperature of 103.4, he has to go to hospital. Very surprised to see Edward Geddes appointment.[75]

21.7.17

I was up early & out with Jourdain round the trenches I left my HQ at 9.30am to go to the trenches but did not get there till after 1pm having a good deal to do en route. Weather keeps very fine. I think.

22.7.17

Bicycled over to the gunners to arrange some details & had lunch with them, got back at 3pm. Very busy since Jourdain came to tea & some of the Divisional staff. I have to be up at 3.45am. Brierley warned me not to let anyone ride the horses, it is all very fine but they are part of the establishment they are not really his. However I will do what I can for him.

25.7.17

I have had disturbed nights lately & last night only had about 3 hours sleep I went out early & met another brigadier & had a chat & went round some trenches & back at 9am. Then I went off with Follett & eventually got to HQ for lunch, then a conference & back for tea. Follett looks worried & does not cheer up at all. Did I tell the Divisional commander was not a Bosche. The Russians seem broken don't they?

26.7.17
Everything goes today I expect & one Mollett comes to this place so we have Mollett & Follett!! It pelted with rain last night & the men got very wet digging but it is a fine & drying day now with sun & wind which makes all the difference I was so sorry for them last night I was out with them from 10.30pm to 2am.

27.7.17
Took Campbell & myself to Divisional HQ to meet Corps commander after that I saw Uniacke & Jourdain. Brown Clayton was in today, he says there was a rumour that the Sein Feiner's would dump all the loyalists in the south of Ireland.[76]

30.7.17
When you get this we shall either have been successful or not. It has been hard work & many times I have been in despair but I see I must go on & not give in now whatever. The gunfire is good & the Bosche trenches are no more. Still he is a good fighter & we may have trouble pushing over the canal, the other day we were forward & yesterday I was walking about in no mans land. All hope that all is well. My staff have been grand none could have done better & Campbell & Norman of course absolutely heroic. I had a pained sleep last night.
9.30pm
Just moved to my new HQ & go to another meeting at 2am I wonder how many of us shall move on tomorrow. Very quiet tonight which I don't like the Bosche will smell a rat. Well I hope Henry could take hold of the country & get things going. He might do something but it seems too late to start after 3 years of war.

31.7.17[77]

'Capture of Pilckem Ridge'
New dugout made for a double battalion HQ was nearly knee deep in water. Some of the troops in trenches for 2 nights already, artillery fired away as usual. The German reply was not so serious as usual. At 3.30am the barrage & bombardment opened with a beautiful display of burning oil drums & some other fearful forms of frightfulness. I did see the fellows go over & anyway it was not too healthy outside my dugout. The line moved into Battle HQ at 2.30am, all went well except signal communication which was a disaster eventually I got the message via telephone I went to the front line & everything was chaos though the concrete dugouts had withstood the artillery fire in a wonderful manner. Everything looked the same dull & uninteresting and many of my old landmarks have gone.

I reached the spot where I expected to form my new HQ but there was nothing there to be seen but another dugout. The telephone had moved on so on I went but we very soon found we were in a very unpleasant spot sitting in an open shell hole near the railway. I was close to Pilckem & a kindly subaltern told me of a good strong point to which I moved. All round us was the chaos of battle, equipment, rifles, ammunition & every conceivable thing lay in piles outside the door. And do dugout was not complete without one or two corpses inside & a collection of wounded inside all Bosche. I heard stories of the fight told to me by an excited subaltern. At some point a corporal had led two men & rushed a dugout whence MG's were firing, bayoneted the inmates & captured 2 MG's.

There were very few of our casualties to be seen but more were coming back from the next objective, and there was an anonymous message that the '15 RWF' were held up at some old barns. It had only been a short time and opposition was soon overcome. As the line of the Steenbeck was approached more & more blockhouses appeared but my brigade had gained all its objectives & did not go as far as that. In the afternoon & evening shelling became more intense. Now men fell & conditions became very bad but nothing really dampened the spirits of the men. The officers too were magnificent they seemed to have suddenly developed & have gained confidence in themselves & to have realised the power to command the men & help them in difficulties.

The night was spent in brigade HQ. Subsequent days contained more of the glory of war but called for the highest military virtues, patients, endurance of the wet ground where little shelter existed & where the rain rapidly filled up the trench as soon as it was dug. Every day I inspected a collapse, numbers of men were falling exhausted but instead their spirit never flagged & with the return of the sun & the idea of relief they soon began to look more cheerful.

1.8.17

4.30pm

My fellows fought splendidly yesterday and I have no doubt the prime Minster that due prominence is given to it in the press. I got my HQ into a strong Bosche dugout and later on Campbell came & shared it and we had a great meal & a good sleep. The men are very wet in the trenches. Follett came round about 11.30am & had some breakfast. I didn't feel nearly as excited as I thought I should getting into this hill we have been looking at for 11 months. I had a narrow shave a sergeant alongside me got a nasty splinter in his arm I bound him up whilst doing so another shell pitched within 5 yards of us & never touched us. The rain is very disheartening I still have suspicions as to the strict neutrality of the almighty. Well I think if he is against us I think we deserve it.

2.8.17

My feet are still wet & boots are caked in mud so that we really have no interest in taking them off. The men are wonderful but the weather is still bad still although there has been little actual rain. The more I looked round the more proud I am of my fellows, they did and are doing splendidly. Norman[78] wounded is a great loss I am afraid he is bad I wonder who the officers were who had the incompetence to deserve this Brigadier!! I have a nice gunner here called Knevett by name. He and Brierley take great care of me & feed me at intervals! I had some sleep last night. There was a dense howl of gunfire at the present I hear the papers have a piece on us. I have more boils on my forehead they have some from mosquito bites. I think I will finish this now communication is precarious in the mud.

There were some cheery incidents in the fight, a corporal & 2 men charged a fortified house in which there were two machine guns. They bayoneted the occupants & captured the two guns. There were other similar incidents which shows my fellows were advanced in their military education. Mostly due to Norman who set a good example & taught them in those few courses at the Brigade school I am so glad they have had the experience they will be able to teach others.

4.8.17

Weather much improved. Wonderful I kept my boots off last night I stuffed paper in them & today they are all right again I hope I shall have a definite change for the better and that the mud will subside. The thermos flasks are awfully useful. Brierley having refused almost any sleep has now gone to the other is extreme & is very dozy. I am awfully fit and not a bit tired send me some café au lait & Bruno, if you can get them. It was extremely difficult moving up to the position. Had the enemy shelled the ridges & put over gas shells in quantities it might have delayed us so that we could not get to the assembly positions in time.

Did I tell you we broke one of the crack regiments the famous 'Berlin Cockchafers'. My officers have been superb & some have come out most determined too so I think staff work went well. The breeze here is no doubt more healthy & drying but it blows the candles about abominably. Our meals are simple bully beef, jam and a tin of salmon or something nothing hot but tea, we eat plenty & things are not too bad.

5.8.17

Marden came up last night & we had dinner with him. He did not appreciate the mud. They gave us a good dinner. About 1am Brierley & I came down. My feet were sore but I am very fit. The men were wonderful I saw them on my way back, singing, joking, thy all done well, had clean clothes, dinner, free cigarettes etc. I came on in a car here picking Vernon up on the way. We got here about 5 to find a lady drying her ham in the kitchen. It was a wintry night & we were chilly & very glad to see the cheery fire in the kitchen.

At 5.45am we had a good breakfast & got to bed at 6.15am but I had to get up at 8.30am to go to see the troops get into the train. Mollett thought it would be better to come straight here but of course it really gave extra trouble going back. However I saw the Major General, he is very pleased of course. I am having such a lot of trouble with Campbell he is so injudicious & say things he ought not to. The General said Campbell abused his position & he had been insulted because he dined when their dinner was late I think this is the case. My opinion then was that he was out of line, he told Price 'I better go up with him Price-Davies is sure to make a mess of it', I don't believe for one minute he said such a thing in earnest I am told now that he fainted last night coming down & another officer commanding a battalion not a popular CO fainted & went to hospital.

Everyone wanted to know if I had been wounded & brought a paper to send to me in hospital. Norman lost an arm & is very upset about it, he was such a keen soldier & will be a terrible loss. I met the Army commander's car today, they stopped & congratulated me etc, he came round twice this afternoon. I shall take a good rest tonight. The men were off to sleep the second they got to their tents. It is warm and sunny so I hope things will dry up. The rain lessened my casualties a shell would have hit me I think if the ground had not been soft. I sent you the little story of the battle yesterday. I've just been saluted by the Prince of Wales, he did quite nicely.

5.8.17

Our battle has come & gone & we have won it. We had trying times during the preliminary bombardments & suffered casualties from gas shells. A few days before the attack we had to send out a reconnaissance because they the enemy was retiring & we lost a company of the 15th & did little good but the Germans on our left got across the canal & stayed which helped a little.

On the 31st we attacked the Pilckem Ridge at dawn & took all our objectives & the 115th brigade went on beyond & took the line of the Steenbeck. The rain fell & fell & fell & the trenches filled & the men had to stand up to their knees in the water & got no sleep or very little sleep. However they kept wonderfully cherry & we came out of the line the night of the 4/5th August & went to Proven.

All rather tired Brierley fainted & I got to Proven at 5am & then had breakfast & a short sleep & I came back to Elverdinghe to see the men entrain. The battalion we fought was the 3rd Guards Regiment, The Berlin Cockchafers. They are a fine lot & it is my thinking that they did not put up much of a fight in spite of heavily concreted blockhouses which withstood all out bombardments.

6.8.17

I am so distressed at you not getting my letters you ought not to have been without news of me. The letter certainly did not get back I am afraid something must have happened to the runner. A regular to command in Norman's place. I now hear that Norman has had his arm amputated. A little fellow HG Jones who was on my staff & then went to Divisional HQ has had his leg shot off below the knee & by some miraculous chance he did not die & I am told he is so cheery. Another man got a slight wound, made no effort to live & died. On the way a military policeman & I got stuck by a side road & we could not push the car out anyway. In the end a kind man came along with a horse & pulled me out, he had to pull me nearly a mile. This morning there was a short conference at Divisional HQ. The Divisional commander was 40 minutes late, which was unnecessary, especially as Marden had got to bed at 3am.

Hubert Gough came to tea.[79] He is very much the same, very cheery but nevertheless emphatic in his opinion about people & does not hesitate to express his opinion but does it quietly, he is very pleasant.

I went round with the Corps commander today & then round myself to say a few words to the battalions. They are all in the best of spirits. Montgomery arrived tonight and had dinner here.[80] Would you do something for the man who pulled me out of the mud, cigarettes, magazines or something of that sort. Address AJC Mirson, 46th Mobile Section, & say from General Price-Davies, thanks for pulling him out of the mud. I should say 5/- would do it.

9.8.17

I feel rotten with my cold. The usual places in the chest but I have it in the head too. There is a regular epidemic. Taffy has been here for lunch & stayed till after 3.30pm, he looks very well. He hardly asked about my show at all, all he said was 'Your fellows did very well didn't they', seems queer he didn't ask me anything about it.

I am afraid my notes are nothing more than personal reminiscences I hardly told you anything of the fighting. Some of the people have such vivid imaginations it is hard to get at the truth. My casualties were fairly heavy all round but spread out over some days. I was in the line from the 20 July I was the only Brigadier up & my battalions were changing every few days. Then I was to have 48 hours break but then this idea came along that the Bosche was off & so I never got out till the 4th so I had a doze of it, as it wasn't ordinary warfare.

9.8.17

I was greatly relieved to get your letter & to know that you got my wire letter I don't think it was any good sending a line until I came out of the danger as there was a chance of a shell in these parts I have such a lot of letters to write but hardly have time I can spare. We had a dinner last night all the Co's who were with me in action, except Hibbert the MG man who was in bed ill.

Brierley is silly over horses too he does not like these people riding them but they are the brigade majors not his, so Vernon told him he could ride them if he had to.[81] Some of the horsy men are very conceited I think I wonder what Henry will do I gather from Ada's letter that he has something in mind.

Yes we knocked the stuffing out of the Berlin Cockchafers & many men behaved with the greatest gallantry I hope they will get a lot of decorations. A guardsman annoyed Campbell & me last night the way he talked insinuating that the Guards had done everything. I got a letter from Tim Bridges, Hubert Campbell is with him.[82]

12.8.17

Mollett is an RC I find he doesn't look like one! Follett & Jourdain & Uniacke came to dinner last night. As they had a nice closed car I got them to give the

CO's a lift home as it was raining. I rode over to lunch with Taffy yesterday he has a jolly little cottage which does for him & his Doctor & Adjutant. And I then went to the 115th Brigade on the way back & had a talk to Gwynne Thomas & had tea there.[83] He was always friendly, an oldish man, he seems to like getting up early & expects everyone else to do the same I have all my battalions close to me which is a change, as a rule they are scattered, they are all in tents.

A lovely day & church went off well & Llewelyn Gwynne, Bishop of Khartoum, was very pleased with the attendance. The tune I liked very much was Aberystwyth. Vernon tells me it is in the Welsh Hymn Book. The Divisional commander went to Boulogne for the day yesterday, queer taste.

Just back from dinner with Hubert. He really could not be nicer than he is now. It is as if all those years had disappeared & we were together again as we were in S.A. Hubert has not changed, he asked me to go up to his room whilst we dressed & we chatted away like old times. We had a very good dinner but afterwards Hubert was busy & we had to leave the mess. It is a very busy time for him now of course.

13.8.17

I was out watching training all morning. Mollett has had a row with Uniacke but I think it will blow over all right. It is cloudy today but so far has abstained from raining I hear from all sides that the Germans are fighting boldly. Algie Carmichael said that his men had to kill them with spades. I shall be out tomorrow if it is fine I am taking the brigade out to a new bit of ground.

15.8.17

I am glad you liked Brierley. He is a bit proud that class of people annoy me I like people more humble! However he is a very good staff officer & I'm lucky to have him. Marden is getting a Division, I'm glad it is high time but I am very sorry he is leaving as he is a great standby when he is a senior Brigadier, he carries more weight with the Divisional commander.[84] Now we are getting, who do you think Harman, you remember him & how he flew round the women.[85] Marden did very well in the attack.

15.8.17

The rain is exasperating & will ruin offensive. Tomorrow 20th division will attack & then it will be our turn again but at present we have no men!

Brierley is on leave, Uniacke 14 RWF is on leave. Peace doesn't look very near. There is no doubt that German morale is worse than it was & that they don't fight it as they did.

I dined with H Gough the 5th Army Commander. It really was like old times & he was quite charming to me. He is very much changed in one-way much more tolerant & talks less emphatically & with less excitement but that is still to the good.

19.8.17

We have moved & it isn't a very dangerous place I cant remember when I last wrote but when I think before my reconnaissance I carried out & saw a lot of dead men, one man who had not a stitch of clothing on I never heard of that before but haven't seen it I wonder if the clothes got burnt off I expect so.

We started off from camp at 5.30am & got back at 3pm. Then at 5.30pm I made off to watch a show. It was a very good troupe, 6 of them including a good female impersonator. We had a great dinner & champagne.

Hard to know what Henry might do when I don't know what he could get if he tried but I think he might accept Home Command, as there appears to be nothing handy.

You've never seen anything like the balloons & aeroplanes that are up tonight. I went round the battalions this evening, Jourdain talks so much I could hardly get a word in anyway, & Campbell (an explosion so way off post has blown my lamp out, Bosche I think) is on standby. I have had my wish being in front of the men presenting all these medals. We went out at 5.30 this morning it was lovely but a bit hazy. We walked along the old Bosche line & I had a good look. My they are strong concrete dugouts, the only thing wrong with most of them is that the whole trench has disappeared & so the dugout was full of water. But if the new trench was made and water drained they would be as good as new. We got back and had breakfast. I went out with some of Campbell's fellows training I am rather mad that his battalion which did its bit like the rest has not done too well in decorations.

21.8.17

We are doing great training & built two rifle ranges & we are all enjoying the fine weather. Isn't it splendid the Italians having these attacks, all help & I am particularly pleased at the Austrians poor things. The Russians & Rumanians are doing better at the moment too.

23.8.17

Yesterday was a very tiring day I went to see Harman & walked over the country & had a good look at it & then came back. We really didn't walk far but I felt quite weary it was a slack sort of day & I felt tired before I started. With my glasses I saw some Bosche who were being shelled. Poor things were running in all directions not knowing where to go.

Uniacke was very seedy, he has a bad inside from a wound & he has got to get rid of the poison in it. I shall try to get month's leave or a job at home or something this winter, 2 years with the brigade is long enough. The Divisional commander is sound there is no doubt about that at all!! He has been of the greatest assistance to me with advice. Because they don't like him or Pryce they look for trouble & of course some of Pryce's ideas are impracticable & that makes them think everyone is wrong, but it is not so.

A good thing to keep on at the Bosche & make him see that it is not so very hard for us to capture a few thousand prisoners.

25.8.17

I got a bit of energy & worked till 1am & got some good work done. At that hour an unfortunate individual arrived who had been told to see a neighbouring brigade & wandered about for 2 hours. I sent a runner with him so as to make sure he didn't get lost. Brierley was up early & went to look at the country. Mollett & I presented medal ribbons I have had 65 awards but it is extraordinary how few there were present. Some are wounded & away on leave & on courses & so.

Henry going to America I don't approve of that anyway. Very sad Henry going off alone.

Gwynne Thomas is a queer card so appreciative when I went round the other night before dinner he said he it is so friendly of you coming round like this & persuaded me to have a drink! I felt I couldn't refuse. Then he talked about the battle, I had sent my account of it, which he affected to believe, and then he said, 'by Jove you did do well.'

27.8.17

I went & saw how two of my battalions had fared in the rain. On the way I called at battalion HQ in another brigade commanded by a man named Edwards. He was in bed but said that he would come with me if they& I would stop & have breakfast & then the brigadier came & had a lot to say & then there was some shelling & finally we got started. We went about ½ mile & it began to shell again so we went in behind a dugout I got rather tired with that & suggested we should look at the country over the top so we got up and started to look and a splinter got into Edwards bum. How it hit I can't imagine but it spoilt my day.

Medals are largely a matter of how the Co writes the story out. The strictly truthful Co's gets fewer than the one who exercises a little imagination I rewrite several myself & got all I wanted except one and am struggling for it. Poor Humphreys was hit yesterday I don't think he is very bad but it is in the leg & he will be some time before he is about again. He is a very great loss. Two of my observers were with him & hit also. He was a very nice lad & very good at his job in my HQ for a long time.

29.8.17

The weather is vile Harman & I walked to Divisional HQ for tea & the General had a little conference with us. We neither of us knew why we had been summoned & they of course thought we knew, so it was rather amusing. The Divisional commander gave me some instructions. Then two Co's came to see me & I gave some instructions & then I came away. Jourdain I'm afraid annoys me, he seems to have no ideas & be rather inclined to slide & hope for the best. The thing I was trying to advise was dry clothes for patrols but he wouldn't help in any way & only seemed to have objections so I was rather short with him. I'm afraid perhaps I expect too much from my Co's but somehow so often they don't seem to please me I suppose it is my fault but it made things very difficult.

The man who was wounded with me the other day will be back in a day or two but can't sit down at present!

30.8.17

We are now in very confined quarters but safe. We have a portion of the dugout with bunks in 3 tiers arranged along the walls & we eat & sleep & work here, part of the room is secured for signals. I was up at 3.45am & went out with the CRE & had a good reconnaissance with him & 2 Co's & got back for breakfast. As we have no daylight in here I find my lamp invaluable. The weather is still beastly I do wish it would get hot again & dry up the place or water will be upon us. I don't relish the idea of next winter I think the Bosche must stop & not go on fooling about pretending he is going to win the war

31.8.17

Brierley & I went round the battalions & got back at 2pm & had lunch & then went out with Montgomery at 3pm round his dugouts & got in at 6pm & had tea. Now I shall out about 11pm & shall not be in before 3am so I shall be dead. Prince of Wales was in this morning very chatty.

1.9.17

I had a conference yesterday at 6pm & we had a great chat about things. Yes poor Norman was wounded in the arm, and then a shell caught him as he was coming down. Gwynne Thomas has Ford's brigade. He was in the Devon's & went to Indian Cavalry. He has two wound stripes & is a stout fellow I believe.

The Morning Post account of the battle is all wrong I am told. I am writing the Official account of the battle it is not easy. I wish I knew all about Henry's idea I wonder how he would like Eastern command. Yes a billet in his command would be suitable.

I am writing a letter to Henry I expect he is wanting me I have just had the sweetest letter from the mother of a man in my machine gun company thanking me & the Divisional commander for a Distinguish Service certificate, which we both signed. Colonel Norman is in the 'Russian Hospital' in South Audley Street.

3.9.17

I went out at 8.30am to go round with a battalion commander but when I got there he had just had his second in command wounded & could not go round with me.[86]

4.9.17

This evening Hull & I went round & looked at our trenches from the Bosche lines which was very interesting. Very hot in this tent. Just waiting for new medal ribbons to be brought in & then I shall go round the battalions. Campbell has just been in & we had a talk, he is very frank & one is very inclined to confide in him but as a brigadier one has to be careful & so I don't talk too much. Still it makes me feel very sad that I don't appear to be able to get on well with people like Flower who are good soldiers. What I think is at the bottom of it, that I had little experience I was not in a position to teach but only able to find fault I knew what had to be done but not always how to do it. If those fellows had a brigadier who had experience as a battalion commander things might have been different. Its not that I get in with this fellow or that fellow but that there are so many with whom I don't hit it off, Hodson, Jones, Flower, Uniacke, Jourdain & to a certain extent Carden now that is a serious business & it seems to me it can't be all their faults. I have just written to Pryce Jones & said I want a months leave this autumn or winter & I'm afraid the General won't let me go just now.

The CRE has died too, I feel that very much I liked him so much he was a very good man & absolutely devoted to his job & duty.[87]

I got up at 12 but got a message not to go as there was shelling. However I eventually started off at 12.45 only to find when I got there the Bosche was active & I remained with the people I went to see till 3 when things seemed quieter & went out & did the job & then left them & then an unlucky bit of shell came over & I heard shouting & went over to see what was up & found that both officers were wounded (one has since died) I got stretcher bearers & then came back.

4.9.17

We have been in the line for 6 days with HB at St Iang Farm & with our line in from Langemarck. There has been a great deal of shelling on both sides & I have had over 100 casualties. The concrete dugouts are useful but are also shell traps as the enemy shells all round them & we have had casualties from shells bursting out the doors & from dugouts having eventually been blown in. Going round has been difficult & last night after waiting & waiting for a suitable time I got out with Lloyd 13th RWF to see a trench he had dug & on the way back just as we had parted he got badly wounded & Pritchard who was with him was killed.[88]

We are relieved tonight & we seem to be off to XI Corps (Haking) near Armentieres.[89] I have lost my nerve to a great extent which is most annoying I find I am all right in action but I dread going into danger & find I avoid dangerous places more than I ought. When I think of those who have to be continuously in danger all the time I feel ashamed but I suppose it can't be helped though perhaps if I get the chance it would be wise to take some other job as the effects on the troops cannot help but be bad if they see I am afraid.

Campbell & Uniacke just been on leave & Jourdain has just gone. The two latter are seedy I am afraid I don't hit it off with them Jourdain to my mind does not pay enough attention to detail. Uniacke is poor about his staff work & at the same time does not take the time to read his own orders.

5.9.17
Went to see Gwynne Thomas who was cheery as usual, Taffy came to lunch, I'm afraid he tries me sometimes with the little details of his show I sure he would be tired if I did the same to him. He assured me greatly that I was lucky to see him there because a shell had fallen near him the other day. This made me smile after the shells I have encountered during the last few days.

6.9.17
Raining now hard again, it has been a nice day I saw Campbell & his battalion in the afternoon, they are all so keen and a great pleasure to work with. After that Brierley and I went for a ride, after tea we played badminton.

7.9.17
Hull is going on leave, Humphrey's, Captain Vulcan Williams, Captain Paine, Lt Morgan (a little Tiger) & Lt GEJ Evans are all in the 3rd General Hospital, Wandsworth.[90] Could you go & see them and take something from me.

Hereward sent a car for me, he is very well but worried with so much work I had tea with him & then he brought me back as he was coming this way. John Brough must have been clean off his head.[91] Hereward can give no reason for shooting himself. He went out onto the training ground sent the car away, got into a ditch & shot himself with his revolver I felt very sad when I left Hereward I don't know why.

I am going to the Divisional commander to dine with Hubert on Tuesday but I am afraid I won't see much of him this time. This is a noisy place a few nasty shells at night & I shall be glad to get away from it.

8.9.17
Misty today but now very sunny, we are having a little badminton this afternoon. The flies are bad here. This morning I gave some ribbons away on parade. Great excitement as one of Campbell's men has got a posthumous VC.[92] I wish he had known it this morning, as it would have been read out on parade. The Prince of Wales has not grown up, quite a boy still.

10.9.17
Rather a disturbed night last night, some shells came unpleasantly near before I went to bed & bits clanged on the roof, however once asleep I was alright. I met Colonel Hardress-Lloyd this afternoon.[93] He was quite chatty much more so than he used to be. He asked after Henry.

I'm presenting the silver bugle to the 15th RWF tomorrow, one won in a competition in the winter. I told you about Lloyd getting killed. I'm getting on alright with Uniacke at present & hope it will continue. Montgomery is very tame. There is to be a long conference at divisional HQ tomorrow & I go straight to Hubert from there for dinner.

11.9.17

We had such a lovely camp here with a lovely grass patch for the badminton. There is a lot of them playing now I was out all morning looking at training & also after lunch rode over to Divisional HQ for a conference. The ADC said it would last till 7pm & that I had better come for dinner. However it was over by 4.15pm. Harman & I played Pryce & Follett a frame & got badly beaten. Then I came away & now off to join the divisional commander & 7 the Corps commander.[94]

10.45pm back from dinner. The divisional commander wore a belt but Pryce & I didn't get there about 10 minutes too soon. It turned out there were very few dining. No one at the ends of table & on our side we were spaced out very far. Hubert talked and though I sat next to him I did not get much chance as he had to entertain the Divisional commander. After dinner I talked to Neil Malcom[95] about my first divisional commander & it was rather interesting to know what Haig's opinion of him was! Hubert frightfully pleased that Kerenski[96] assassinated and the soldiers going to Petrograd.[97]

13.9.17

Campbells battalion very concerned that I may go home for 3 months & return to another brigade I don't know what the others think, I would take a billet at home for the winter if it were offered me. That of course is different to trying to get a billet. Of course in any case people will probably say Henry worked it for me!! But it would be very selfish of me to mind a little thing like that.

A quiet day yesterday Mollett & I & two Co's off in a car to look at some trenches. As a matter of fact I did not get much beyond brigade HQ. We started at 8.30am & did not get back till after 9pm. I'm having a conference this afternoon I have such a lot of new officers. We have a desperate lot of boys to get to know, we shall have to work away at them.

14.9.17

Yes I think Hebert Campbell has been badly treated I will write to Henry I must write to Tom Bridges too.[98] My march went off very well & the weather kept fine which surprised me. Two battalions have drums & bugles and make a great noise.

15.9.17

I met Shoubridge, you know he commands a division. He stopped his car & got out to speak to me. He was in tremendous form. A long letter from Herbert Campbell I must see what I can do for the fellow. Poor Brierley has heard that his brother in India is dying of consumption. Our march today worked well, one battalion annoys me they have so many pulling out I hear Evan Williams has a brigade at last.

16.9.17

I have been riding Molletts horse yesterday & today I was on the go all the time watching the march, all our arrangements went A1 in fact we have so pre-managed all the marches well since Brierley came, but I scrutinise the rides closely. That is the difference between a brigadier & a Divisional commander, a brigadier is his own chief staff officer.

18.9.17

The Divisional commander says he will put in for me to go home for 6 months. Evidently Cavan has written to him! So I have agreed but it complicates things as they say I cannot have leave from home if I am going to be transferred home.

19.9.17

The Bosche didn't see when those fellow who were killed because it was dark I thought I told you about it I had been trying to go & look at a piece of work the night before but 3 people got wounded at the battalion HQ as I arrived there & so the CO was too busy to come & at 4am he telephoned again to say there was too much shelling. The next night I was determined to go, it doesn't do for the men to see the senior officers are continually being put off by shelling I waited an hour & a half but in the end had to go much against Lloyds wishes but he is not keen on that sort of thing, and I had no whisky to put some spirit into him. A rumour got about that I was hit but Campbell says the men don't think I could ever be hit!!

19.9.17

I feel very unsettled I now hear that no application for leave went in for me but they have applied for me to go home for 6 months. Will you let Henry know the result of this letter & thank him, also ask if he can get me into his command. Well that's the end of the Welsh Division for me I don't mind leaving the divisional staff but I shall hate leaving a lot of my brigade. I wonder what will become of them all. Pryce-Jones thinks the application should go through as quickly as an application for 6 months leave could but it has to go through the Corps & Army to GHQ & you know what that means 2 or 3 days at each HQ it goes through & then it has to toddle much the same on the way back I shall hear nothing for 10 days.

20.9.17

The Second Army seem to have done well in their attack.[99] We are very nervous when the rain started last night again! I was out from 9.30am till tea. Going round I had to crawl a lot to prominent places without being given away & it was very prickly there being a lot of thistle.

21.9.17

A lovely day, first off I had a hours work before breakfast, now I hear that the Corps commander will be here at 12.15. Grand day to be out I hear the Second Army have got 700 prisoners.

22.9.17

I don't know what is the matter with people I have been struggling with Uniacke for several days to get him to use a certain plan & we have explained & drawn plans & referred him to go to graphs & still nothing happens & so today I had to take him there so I was nearly late for the conference at divisional HQ. It lasted till tea time the divisional commander says he asked for my move home to be hurried up because I deserved it & because I want it, I think they want to get rid of me now I have had one or two little troubles with Divisional HQ over the most absurd piece of red tape.

Vernon & I started at 6.30 this morning & went to see our transport line, we did two battalions & got back at 8.30am & now I am off with Brierley on another job & taking sandwiches & I hope to be in for tea. The day is simply glorious, Bosche aeroplanes very busy today for some reason. The battle continues and the weather is perfect for an offensive.

The Divisional commander dislikes the idea of Campbell commanding that he has brought in a CO from another brigade to command in my absence. Campbell of course does not mind, but the brigade as a whole will feel it.[100]

It would be very kind of Henry to find out what is the policy about leave. The Corps commander missed me again. He is most anxious to see me before I go. He said he was coming at 12.15pm yesterday & I marched back & got here at 12 to find some mistake & he had come at 11.15am & gone again. He said I was going home on the 25th but I think the old boy is muddled, as no one knows anything about it I have written to Tavish to find out.

23.9.17

I went out with Brierley, we called on a gunner he had his carpet slippers on. His name is Pottinger, a nice man.[101] Then we had a lot of walking round back trenches I found an OP whence we studied the country & ate our sandwiches & apples of which there was a good number at the derelict farms. Then we continued & got back at 5pm having been on our feet & horses most of the day, I get up early tomorrow to see the commander of the transport lines I think the Divisional commander thinks I require a rest.

25.9.17

It was very misty this morning I was starting off when the Divisional commander pulled me up & took me to see something & then Campbell at 11am & walked round the trenches till I had lunch with him. Then off we went again. His energy is marvellous & he is so keen. Tavish says there will be no delay in getting home once my name gets to GHQ so I imagine I should hear soon.

26.9.17

Brierley & I started out soon after 9.30 & met an officer & went round his trenches. It was very hot & Brierley got very thirsty. We got a very nice drink of lime juice & good water at a company HQ & then lay down in the shade for a smoke before going on. Brierley suffered from headaches from his steel helmet.

27.9.17

2nd Army seem to have done well again I hope this fine weather continues for them. Hastings Andersen of the Army was over here today but of course I was out.[102] In fact the visitors appear to be endless but I saw some of them. Bond came over with Andersen he was on 2nd Division staff with me. I have a great fellow on my staff, a gas officer his name is Ebenezer Thomas![103] The Divisional commander & his staff shot partridges today, they got one, there was a great number about.

So glad I may be under Henry though the east course is the dangerous side!! I wonder how the prisoners depot will do when you are gone I hope they will realise all you have done. The days go on & still no news. It turned fine again after breakfast I rode with Vernon to see the billets when an amusing incident occurred I was watching a party drilling when I suddenly saw a company shambling along in an awful formation I galloped off after them in great wrath & Vernon caught me just in time to tell they did not belong to my brigade.

28.9.17

I tried to write you to go to Cookham if I don't meet you at Victoria. I shall probably have to come up to town to report to WO I think that is the rule I have just been presenting medal ribbons, one man now has a DCM, an MM, & a bar to the MM, pretty good. Another lovely day I am glad 2nd Army have such luck. I hope Hastings sees my message today.

I find my application has passed through Army so surely I should not have long to wait now. I had a great day with Campbell I went up at 12.30 & ate my sandwiches on the way. We started off & picked up Wayne Edwards & we went up an ammunition trench with the intention of going to the right I need hardly say we went to the left. We went off for a minute down a side trench leaving a runner behind and then got absorbed in a discussion in which they both told me I was wrong about a certain trench so we all had to go all the way there then I found I was right. By the time we thought tea would be a good plan & we had tea with Wayne & his subaltern.

Campbell had gone to his front line at 6am & had got back to his HQ at 10, so we had a strenuous day. He really is wonderful. I found the CRE here for dinner & had a chat with him.[104]

29.9.17

I had a conference at 11.30am to 1pm. At 3pm Vernon & I went for a ride to see something I came back for tea & after to an OP as the night was so good I remained there until the light got bad & then went to see Montgomery.

Thompson came to see me to say how sorry he was I was going etc, etc. He has 2 sons in the Army one out here & one in the Indian Army.

1.10.17

I went out at 9am meaning to get back at 4.10pm, Montgomery & I had a great round. Then the commander arrived he is an annoying man as he makes you have all sorts of things done you don't want to. After tea we played badminton & after dinner Campbell came in & kept talking till 11pm & then I got at my papers the first time today. I have written to Tavish to hurry things up I seem to have a great deal to do & I am not making headway I don't seem to get the assistance I want but perhaps it is my fault for not setting about it in the right way. I am very anxious to get away.

Things have changed since my last entry. We hold a very extended line below Armentieres. It was very interesting & a great change to see grass & trees instead of shell swept battle front where everything is blown I felt things were not going very well between me & the Divisional commander. Relations are a bit strained & Blackader was wanting a rest & seemed disinterested to take anything seriously I had a row with Follett in which I don't think I was in the wrong & some unpleasantness with the 115th brigade was really due to the Divisional HQ for not settling a question & leaving the brigadiers to settle it between themselves so I felt on the whole as if it would be a good thing if I got away somewhere else.

There were great delays but eventually I came home on the 15 Oct & joined Teenie at Sonnybrook, Cookham Dean, a jolly little place lent to us by Hubert Campbell. We took Henry's Studebaker down & had a little petrol for it which was very useful & a great amusement I was told I was to have a brigade at Crowborough in Henry's command (Eastern) & we ran down there for a night to get a house. It is lovely country but houses are scarce there, we very nearly took one however luckily not quite for unexpectedly the War Office decided I was not to go to Crowborough but to Colchester. Nothing could be done because it had been arranged at a meeting of the Army Council!

Henry was busy at this time writing a memorandum for the war Cabinet which finally resulted in the formation of the Inter-Allied Council or whatever they choose to call it which is to settle the higher strategy of the campaign. Henry is to be the soldier representative & he left London to go to the Italian front to see what is to be done. He is very concerned about the recent Italian trouble.

NOTES

1 The failure of the potato crop combined with the British naval blockade led to the German military to make conditional peace proposals at this time. These were strongly rebuffed by the allies and led to a policy of unrestricted submarine warfare of all shipping whether hostile or neutral. This became one of the factors that would cause America to enter the war on the side of the allies.

2 Lieutenant Theophilus Beynon MC, 13th RWF, served with 113th Trench Mortar Battery.

3 This German withdrawal to the Siegfried Stellung later became known to the British as the Hindenburg Line. The German high command's original plan was for a belt of fortifications stretching from the Belgian coast, 300 miles to the Moselle. The average position was to be 1 mile in depth, to be extended to 4 miles in due course.

4 Lieutenant Colonel William Charles Eric Rudkin DSO, GOC 122nd Bde, Royal Artillery. Temporary Brigadier General CRA 57th Div. August 1918. CMG 1918. Wounded twice and MID seven times. ADC to the king 1919.

5 Brigadier General Spencer Edmund Hollond RB (1874–1950). BGGS XVIII Corps.

6 Captain Thomas Elias, Adjutant 15th RWF. Relinquished his commission March 1918 due to ill health contracted on active service.

7 Brigadier General John Randle M. Minshull-Ford MC, RWF (1881–1948). 115th Bde. He was wounded at Neuve Chapelle. DSO 1917.

8 Brigadier General Edward Leonard Ellington CMG (1877–1967). BGGS VIII Corps until November 1917. He was later knighted and became marshal of the RAF.

9 Lieutenant Colonel Compton Cardew Norman joined the RWF as a second lieutenant 4 January 1899 and served in the South Africa War, where he was wounded. He was attached to the Loyal North Lancashire Regt and wounded again in June 1915. He then served with 1st Bn RWF and was promoted to major 1 September 1915, then Temporary Lieutenant Colonel the 15th RWF (The London Welsh).

10 Colonel G. de Houghton KOYLI. His brother, Captain Vere de Houghton, Adjutant 1/5 Lincolnshire Regt was killed in action, 11–13 October 1915. Commemorated Loos Memorial Panel, Pas de Calais, France.

11 Lieutenant William Bevan, 15th RWF.

12 Lieutenant Colonel Charles John Markham, 1st KRRC, later Brigadier General 42nd Inf. Bde, 14th (Light) Div.

13 60th refers to the KRRC.

14 Lieutenant Colonel Harry Vivian Robert Hodson, North Staffs Regt, 14th RWF.

15 General Sir Francis Lloyd, GOC London District throughout the War. *See* Richard Morris OBE, *The Man who ran London during the Great War* (Pen & Sword, Barnsley, 2009).

16 Temporary Captain Richard Meredydd Wynne-Edwards (16 July 1916), 13th RWF. Awarded the MC & Bar, and also received DSO for actions at Mortho Wood, 7 October 1918. (LG 1 January 1919.)

17 Lieutenant Colonel (later Brigadier General) Frederick William Sheppard Hart Cavendish (1877–1931). British Liaison Officer at French GQG.

18 Colonel Eric Dillon was one of Wilson's liaison officers during the war and later private secretary 1919–20. *See* Brigadier General The Viscount Dillon CMG, DSO, *Memories of Three Wars* (London, 1951).

19 Lieutenant Colonel Archibald Neville Gavin Jones, 16th RWF, formerly a Captain Jacobs Horse, Indian Army.

20 Brevet Colonel Ernest Napper Tandy RA (1879–1953). Staff Officer GHQ. First-class cricketer for Somerset.

21 Lieutenant Colonel Robert Spencer Follett RB. Staff Officer 1914–19.

22 Brigade Major Fergus Brinsley Nixon (1880–1969). 6th (Inniskilling) Dragoons, 114 Inf. Bde.

23 Lieutenant General Charles Lewis Woollcombe (1857–1934). IV Corps Commander.

24 Lieutenant Colonel Edgar John de Pentheny O'Kelly DSO, 16th RWF. Wounded with 10 Manchester Regt in Gallipoli 1915.

25 Lieutenant Colonel Gordon P. McClellan, GOC 121 Artillery Bde, 38th Welsh Div.

26 Lieutenant General George Sidney Clive (1874–1959). Grenadier Guards Staff Officer. Head of British mission to French HQ from 1915. Later Military Governor of Cologne; Brigadier

General Charles Richard Woodroffe RA (1878–1965). Attached Japanese Army 1907–08. DA & QMG 1917–18; Lieutenant Colonel Randall Charles Edward, Coldstream Guards.

27 Major Wynn Powell Wheldon DSO (1878–1961). 14th RWF, commanded battalion 1918. Wounded at Foret de Morval four days before the Armistice. He was later knighted for his work in Welsh society. He was the father of Sir Huw Phrys Wheldon OBE, MC, BBC broadcaster and executive (1916–86).

28 Brigadier General J.R.M. Minshull-Ford DSO, MC, RWF, 91st Bde, 7th Div. Was later Lieutenant Governor of Guernsey & Alderney 1940 (escaped just before the German troops arrived).

29 For a very good account of the Battle of Arras see J. Nicolls, *Cheerful Sacrifice* (London, 1990).

30 Lieutenant Colonel G.P. Macclellan DSO, GOC 121st Bde.

31 Major General Thomas Herbert Shoubridge, GOC 7th Div. (1871–1934).

32 Lieutenant General Sir Thomas Leithbridge Napier Morland KRRC (1865–1925). GOC X Corps.

33 Major General Edmond Guy Tulloch Bainbridge (1867–1943). East Kent Regt, GOC 25th Div.

34 Major General David 'Soarer' 'Barbara' Graham Muschet Campbell (1869–1936). 9 Lancers, GOC 21st Div. Won the Grand National in 1896 on *Soarer*, which became one his nicknames. Later Governor and C in C Malta.

35 Lieutenant Colonel Henry Cecil Lloyd Howard, Staff Officer France until November 1917, then transferred to Italy until the end of the war.

36 Lieutenant Colonel John Lawrence Buxton DSO, RB, Brigade Major (1877–1951).

37 Captain Henry Howard Paine MC, 16th RWF. He won his MC for gallantry at Pilckem Ridge, 31 July 1917. His brother, Captain William Arthur Pain, was in the same battalion and won an MC commanding D Company, 30 September 1918 at Delville Wood.

38 Red tabs refers to red collar tags, which were attached and worn by senior officers.

39 Lieutenant Colonel John Edward Henry Davies DSO, 130th Field Ambulance, 38th Div.

40 Lieutenant General Sir Charles Macpherson Dobell (1869–1954). He was involved in the two Battles of Gaza, which proved to be heavy failures, and as a result he was made a scapegoat by the commander Sir Archibald Murray and posted to command a division in India.

41 Brigadier General Sir George Ayscough Armytage (1872–1953). GOC 117th Bde, 39th Div.

42 Lieutenant William Hughes Jones transferred to the 16th Bn on 19 December 1916, he was later attached to the Ministry of Labour.

43 Lieutenant William Howard Jones, joined the 16th Bn in France in March 1917. Killed in fighting, 21 June 1917 aged 28, and was MID. Buried Bard Cottage Cemetery, Boesinghe, Belgium.

44 Captain A. Smith MC, GSO 2 July 1916–May 1917.

45 Captain L.B. Brierley MC, RE (TF). Brigade Major 113th Inf. Bde May 1917.

46 Bazentin was one of the positions fought over during the Battle of the Somme. There was Bazentin le Grand and Bazentin le Petit, both are on the Bazentin Ridge just to north of Mametz Wood.

47 Lieutenant Colonel George Kendall Priaulx DSO, 11th Bn KRRC. Killed with most of his staff when a shell found the battalion HQ during the attack on the Libermont Canal, 25 March 1918.

48 Captain John Chamberlain MC, 3rd Bn South Wales Borderers attached 24th Bn Welch Regt. Killed, Monday 14 May 1917 aged 35 years. Buried Ferme-Olivier Cemetery, Belgium.

49 Colonel (later General) Huguet, Chief of French Mission to BEF in 1914.

50 General Henri-Philippe Petain had replaced General Nivelle as Commander in Chief of the French Armies on 15 May 1917. His first task was to quell the mutiny that had affected altogether sixty-eight divisions of the French Army.

51 Lieutenant Colonel Charles Finlayson Hunter DSO, 4th Dragoon Guards, AQMG British Mission to French GQG 1917–18.

52 Lieutenant Colonel William Edward Rothwell DSO, OBE. Royal Inniskilling Fusiliers. Commander of Second Army School of Musketry.

53 Major General Sir Geoffrey Percy Thynne Fielding, GOC Guards Div. 1916–18 (1866–1932).

54 General Jan Christian Smuts (1870–1950). He had fought against the British in the Second Boer War but was so highly thought of that he was invited into the British War Cabinet.

55 Lieutenant Colonel William Charles Eric Rudkin CMG, DSO, GOC 122nd Bde RA; Lieutenant Colonel J. Kennedy DSO, MC, DCM, GOC 13th (2nd Rhondda Batt) Welsh Regt; Lieutenant Colonel Charles Darley Harvey DSO (1881–1929). GOC 10th (1st Gwent) South Wales Borderers. Died in a car accident January 1929.

56 Lieutenant Colonel Harry Vivian Robert Hodson, North Staffs Regt, GOC 14th RWF.

57 Brigadier General Cyril Aubrey Blacklock DSO & Bar (LG. 3.6.16 & 14.11.16). GOC 182nd Bde, 61st Div. January 1917. Officer KRRC 1901 and saw action in Second Boer War. He resigned his commission in 1904 and went to Canada. He rejoined the 10th KRRC in November 1914 and by October 1915 he was GOC of the battalion. He was promoted major general in 1918 and was GOC of 9th Scottish, 39th and 63rd Royal Naval Divs during that year. CMG 1918. CB 1919. He was relinquished from his commission in 1920 and returned to Canada.

58 Major Robert Spencer Follett DSO, RB, appointed GSO 2 May 1917.

59 Brigadier General Percy Pollexfen de Blaquiere Radcliffe DSO (1874–1934). BGGS Canadian Corps. He took over as Director of Military Operations 1918. Later GOC 4th Div. and GOC Scottish and then Southern Command.

60 The Battle of Arras opened on 9 April 1917; Vimy Ridge was the sector successfully attacked by the Canadian Corps.

61 Lieutenant R. W. Brierley, 21st (Empress of India's) Lancers.

62 Lieutenant Colonel Archibald Herbert Leggett (b. 1877). GOC 156 Inf. Bde 1917–19. Educated Clifton College. Joined army 1897 served in South Africa. Instructor Sandhurst 1903–07. Served in Japan 1908–10. Retired from army 1913. Commanded 5th Bn (TF) Royal Scots Fusiliers 1915–17. DSO 1900. CMG 1918.

63 This entry in the diary was found on this date but may have been written later.

64 Temporary Brigadier General Thomas George Cope DSO & Bar, RF. He took command of the 115th Bde on 9 June 1917, he went sick on 14 July 1917. He later commanded 176th Bde, 59th (North Midland) Div. in the latter stages of the Third Battle of Ypres. He was wounded twice during the war and was awarded DSO and Bar. CMG 1919.

65 Lieutenant General Sir Walter Norris Congreve VC, GOC XII Corps, was wounded 12 June 1917.

66 Lieutenant Colonel H.E. ap Rhys Pryce CMG, DSO GSO 1 38th Welsh Div.; Lieutenant Colonel H.M. Pryce-Jones DSO, MVO, MC, AA & QMG.

67 Brigadier General Montague Leyland Hornby DSO, 116th Bde, 39th Div. (1870–1948).

68 Major William Redmond MP (1861–1917). He joined the 6th (S) Bn Royal Irish Regt in February 1915. Killed at Dranoutre during the Battle of Messines, 7 June 1917 aged 56 years. Buried in the garden of the convent at Lucre. *See* Desmond & Jean Bowen, *Heroic Option, The Irish in the British Army* (Pen & Sword, 2005).

69 Lieutenant General, 10th Earl of Cavan, Frederick 'Fatty' Rudolf Lambert, GOC XIV Corps (1865–1946).

70 Lieutenant Harold Williams, 14 RWF.

71 Lieutenant Colonel Cecil Champagne Herbert-Stepney KRRC, GOC 16 (S) (Chatsworth Rifles) Sherwood Foresters.

72 The Battle of Spion Kop took place on 24–25 January 1900 during the Second Boer War.

73 Lieutenant Colonel Evelyn William Pierrepoint Uniacke DSO. Served with the King Edward's Horse, he was then attached to the Royal Irish Fusiliers where he was awarded his DSO at Hulluch on 27 April 1916, and he was gazetted to the 14th Bn RWF on 14 July 1917.

74 Lieutenant Colonel Henry Francis Newdigate Jourdain CMG (1872–1968).(Connaught Rangers.) GOC 16th RWF appointed June 1917. He was the last colonel of the regiment before it disbanded in 1922.

75 Sir Eric Geddes (1875–1937). He was a railway expert who Haig had appointed Director General of Transport in France 20 June 1916 to 7 July 1917, then Lloyd George transferred him to the Admiralty, where he implemented a convoy policy over the head of firm professional naval opposition. This probably brought about the dismissal of the First Sea Lord Sir John Jellico, during Christmas 1917.

76 Sinn Fein was to become the political wing of the Irish Republican Army; Lieutenant Colonel R.C. Browne-Clayton. Major South Irish Horse, GOC 16th (S) (2nd Birkenhead) the Cheshire Regt.

77 This was the start of the Third Battle of Ypres, also known as the Battle of Passchendaele.

78 Lieutenant Colonel Compton Cardew Norman CMG, DSO, Legion d'e Honneur. 15th Bn RWF, went on to command the 17th Bn RWF from July to September 1918 in France.

79 General Sir Hubert Gough, GOC Fifth Army. He was in command of the unit in South Africa when Price-Davies' actions resulted in the award of a VC.

80 Lieutenant Colonel Robert Hamilton Montgomery, new GOC 15 RWF (London Welsh). A regular officer the Welsh Regt.

81 Captain A. Vernon-Jones.

82 Major General George Tom Molesworth Bridges (1871–1925). GOC 19th (Western) Div. He lost a leg during the Passchendaele Offensive. Head of British Mission to USA 1918. KCB 1925.

83 Brigadier General G. Gwyn Thomas CMG, DSO. Indian Army, GOC 115th Inf Bde July 1917 to April 1918.

84 Major General Thomas Owen Marden (1866–1951). Welch Regt, GOC 6th Div. 21 August 1917 until the end of the war.

85 Brigadier General Alexander Ramsay Harman DSO (1877–1954). Worcester Regt, officially took over the 114th Bde on 19 August 1917. He remained in command until August 1918.

86 Major Frank Stewart Lloyd, Second in Command of 13th RWF. Wounded 4 September 1917, died of his wounds 5 September 1917. Buried Dozinghem Military Cemetery, Westvleteren, Belgium.

87 Lieutenant Colonel Brian Surtees Phillpotts RE. Severely wounded 2 September 1917, died 4 September 1917 aged 42 years. Buried Dozingham Military Cemetery, Westvleteren, Belgium.

88 Second Lieutenant John Pritchard, 13th RWF. Wounded at Mametz Wood, 11 July 1916. He returned to the battalion and was in action around Ypres where he was killed, 4 September 1917 aged 23 years.

89 Lieutenant General Richard Cyril Byrne Haking, GOC XI Corps (1862–1945).

90 Lieutenant Guy Ernest Evans, 14 Bn RWF, wounded 2 August 1917.

91 Lieutenant Colonel John Brough RA was a leading exponent of the new Tank Corps who had reservations as to their deployment during the Battle of the Somme. In 1917 he was transferred to 61st Div. and then onto the staff of Fifth Army. Killed himself after presenting his plan for the deployment of the tanks, 29 July 1917 aged 45 years. Buried Longuenesse (St Omer) Souvenir Cemetery.

92 Corporal James Llewellyn Davies from Nantymoel, Glamorgan, 13th RWF (b. 16 March 1886). He captured two concrete pillboxes in succession, the first with a bayonet and the second with grenades and, although wounded twice, he then dealt with a sniper before dying of his wounds. Buried Canada Farm Cemetery, Belgium.

93 Colonel (later Brigadier General) John Hardress-Lloyd DSO (1874–1952). 3rd Tank Bde, 4th Irish Dragoon Guards. He was awarded a Bar to his DSO and Chevalier to the Legion d'Honneur in 1918. He was a world-class polo player and represented both Ireland and Great Britian in the Olympics.

94 Lieutenant General Sir Thomas D'Orly Snow (1858–1940). GOC VII Corps. GOC Western Command 1918.

95 Major General Neill Malcolm MGGS Fifth Army (1869–1953).

96 Alexander Fyodorovich Kerensky (1881–1970). In July 1917 he became prime minster and insisted that Russia remain in the war. In October 1917 the Bolsheviks led a coup d'etat and Kerenski fled, first to Paris and then to the USA.

97 Petrograd was later to be renamed Leningrad, and had originally been known as St Petersburg.

98 Brigadier General Herbert Montgomery-Campbell RA (1861–1937). CRA 46th Div. 1914–18. Price-Davies served in this division from 1915. His reference I presume is to lack of decorations for this officer in relation to his time with the division. He was wounded 12 March 1918.

99 The Battle of Menin Road Ridge 20–25 September 1917.

100 Lieutenant Colonel Robert Ormus Campbell was acting GOC 113 Inf Bde 15–17 October 1917; Brigadier General Henry Edward ap Rhys Pryce commanded until 19 November 1918 when Brigadier General Adrian Carton de Wiart VC took over.

101 Temporary Lieutenant Colonel Eldred Charles Pottinger RFA (Reserve of Officers).

102 Lieutenant General Sir Warren Hastings Andersen, Chief of Staff First Army 1917 (1872–1930).

103 Lieutenant Ebenzer Thomas, 16th RWF. Joined the battalion 11 September 1917 & demobilised in August 1919.

104 Lieutenant Colonel T.E. Kelsall DSO, RE, divisional CRE.

Five

1918

His letters resume in April when he moves across to France in command of 8th Infantry Brigade, 3rd Division. However, his time in that position would only last a few days as he is promoted to become major general liaison officer Italy. He was appointed to his position by the new CIGS Henry Wilson, who wants to have his own man in this theatre of operations. In Italy, he works under the command of Cavan, but at the same time he passes on information about the current military abilities of the Italian and French allies. To do this, he travels all over the fronts held by both the British and Italians, making a comparison between the forces with the respective differences of terrain. His journeys up to and through the mountainous front which the Italians hold, shine a great deal of light on how difficult it was to fight in the mountains.

Much of the correspondence was sent as 'secret', informing the CIGS as to the relevant merits and progress of the joint coalition of forces, and the views of the commanders. Much of what is passed on gives the reader an insight into the strategic pressure of fighting away from the Western Front and show how difficult this was. Inevitably, his close relationship with the CIGS leads to Cavan feeling isolated and unable to command as he would have wished. His position as a go-between reveals how difficult it was and how much diplomacy was required by him to try to make compromises, whilst keeping the confidence of all parties concerned.

Frustratingly, all correspondence finishes just a few days before the armistice is signed. However, it remains a fascinating period, showing the tensions that existed on the Italian front at this time. It also provides an insight into how the Italian forces were commanded and what they in turn expected of their allies. Another aspect was the growing ability of British forces to adapt and prosecute a war in an environment which differed considerably from that of France from where they had come.

20.4.18

Versailles

More changes. We finished our happy existence at Colchester though it was marred by the departure of General Dallas and the arrival of General Bingham.[1] On 21 March the Germans held their great offences on the

Cambrai front. The 5th Army just North of St Quentin did not hold & this caused the withdrawal of the 3rd Army (Byng), which was north of it.[2] The Somme was crossed & Amiens threatened & we lost the use of the railway through that place. Gough was subsequently sent home.[3] The Versailles had worked out in detail an attack of 6 divisions (as a matter of fact the Germans attacked with 15). However the higher command could not agree to the formation of the reserve & disaster was the result.

Every available man was sent feverishly to the front in France. All my men were taken. Many considered they had a grievance as they had to go without going on leave. They went on strike & things looked ugly I am thankful to say after I had talked to them they saw reason & went off all right.

I was not left alone for long at Colchester & on Tuesday 2 April I crossed to France & on the 3rd I took over command of the 8th Infantry Brigade,[4] 3rd Division. Deverell[5] commanded the division, I had Gosling as Staff Captain, Graham as Signals, Broadwood, Quinn & a Major Taylor, 2nd Royal Scots, Gallat, 1st Royal Scots Fusiliers, Gordon & 7th King Scottish Light Infantry, Johnson. The Brigades having been reduced to 3 battalions we were near Bethune, Vandecourt & Dronion, and Fongueriel etc. Then the German offensive between Armentieres & La Bassee Canal commenced.

On the 10 April we were moved to Hinges that night & relieved by 154th Bde in front of Locon. That night I heard I was to go home & Bertie Fisher relieved me on the 11th in the middle of a fight & I slept that night in Bontope.[6] Henry wanted me as a liaison officer in Italy My feelings were mixed I had not done well in the fight so was glad to leave the brigade but I felt no one ought to be getting a soft job at such a time of crisis. I hardly dared look at anyone in the face what would people think of me. My nerve had gone too & was very shaky during the fight so perhaps again it was right for me to be out of it yet there were others who had many hard months & deserved a rest. I was about as miserable as I could be. At this time I heard the news of the death of 'brother Prialux'.[7] I got home on the 12 & stayed with Henry. A chat with him put me in better spirits & I decided that anyway it might be all for the best I was in & out of the W.O. picking up the thread of things. On the 17 April went to see the Italian Ambassador, he was very charming & on the 18th I went to Windsor to see the King. He was very affable & we talked for about 20 minutes. He was much concerned about events being anxious that Italy should remain in the war, holding the opinion that we were 'done' if Austria could bring her whole weight against us. I had lunch Lord Minto, Lady Airley, Lady Joan Mulholland,[8] Sir Douglas Davison[9] & Sir Derek Keppell.[10] I also saw Colonel Willoughby, Viscount Kalentia, Clive Wigram[11] & others.

April 19th left Charing Cross at 10.30 & crossed to France, at Boulogne I was met by a Rolls Royce & taken to Versailles I had a talk with Tavish at Montreul on the way. He is against using Italian divisions on the battle front. This is important as it is part of my mission to get Italian divisions over here. I arrived at Versailles at 11pm & stay with Sackville West in a charming house I have a bedroom & bath to myself.[12]

20.4.18

Walk to the office with Tit Willow I see Studd, Bell, Green & read some papers. Their HQ is the Trianon, a fine building. To lunch with Ma Stead, in charge of propaganda, Colonel Stern[13] (Tanks) Wicks (Cipher office) & Colonel Brigand. I was to dine with Hereward Wake & went to his mess but he had not got back I dined with Major Lord Charles Bentinck, Green, Ross, Wicks, Benor & Bevan.[14]

21.4.18

Walked to the office in the morning & lunched with Hereward. He is concerned about the state of affairs. He fears we are not strong enough to withstand the next attack by the Bosche. The result will be he considers that we shall be practically knocked out & will lose the channel ports. The French seem to be disinclined to take over their share of the fight, which so far has fallen almost entirely on us.

22.4.18

Hereward came to dinner I have not mentioned that I am a new temporary Major General I am glad of this chiefly because it will be definite promotion & not merely a change of job & will perhaps reduce the caustic remarks that are bound to be made at my leaving the battle front after having had 6 months at home.

Letter to the CIGS Sir Henry Wilson

British Military Representatives
Supreme War Council
British Section
Versailles

23.4.18

Going with Green to GHQ. I am not sure how I stand now with influence to inducing the Italians to send more divisions to France. So long as we can offer them a place of honour in the battle under British Command the way seems fairly clear.

Now however, one could be asking them to go under the French command with the probability of a inglorious career in the Vosges. How can one appeal to them on these grounds? I shall wait therefore before tackling these arrangements until I hear from you – no time will be lost as you can easily wire me. That being so I shall apply myself chiefly to getting Cavan a mixed army & probing deeply into the question of putting up an offensive I have been very happy here everybody has been most kind T.W. especially hospitable.[15]

Wire To – P.D.

24.4.18

SECRET

From – C.I.G.S.

HW 33

I have now asked Foch if he would take two more Italian divisions and will let you know directly I get reply. Would Cavan like me to write to Diaz suggesting that Cavan be given an army of 3 Corps – one corps to be commanded by a British General and the other two corps to be commanded by Italian Generals and each corps to consist of one British & two Italian divisions.

Wire To – P.D.   G.H.Q. Italy.

25.4.18[16]

SECRET

From – C.I.G.S.

HW 33

The French are going to give the Italian divisions a short rest and some training before pulling them into battle & I understand the Italians are pleased with the arrangement so that is all right. I have now asked Foch if he could take two more Italian divisions and I will let you know directly I get a reply. Would Cavan like me to write to Diaz suggesting that Cavan be given an army of three corps – one corps to be commanded by a British General and the other two to be commanded by Italian Generals and the corps to consist of one British and two Italian divisions.[17]

25.4.18[18]

My dear Henry

I've sent you my first report. It reads to me a colourless report & is a poor thing after you injunction to have determination. Cavan & Radcliffe have very definite ideas, however & we must look round before butting in too much.[19] However I thought it best to know the course of events.

2. I found it had been arranged for me to live with Dick Crichton – GSO.1 Training. He is at Thiene about 6 miles from GHQ of course I shall be very happy living with Dick but I am doubtful whether it is the best place.

3. I presume after reading Cavan's letter you will take Williams away I don't think it could be very good leaving him here & I doubt if there is much to be gained in having two of us. We either go round together or go round after each other & bore the people by asking the same questions twice.[20]

4. Cavan was not sure about promoting Radcliffe. His theory is that other attaches' are not Major Generals & sees no reason in that case. He will in no doubt write to you.

5. As regards my reception Cavan was of course charming & quire frank & told me everything but even he does not understand the need for liaison & said so.

Radcliffe has been quite nice in fact he said he was glad I had come as I could take stories home & save him writing.[21]

Letter to CIGS

26.4.18

My dear Henry

As I wired to you today Cavan has gone away. He went to see Lawson & comes back tomorrow I am to dine there & talk after. The French difficulty may induce Cavan to shy off, he knows the Italians would not like a similar arrangement with the French & fear the latter would demand it. Gathorne Hardy argues with me that all arrangements ought to be arranged at once ready to put in place immediately it is considered the right time has come.[22]

Cavan formed a Corps of one British & one Italian Division as being more in keeping with the Italian aspirations but that is merely a detail.

I went round the 48th Division today with Williams & Cecil Howard.[23] Williams has a good knowledge of the country & has these confounded names at his finger ends. It was well worth the visit. What puzzles me is the Asiago plateau is really a valley! It is a great good piece of country looked down at from one side & from the still higher ground which the Australians hold on the other side & which by the way looks as if it would take some climbing to get up. What struck me was the formidable nature of the undertaking they propose. It only shows the contempt in which they hold the Austrian. The situation is so unlike anything one has seen before. People go without danger into no-man's land by day & they are even going to propose gun positions in no-man's land!! Tomorrow I go to the left top see 7th Division.

Wire From: P.D

28.4.18

To: C.I.G.S.

Re-your HW 33.

I was told yesterday by Lord Cavan that he was against altering organisation until enemy intentions on this front are clearer. He is away at present but tomorrow night I will see him and wire again.[24]

PRIORITY

28.4.18

Wire From: P.D.   Despatched 2am

To: C. I.G.S.   Received 7.30am

I have discussed re-organisation with Lord Cavan. At present he does not favour changes. He will write fully and send letter to you on Monday by Colonel Williams. Will Col. Williams return here?[25]

28.4.18

My dear Henry

What I must try to find out is how far Cavan fears are groundless but in the face of it, it seems very difficult business. He had another idea last night i.e. to carry out a modified offensive, say to include the Asiago & Camperovere. This will cost probably 1,000 casualties & if really successful the British force could be withdrawn into reserve and be formed into a reserve army with the Italian reserve divisions. They would remain in reserve during the dangerous season i.e. till about October & then return to the line. This has various drawbacks – it would probably not appeal to the French or possible to the Italians either to curtail the offensive & as he points out in his letter the only real way to spread the gospel is for the troops to continue to hold a portion of the line.

I hear a great deal of chat one way or another. The Wullyites are saying that Wully wanted to withdraw troops from Palestine & other side shows & that the politicians would not let him & that now the very thing he said was necessary was to be done I don't know whether to write to you these private chats or not I am rather afraid they may give you extra trouble to read.[26]

I suppose Trenchard will return now. There was great feeling everywhere over his resignation & great rejoicing now that the problem has been done down.[27]

About Williams Cavan told him he had recommended there being only one liaison officer. He was badly wounded in South Africa & so cannot stand any hot climate otherwise he can stand a fair amount of hard work.

I had a chat with Shoubridge yesterday, he was most friendly.[28] He is a great Britisher & thinks we don't make enough of ourselves & that the English Generals & soldiers are quite as good as the French & that we should not give in to the French demands on all occasions I tell you these bits of chat to keep you in touch with the Army![29]

30.4.18

My dear Henry

I am still going along in spite of Cavan's letter, to try & get this Army going.

Gathorne Hardy is all for it and so is Delme Radcliffe I saw the latter today and he will find out for me whether Giardino has mentioned the matter to Diaz or to anyone in the Commando Supremo. If he has then it will help us. I am in hopes in any case that we might arrange to form an Army as a reserve Army at first as Morrone is easiest to kick out.

The reorganisation of the higher staffs will be difficult which will probably take time to arrange.

2. Delme Radcliffe seems to be very hot on bringing off an offensive chiefly because of his extreme optimism regarding the disaffection amongst the Greeks. There is a danger that he might precipitate matters. A declaration from Versailles would therefore be of help.

3. Thanks for your letter of the 22nd I know you would be disappointed at the attitude of G.H.Q. France.

4. I spent the day in the training area where the schools are I went with Gathorne Hardy & Crichton. The Italians are not playing up too well as they don't take up all the vacancies allotted. G.H.Q. will take this up.

5. I get asked many questions – for instance – Douglas Haig objected to taking over the extra line from the French which gives us more than our share & from Studds lecture V would have liked the French to have taken over from us. Who therefore decided we were to take the line over? Presumably Lloyd George in which case it was against the soldier's advice.[30]

4.5.18

My dear Henry

Yesterday I spent on our own mountain I'm getting hold of the names now. Today I went on expedition with P.T. to PASUTIO.[31] We went to the H.Q. of the 55th Division. The commander seems very keen and is an ardent machine gunner & has been carrying out actual firing experiments. He is most friendly. From there we went up by teleferic (PT hates the teleferic & the mountains!) to PICENO brigade H.Q. at PORTE PASUTIO – a collection of huts in the snow which look as if they would fall down the cliff at any moment. Colonel Brigadier Lungio Amantea commands he was for a time the Chief of Staff 5th Army. He too was friendly in fact they are all as nice as can be & not so suspicious as the French I should say. They seem to be inspired with the right spirit and to understand the principle of defence but of course it may be all talk, what little we saw seemed alright. The machine gun emplacements seemed to be in the right places. We could not get to the front because of avalanches. They gave us the most excellent lunch & then at 1.30 we started to come down. It was a great procession 2 shoveller's in front to move the snow a guide with a lantern, we had to go through 50 tunnels then me & an Italian officer then another lantern & P.T. and another Italian officer. On the way we visited some batteries of 75's & heavy guns, great long guns about 6ins, how they got them up I can't think as they are too heavy for the teleferic. The path down had been cut out of the face of solid rock of Formio Alta & was mostly tunnel. We were still about 500 ft up when we heard a Beseglari Band far below us, and we could see them marching. Then they took to a path & went along in single file, still playing & finally drew up in front of a hut. Then we heard 'God save the King' which we discovered was for the benefit of the American Red Cross I don't know what the Yankees thought of it! When we got down the band was in front of the American canteen where we had some coffee whilst the band played 'God save the King' again, the Italian anthem and the Marseilles.

I have not yet thought of any way to get at the training of the Italian Army. Cavan and Delme Radcliffe are all anxious about it & busy over it & I can't quite see any way I can butt in just at present. First of all I must try to get to know people, and I fear they all regard me as an unnecessary extra. Cavan wants to consult me over a letter he is writing to you so I have to be up there at 8 tomorrow. This is a good sign. Radcliffe took me out to dinner with the King I didn't cut much ice there I am afraid. The King is wonderful he knew at once the towns my relatives come from. He is a nice little man but does not get through his dinner quickly? I enclose a map of the objectives. This is practically what I wrote to you officially. The Bosche seem to have taken a nasty rap in France I wonder he puts in so many of these small attacks instead of putting up a big show, or a quick succession of small ones.

I am so glad you wrote to Tavish I though it much best to let you know how things stood.[32]

5.5.18

My own darling

They have been treating Norman badly. The Inspector General of infantry reported badly on his battalion. It makes me wild.

That hat of mine was an awful extravagance but it cuts much ice with the Italians I think I wore it to dinner with the King.

Great letter from Campbell I was talking about him to Gathorne-Hardy & also HRH/POW.[33] There is no doubt his rudeness & antipathy to the staff made it impossible. It is a great pity as he is such a fine man.

I have written steadily for 2½ hours & I have a good deal more to write I went up to GHQ with Dick this morning. The Corps commander had just got up and was in his pyjamas & very sleepy! I had a chat with him, he certainly seems to tell me everything but I still think he does not see the necessity for me! Now I will answer your letters there are 12 of them. Henry wrote to Douglas Price to try to get me the Legion de Honour. It would be nice to get it & good of him to bother about it. Vernon Jones said Rex had seen Follett I have written to the latter to find out what happened to the Old Division. Campbell's account did not seem good but he is not always to be depended upon.

5.5.18

My dear Henry

How awfully good of you to think about a Legion for me I certainly should take it above anything I am getting along very happily with Gathorne Hardy & Cavan etc. The former thinks we cannot influence the Italian training any more until we are an Army & of course that cannot be at present I am going to see Grappa tomorrow & going up another mountain with the Prince of Wales on Tuesday.

Cavan had some little difficulties but I think they are over now. I think he feels is that decisions etc are only sent him through Montuori (the same with the French) & he thinks he & the French should have different treatment than the ordinary Corps commanders I think this is reasonable as he might want to communicate with you.[34]

Post didn't go after all. I suppose nothing more is being done for the present about the matter you wrote to Foch about?

We are wondering very much about when the Bosche is going to put in another really big attack in France I can't understand what he is at. Is he really bothered about Austria? If so I should have thought a successful offensive could have been the best for him, or is he wondering if his offensive is going to be successful?

I see the Executive Board at Versailles is abolished, that means I suppose Versailles remains as it was? M branch seems to be the only one that produces any useful results as no one takes any notice of what the other branches do that is the impression I got. I suppose if Cavan gets an Army Gathorne Hardy will be a Major General I think it is time he was. Cavan flies a union jack & he is C in C & his HQ is called G.H.Q. so the Chief of Staff should be a Major General.[35]

6.5.18

Thiene

We duly arrived on 25th April I am about 6 miles from GHQ & about 30 miles from Delme-Radcliffe's British Mission. Radcliffe took me to see the Italian Grand supreme & I also dined with him & the King.[36] The King speaks English very well & he is a very simple little man. He lives simply & dinner was quite short. I have spent my days so far going up the hills on our front & also the Italian front. I don't feel as if I am doing much good. No one here wants me or cares to ask me for assistance. Cavan & his staff & everyone else have been very nice to me & Cavan certainly tells me about what he has been doing but he could manage quite well without me I am sure

6.5.18

My own darling

I went over to see Delme Radcliffe today I went with a Colonel Mitchell[37] who is the chief intelligence man & then had my car to bring me back I had a chat with Delme but nothing satisfactory he is going home tomorrow so I gave him a letter for Henry. The King went to see Dick's school today & appears to have been very impressed.

Tomorrow I intend making an excursion to Mount Grappa but I have had great difficulty in getting PT on the telephone & I can't make the arrangements without him. Henry seems to be continually in France now I hear French goes to Ireland. (Sir J. French was Lord Lt of Ireland 1918–1921) I wonder how that will do? A good job to have a soldier there. Wully takes his place.

7.5.18
My own darling
I started off before 8am & went to an Italian Army HQ where I saw the Corps commander. He was recently at Versailles & knows Henry & he was of course delighted when he heard I came from him. We had a chat I get on so much better when I am alone with these people. We conversed in French! Then Goldsmidt the British officer & I went up a mountain motoring to the top but when we got to the top we were in a cloud and got no view.[38] We saw some interesting things all lit by electric light & the sapper Colonel there let us eat our sandwiches in his hut & gave us soup & coffee. We hadn't arrived there till 12.30. so you see it was a long day & on the way back we went to Divisional HQ. The views from there down were marvellous I got back about 7.15pm. It was chilly & I had foolishly not taken my coat. There were some lovely old villas I passed today. They looked so peaceful. The old statues looked very quaint, I don't know what gods they are but they all look alike.

7.5.18
My own darling
Such a wet day poured nearly all day & there are floods out everywhere I did not go up Mount Grappa in consequence. In the morning I went round to see a brigade but found no one there. Delme Radcliffe & PT & Stanley (Lord Derby's son) came to lunch. After lunch I took Dick out & we did liaison with the Division I tried to see yesterday. General Lamberts[39] brigade was our first call, he was having a conference! He seems nice & said he had met us in Ladysmith. Then we went to the Division & saw the GSO1 Col Sandilands,[40] he was nice also Gen Babington.[41] Then we went to see Gen. Gordon[42] & found he had a conference too. However we waited a few minutes & it was over. Gordon was very pleased to see us & gave us tea & we had a long chat.

9.5.18
My dear Henry
There are still some points I didn't understand about the extension of the line but I am not going to bother you about them till we meet. I wired you tonight because I thought you might have a chart with Delme Radcliffe now he is at home. If we don't get busy with this reorganisation I'm so afraid it will

die a natural death & I am sure it will take a long time to organise again, so why not begin now.

I had a day with the French today which went off very well General Benfait I found him very friendly I think he likes the English. He comes to the 23rd Division & so he is very pally with Babington.

Hereward thinks that the Bosche will attack in 3 or 4 weeks on a front of 80 kilometres with 110 Divisions. Jolly for a little British Army! He & Tit Willow don't see eye to eye as to their functions I think Hereward wants a job away & hails after a Brigade in France.

Dick says the training of the 11 Italian Divisions is progressing at the schools.

10.5.18

I have visited in addition to our front I have visited Pasubio here we could not see the front line due to the danger of avalanches. We lunched with the Picena Brigade Colonel Brigadier Amantea 55th Division,[43] after that we walked 12k on a path along which they had over 50 tunnels & was cut in the side of the rock. The marvellous thing is the way the Italians have hauled up their heavy guns into the most inaccessible peaks

I visited General Giardino 4th Army & went up Grappa with Goldsmidt but could see nothing when we got there.[44] We saw however two long tunnels, 9k long, which runs through a spur & has openings to right & left through which guns shoot & there are 5 battery's there now & they propose 25.

Front held by Italian 12th Division immediately on British left.

We went along these fronts' trenches for a short distance looking across the Asiago to the Austrian trenches on the other side. Fine paths cross the precipitous sides but the impression we got was that some resolute men might cross & penetrate the defences (Italian), which might lead to disaster.

Front held by the 23rd Division on our right.

The trenches are not deep enough & there is insufficient protection against shellfire.

9.5.18

My own darling

I had a jolly day today, first I went to GHQ & chatted to Gathorne-Hardy & then went up to the mountains. Then I saw Sladen (RB) who commands a brigade, he seems very nice.[45] I then went to another brigade but the brigadier was out, he was expected in so I stayed to lunch but he did not come. The French interpreter wanted to go to a French canteen near the HQ of a French division so I took him & his servant along, as I wanted to go to the HQ myself. The General was out but they arranged for a guide to take me to the mountains to look at the view. On our way we met the General coming down, he was very genial but for some reason or other I was tongue tied & could not get a word of French out. We had no sooner parted when some shells came over which fell quite close to the general who was then just out of sight. I tried to see if any damage had been done but heard a laugh & knew all was well. I had an interesting afternoon in the French trenches. At some places the officer who guided me went to look for the way & when he came back he said it was too 'degoutant'.[46] The officer had appeared grumpy at first but got quite friendly after I had tried my French on him a bit. I got quite chatty so on the way back I thought I could go & look up the General again just to show him I really could talk French a little also to make sure he had not come to any harm from the shells. He arrived just after I got there & was most friendly & showed me the maps etc & gave me a cup of tea & then saw me off. I went to see Cavan on the way back & I got here about 8pm.

I got a letter from Henry, he seems to have been busy over in France again I wish they would let him get on with his work. Hereward has written & sent me some papers, which interested Cavan very much. He is very unhappy where he is & is trying to get away he wants a brigade on the western front.

10.5.18

My own darling

There is luck about, Fred Maurice[47] I am so glad he was scored off. I don't know what can have made him do it? I went today & saw PT and had a chat with him & then went & had lunch with Mordant[48] & after lunch we had a look at the country from near his HQ. Then I went with one of the officers Bill Nage by name, an Australian who wears a kilt! We went to see the Italians & went into their trenches. Good trenches but the sanitary arrangements are vile. We saw some lovely country deep ravines & mountains. Tomorrow I have an expedition to see some other Italians. The Prince was going with me but he cannot get away so easily now. I am still wearing winter clothes, except that I wear a thin coat, but it is hot in plains, but I spend most of my time in the hills.

11.5.18

My own darling

Anthony has been in here, he was lucky to find me as I only came back early because it was so misty in the hills I could not see anything. He is quite a soldier now, has an MC & bar so it was a good move sending him to his regiment. Poor little man he is so humble about himself. He is coming to dinner tonight. I was lucky today I went to an Italian camp at 9am & they gave me two officers one talked English & the other French. The Corps commander talks English very well & I had an interview with him. First we went up the mountains but there was thick mist & so we returned to Corps HQ. We spoke French at lunch & I had to talk nearly the whole time! The Corps commander told me I could go there to eat & sleep anytime & that if I had not had my 'breakfast' their servant understood English & would give it me anytime.

11.5.18

My dear Henry

I am not at all sure that I am setting about the business you sent me to do in the right way. The last thing I want to do is bother you with my affairs but as you have sent me here for a practical purpose, perhaps after reading this you should either send for me or tell the Lord to write & say what changes I am to make.

I don't want to come home unless you want me as there is so much to be done & if I am to come home I should like to visit the L of C also if the war permits spend a day in Turin. Looking in my duties contained in o.1/155/444 I have not obtained 'an intimate knowledge of the British line' I have attempted to get a general knowledge of the country more especially of the British & also important parts of the French & Italian fronts. In view of the last paragraph you wrote I thought the more I saw of the Italians the better.

I have quietly worked towards the object you had in view i.e. getting Cavan an Army. All I have done in this direction is to peg away at Cavan & Delme Radcliffe so as not to let them forget about it. Apart from this I don't think my little efforts have as yet been very fruitful.

2. Cavan as you know is very anxious to have the question of the offensive settled one way or another. It is unsettling for it to remain as at present. It was an appreciation of Hereward which fully decided him to write to you on the subject.

3. As regards reciprocal help between us & the Italians GHQ are doing all that they can. Three battalions of the 11th Italian Division are now at schools being put through musketry & they are shown demonstrations etc. It has also been arranged that Italian Brigadiers shall come 7 spend two days at a time at the schools. One of the chief difficulties with the Italians is that the have no idea of punctuality. They are sometimes too early or sometimes too late.

4. The Italian now wish (if the attack takes place) not to wait a day between the two attacks as already planned, because of the difficult positions some of the troops east of us will find themselves after the first days fighting. Personally I think our troops will be in similar difficulty & will have a pretty hot time during the days halt, but Cavan does not agree with me.

Anyway Cavan has been asked what he thinks about going on A+1 instead of A+2 & has replied that either we must go in the same day i.e. A day or we must wait till A+2.

Since writing I have received a letter from you. Thanks so much for writing to Tavish that'll do a lot of good. I told Cavan about Maurice in fact I showed him your letter as I found myself in a position I could not help it. However there was no reason he should not see it, he was glad to see it & said he was 'all fool & all knave' which shows that Cavan something to do with Ireland. He is wild about it & says he ought to be court-martialled.

Gathorne Hardy who was a tremendous Wullygate & I gather hitherto rather friendly with Maurice but I may be wrong he is angry too, but thinks

Maurice was not a knave I gather I did not say very much to him as I did not think there was any question of taking sides. His attitude was rather that Lloyd George intended to deceive by including the labour battalions etc & that all soldier distrust Lloyd George & that Maurice was voicing what he thinks. Of course he did not in any way defend his actions & though it would do good in knocking Squiff down for good. Cavan & Gathorne Hardy are much upset by the tone of the French press.

I am glad you like my letters I am arranging to go and live at the schools with the Italian brigadiers when they go for their two day visit. Thanks very much for the interesting news about Ireland I see your point about the Greeks I agree Radcliffe is too optimistic about the Greeks. The only hope I have is that the propaganda was so effective against the Italians but I doubt such things being much good until the Bosche is beat.[49]

12.5.18

My own darling

A letter from you & a really nice one from Taffy congratulating me on pro-motion. The Kings messenger I met coming out & who I took for a jaunt with Williams knew you well. His name is Bridge, he married Miss Charlton & met you years ago at the Kennedy's.[50] A letter from Henry telling me about Maurice. The whole thing was most second class I can only think that he got worked up to it by the Robertson clique & thought he was doing good ser-vice to the country & himself in trying to get rid of Lloyd George & Henry. Henry says I am to tell Cavan the facts.

I am going to the schools (Dicks) for 2 days. Italian brigadiers are going to be there for 2 days to be shown around & I thought it would be a good opportunity for me to help, to live with the Italians & chat to them. Dick very pleased with the idea.

I have had wonderful letters from Henry. He wrote to Tavish so that is alright. Tavish wrote back a very grateful letter.

Dick took me to GHQ this morning I had to see about a car, something has gone wrong with mine I have a nice driver who apparently wants to stop with me so I shall try to keep him. We went to Vicenza for lunch on the way to some sports. The lunch was bad, we had some fish & it was rotten. Cavan was there & I told him what Henry had said about Maurice. He was very glad to hear the news.

12.5.18

My own darling

I must scribble you a note. I think Sunnybank would be very suitable but transport would not be good. I expect Hampton Court sounds much better. I should like to keep chicken's, Delme Radcliffe has over 4,000 & sends his eggs to Harrods. He has ten acres of land only.

13.5.18
I spent an interesting day with Colonel Joubert 14th Wing RAF.[51] News came whilst I was there that we had brought down 7 Austrian planes & one down out of control. He has 3 scout squadrons, i.e. 18 Camels each. One artillery Corps has squadrons to which is attached 6 Bristols. He would like to do more bombing of aeroplanes behind the Piave or more Bristol fighters or some F.E. for night bombing. The Bosche aerodromes are nestling on the Piave front along the Sivenya & the railway at Sacile for instance is an important one & balloons are on the front north of the Piave. There are aerodromes on the Val Sugana & at Trento. I lunched with the 66th Squadron & went to see the 27th Regiment, 11th Italian Division shooting at the range at our schools, some shot well but they hold their rifles badly.

13.5.18
My own darling
Just a little word as Bridge is coming to dinner & will take this in the bag. I did a jolly days work today & felt more useful I spent the day with the flying officer here. I had lunch with one of his squadrons & went on to the schools & Cavan came later & was very nice to the Italian regimental commander. Dick & I are off up the mountain tomorrow. They say it is usually clear until 8.30am & then it clouds over so I shall have to start at 3 or 4am in the morning.

I really am getting on all right with everyone, my chief concern was that I did not feel I was making headway in what Henry wants doing nor do I feel my way to accomplish much.

13.5.18
My dear Henry
I am writing this letter unofficially as I can put more into it & I find it easier.

I spent the morning with Colonel Joubert, commanding the 14th Wing RAF. He is the most excellent officer very keen & thinks you will agree has produced good results on this front though of course the results may be due to his predecessor also. He attributes his success very largely to the great attention he pays to shooting, he has got his fellows keen about it & has improved their shooting no end as is proved by the number of rounds it takes to down a Bosche. This morning his people brought down 7 Bosche & 1 more out of control with no loss to us. The officer who brought down 3 had been practicing hard on the range for a week.

Joubert is very enterprising & is continuingly introducing new methods, new ways of flying, intelligence, new kinds of maps etc. He says he finds the Italians keen to learn & he does a pretty good liaison with them. I enclose some excellent stereoscopic photos he has taken I think they are most useful. He is most anxious to bomb Bosche aerodromes but he is not able to do so because his machines cannot climb high enough with bombs and the aerodromes behind the PIAVE are too far from his aerodromes for his machines.

I told him everything is concentrated on the French front but I think it is worth mentioning his requirements.

He would like best <u>6 F.E. 6's for night bombing. Failing this 6 extra Bristol's.</u> He has 6 Bristol's & has been promised 6 more. <u>If he had 18 he could carry out day bombing.</u>

Failing these two he might get an aerodrome on the PIAVE front & bomb from there but it is extremely difficult to get an aerodrome & he does not feel very hopeful about it. He says there are great possibilities here for bombing if he could get machines. I spoke to Cavan & he quite agrees to my visiting, but would not write himself as he naturally does not want to ask you for things. In one squadron one officer got down 17 enemy planes, several have got 5 or 6 only one has not brought one down.

2. I saw the 11th Italian Division shooting at the range today. They shoot pretty well but have queer ideas as to the use of the left hand for holding the rifle steady. I am told they did a very good field firing show this morning. Cavan told the Regimental commander this afternoon how pleased he was with what they had done & that he thought it an honour to have them under his command.

P.S. Most of the Bosche aerodromes are on the PIAVE front. By Bosche I mean Austrian of course one gets into the habit of calling them Bosche here.[52]

14.5.18

My own darling

I started off at 8 this morning & and collected an Italian officer from Army HQ, he spoke French much worse than I do & it was a great strain having to repeat every sentence. He was quite nice, we had fair views only & had lunch in the car. It began to rain about 12 & never stopped so in the afternoon we went to see some trenches where they produced an officer who spoke English very well, that only made matters worse! We got back to Army HQ at 6pm where Alfrieri had asked me to tea at 5pm & he was awfully pleased, not so much as my being late, but that his plan was upset because it took a long time getting tea.[53] Their chef is a pastry cook from Milan & we had the most delicious chocolate cake I have had for a long time before the war I think! After that I was presented to Montuori, the Army commander & we had a long talk.[54] That was a mental strain as it was in French & he asked me many questions some of which I couldn't answer.[55]. He was examining me in his questions about the Americans & the number of our troops in France. He was very pleasant & I got back here at about 7.30pm.

14.5.18

My dear Henry

A beastly wet day & poor views I went today to Col D'Astiago which over-looks the BRENTA, with an officer from 6th Army HQ. A nice fellow but he speaks French worse than I do & it was rather a struggle. Also he belongs to the cavalry & as he wore boots & spurs his progress was somewhat slow & the boots did not improve with the wet. Subsequently it was so wet we went into the trenches where we were presented with an officer who 'speaks English very well'.

On my way back I was introduced to the Army commander Montouri & had a talk with him I found it difficult. It was a strain on my French. He asked many questions about the number of British troops in France & about the Americans I hope I did not tell him anything I ought'nt to but I like to be frank as one can with them. If you want a Diplomat here you will have to appoint someone else!

What puzzles Montouri is that Mr Secretary Baker said there are 500,000 Yanks in France & that they were being incorporated into our Divisions & he did not understand why we have not got ahead with it.[56] I said there were difficulties about shipping but he said Baker had said they were coming over all right. Then I said I had no news about it & that I did not quite understand myself why they were not available & that I would find out why when I next went to London. Petain had told him that the Bosche had only 50 Divisions in Reserve & that only 30 were fresh. I told him I thought they could attack with 100 Divisions but he said the balance would be composed by Divisions in the line & would not be so fresh. I did not continue the argument. He seems very happy with his command.

I think things go well under him. Certainly Cavan thinks a good deal of him.[57]

15.5.18

My own darling

I am now in the training area with allied officers who have come to see Dicks school. We have 5 Italian, a French officer, Brigadier Lambert & an ancient British officer who interprets & minutes the show, & sees that we have break-fast.[58] This morning I started off at about 9.30 & went to GHQ & then on to PT & left him about 12 & went up the mountains & was surprised to find it quite fine up there. Had a look at the country & ate my sandwiches & then went to see George Bennett & had a chat & saw two brigadiers & came down to GHQ where I ran across Shoubridge. Got in late for tea at GHQ I seldom have tea now so it did not matter. Cavan wanted to see me, so I was late start-ing to come here & did not get in till 8.45. I have been given a brand new car, a baby Fiat it came down here in very good time & they say it is splendid for the hills, I have the same chauffeur Boyd so that is alright. If I go on a long journey they will give me a Rolls Royce.

Attached to this letter of 15.5.1918 was a newspaper article

Motives for the Maurice Letter
French view of the controversy
From our correspondent
Paris May 8th
The French are following the development of the Maurice controversy with natural interest and anxiety. 'Pertinax' the well-known writer in the Echo de Paris, finds 'the powerful spring moving the whole affair' in 'personal, unpleasant, uneducable hatred borne by Colonel Repington to the new CIGS General Wilson.'[59]

'Pertinax' says that the proof Colonel Repington is the real inspirer of the Maurice letter is the venomous articles published under his name since January. If there is a man who has not the right to attack General Wilson then nit is Colonel Repington. A quarrel separated them in the past when both were serving in the same regiment. The military writer is truly ill advised in subordinating to it his whole public activity. At such an hour his spirit of revenge is inexcusable.

'Pertinax' concludes 'We have no desire to express as to the solution of these persons, but we have right to express aloud our hope that at the Commons sitting no leader or party will be found to reopen the question of unity of command or the military measures taken since March. The splitting up of the command is the direst cause of what happened in France at the end of March. Of those who willed it whatever the motives, falls the responsibility for the reverse sustained'.

15.5.18
My dear Henry
I have just heard that it has been decided to carry out the attack. The date is not yet fixed but will probably be about the 5th. Cavan of course is going to press for a date to be fixed as this uncertainty is upsetting. The arrangements have been proceeding. Rods have been repaired in <u>No–man's–land</u> & battery positions have been prepared there also. An old dressing station has been renovated. As Cavan says this shows that it is not quite the same as fighting the Germans I am very late & must dash off to meet the Italians.

16.5.18
My own darling
This visit has not been well run so I have made a lot of notes & no doubt Dick will confirm it next time. This is the first one. One thing the Italians get up much later & do not understand hanging about till 9 before making a start. Then those who took us round don't take a grip of the party sufficiently

I could do much better! We have just had lunch & I am writing this now, as we don't start again till 2.45. There is an old boy here who used to be in Dublin Fusiliers he has a double name Calbeck or Colbeck or something like that, the first name I have forgotten. He said he stood for Dublin when quite a boy. He was in Dublin some years ago (1903) & has been active in connection with some form of National service. He knows one of the Wilson family very well. I am not sure which? His name is Roper-Calbeck.[60] I found another officer from my old Brigade, Glover, who was one of Campbell's best subalterns.[61] We shall have to have a 113th Brigade dinner.

I think I have done good by coming here Dick is going to alter things tomorrow in accordance with my requests so that is good. We saw the artillery & gas schools this afternoon both were excellent.

In my view today has been a great success & a good thing, we are getting along better tonight. It is a funny business these English officers one can talk Italian & the other two who can struggle in French. There are five Italian officers none of whom can speak English & only two can speak French. One French officer who can talk nothing but his own language. The Italians do most of their talking at meals & do it in their own language & we chip in French occasionally I have just been for a walk with an Italian colonel and had a long chat. I curious thing is that the Italian officers can't stand the priests, they say they bring bad luck I asked a French fellow about it & he said he had often been to mass in this country but hardly ever saw an Italian officer.

17.5.18

My own darling A perfect day, bright sunshine & a cool breeze just come in for lunch after going round the sniping & trench mortar schools. Quite interesting I believe we are to dine with the Commandant of the central schools tonight.

Our day is over & some of the officers have gone off with every expression of gratitude & thanks. The rest of us go tomorrow I am glad I came here because though Lambert would have run the show alright I am in a better position to say probably what is wrong & get it put right. There was a difficulty over mess bills old Roper-Calbeck came in to me about it, so I am paying an extra £1 to lessen the charge to the allies. They probably feed up to 5 or 6 here a day, however it is an improvised mess & they all seemed contented about it. In the last few days I have seen cheese eaten with everything but a spoon, knife, knife & fork, fork I have seen fish eaten with a knife & with a fork.

We had a great dinner with Colonel Woodward I sat between Shepperd & my French friend Colonel Larrier. Shepperd was not very cheery like he used to be though it may be General Davies death (which he told me), which has upset him.[62] He is inclined to stick up for Maurice but I could not stand that & told him one or two facts. Major Betts a great physical training man amused us with his experiences with British teams in Florence & other towns.

18.5.18

Yesterday I had a short time in the mountains at Mount Torre & we had a great view. Then I went to see George Barnett, 48th Division & then to GHQ.[63] Here I was kept by the C in C to give me some important information. This made me late & I did not arrive at Villa Treviso, the training area till 8.45pm. They had all had dinner by then I am attending a visit of allied officers to our school run by Brigadier General Lambert.[64]

19.5.18

Owing to the coming offensive Lord Cavan thought I should go home to explain the plans to the CIGS & also to give his views regarding the subsequent employment of the 3 divisions that constitute the British force. This morning I left him at 6am & went up into the hills. Had breakfast with Shoubridge (7th Div) to get his views. He came to lunch here & we went into the Conference at GHQ. In addition to the British officers General Alfrediere commanding the 26th Italian Corps was there & General Demetrio commanding the 1st Italian Division & his staff.

On the 21st & 22nd I saw Gen Badoglio,[65] Chief of the Italian Staff & Diaz chief of staff (the King is C in C) also saw Scipone & Marchetti & Cavolina. They were very pleased & gave me messages for Henry & telling me the English had create a very good impression in Italy & so on.

I left Vicenza 1.30pm on 21st May & travelled with the Kings messenger (Captain Somerset). Milan was pleasant where we had to spend the night. We were off again at 7am it was cooler until the afternoon. We lunched at Turin

31.5.18

My own darling

England is so peaceful I have just seen two men mowing a golf green, seems unnecessary surely they could do war work. Well Darling we had a jolly time and it was not such a bad parting, when I am on this job & may get back more frequently I hope I shall not have to stay long in Paris, or if I do I shall run across someone I know to go about with. However I dare say I shall be at Versailles a good deal, Paris will be hot.

This will amuse you, we got down at 4.30 & went on board & then there was nothing to do. I got hold of a staff officer Captain Paterson & asked the early trains tomorrow. It is really ridiculous they arrange that everybody misses it. However he said there was a Count Sobanski, a Pole who was being met by a car & he introduced me to him & he says he will take me to Paris. Then I was introduced to a Mrs Leigh & her daughter, they are the people who had UAB on their arms. UAB means United Army Board, it is a group of non-conformist denominations that are grouping up just like C of E or RC. These ladies are running a club in Rouen.

There is a funny little man, he has been quite friendly & I know all about him. He is Barton Hirsch's son. Patterson says it was secret where he was going but he told me but I shall not mention it in case of accidents. He was at

Sandhurst but had to leave on account of ill health. He had appendicitis and the operation was badly done, strange with all that money. Then there is Sir Percy Cox, he wears white tabs and Major General's badges I find he is Chief Commissioner for Mesopotamia where everyone has to have uniform & a rank![66]

3.6.18

There is of course a large amount of traffic through Amiens now. We found a suite of rooms at the Curzon which were not expensive & which were very comfortable & handy, we saw a lot of Henry.

Whilst in London telegrams came from Italy to say the feared attack by the Austrians & the Italians maintained there were German divisions there also. This Cavan would not agree to & Henry did all he could to wire to Diaz & in conversations with De Paravaieni to persuade the Italians to carry out their offensive.

Tim Harrington & P de B Radcliffe now in the W.O. which is very nice I also saw the latter. Maurice wrote to Henry he was given the impression that it was an official letter requiring an answer. It did not foreshadow any action by him or suggest any action by Henry. I crossed to France via La Harve meeting on Major General Freeland going to India to organise railways. Count Sabrawski, who gave me a seat in his motor to Paris.

The offensive in the Soissons & Rhiems had started whilst I was at home & made uncomfortable progress. I arrived in Paris 3pm 2nd June & went to Versailles where the inter-allied council was sitting I saw Henry & dined with Currie, Bell & Heneker.[67] Then went to Tit Willow where I saw the PM, Lord Milner,[68] Hutch, J.T. Davies, Philip Kerr,[69] Du Cane,[70] Cazelet (Tit Willows ADC), Henry, Bliss[71] & Bowlby. I went on with Tit Willow where I slept the night, there was an air raid which was rather interesting.

On the 3rd June I lunched with the PM, Lord Milner, Duncannon,[72] Philip Kerr, Bowlby, Lord Derby,[73] J.T. Davies,[74] Hutch, Stead, Cazelet. Then we all went to the Trianon (V) where a small meeting took place & everyone else hung about a very bad arrangement indeed. Henry says they talked of subjects of which no notice had been given. Great difficulties are being experienced in arranging how the Americans are to be trained & organised. Pershing does not make things easy.[75] Henry advocates cutting back the line to St Omer so as to shorten the line. Foch won't hear of it at any price & one hopes he is right but what will happen if the Germans now attack elsewhere as well, they may & have at least 36 divisions available for it.[76] We are at a most critical time to go through at present the Bosche are having it at present all his own way & we are engaged in squabbling amongst ourselves or at least failing to come to decisions. The French as usual complain they are not producing the men we ought to. Henry I think is not so pro-French as he was! The PM looks nonchalantly well. At tea we saw all the notables Clemenceau,[77] Orlando,[78] Foch, Sonnino[79] & very many others.

7.6.18

My dear Henry

I had lunch with Montouri yesterday which went off all right. Then I attended a demonstration by the 14th Wing dropping things from aeroplanes. Apparently the idea is to throw out tins attached to parachutes. These fall in the enemy lines and contain balloons & gas for sending messages back to us. I should think we should collect a good many lies!

2. I stayed the night with Babington in the hills.[80] It was very cold up there. Babington was very friendly. He talks a great deal about you & tells stories about you. He is great friends with General Benfait (French 23rd Division). He says Benfait is very sick of the offensive being off apropos recent events. Babington made an interesting remark, he said, 'I wish they would give Cavan an Army and then we could have more say in the matter'. His solution was to make an army of ourselves & the French holding that as we are under Foch they could hardly refuse a reciprocal arrangement. This is not a practical solution as it would amount to degumming Montouri. Babington was very disappointed & his division was to be at the offensive. He thinks we had a sitter.

3. I hear indirectly that we are to have some sort of offensive – to the brown dotted line I understand. A pity we cannot do the whole thing. General Hudson the heavy gunner says we shall be 60 to 80 guns short of what it was originally intended to be.[81] There is a conference tomorrow at GHQ.

4. Joubert still hankers after his aeroplanes for bombing. The air people at Hotel CECIL said he could use his REP's but he tells me he cannot do so without taking machines away from other work. He says, however, he can manage if his <u>personnel</u> is increased. He requires a complete RE 8 flight.

He also has an idea he might get 6 Capries I am writing to Carthen (Lt. Col) about these points.[82]

Wire

SECRET

From: – C.I.G.S.

To: – General Price-Davies

H.W. 5.

Your letter June 5th. I think the L of C in the North the most important. Later on you might find time for TARANTO.

The King absolutely refuses permission for our troops to wear foreign war ribbons and so the Italian ribbon is only treated as are all others.

10/June/18.[83]

13.6.18

My dear Henry

I have just arrived back from a visit to wise Bob I'm glad I went & I have learnt a good deal from my visit. I left here Sunday afternoon 9th inst & got to CREMONA about 6pm. They lent me a Rolls Royce for the trip, so comfortable that I could read on the way.

On 10th I visited the hospitals, Veterinary Hospitals & Remount squadron at that place and at VOGHERA & reached TORTONA about 7pm & stayed the night and the next day with the I.G.C. He was so pleased I had come & was most hospitable & he & his staff did everything they could for me.[84]

11th June I visited ARQUATA, General took me round & also gave me lunch. I liked him and thought him a real fine man I saw the reinforcement camps, hospital, bakery, M.T. stores dept, ASC base depot, supply depot, Ordnance depot & workshops, R.E. depot, detention camp, Base depot & Vet stores.

Yesterday I spent all day till tea time at the HQ office IGC & saw all the heads of Departments & got to know what their work is & how things are run. These included A & Q Branches, Supply transport, Medical, Remounts, Veterinary, Transportation, and Financial advisors. After I was going to see the Ammunition depot & was going to stay that night & tonight at ARQUATA when I get a wire from Cavan saying he wanted me back. 'Please return. Important development. Cavan'.

I am very sad as Friday I was going to GENOA & tomorrow I should have done the M.T. Heavy repair workshop (PAVIA) & CAPROVA works (MILAN), blanket clearing establishment TREGOGLIO & proposed sleeping at the new rest camp at SEMIONE on Lake GARDA, returning here on the 15th visiting on route laundries (MANTOVA), ordnance & supply depot (Legragio).

However it is most satisfactory that Cavan should think of asking for me I came straight away leaving TORTONA at 8pm & getting here at 2.45am 285 Kilometres. About an hour must be knocked off for a halt I had a chocolate & biscuits, at MANTOVA a burst tyre (only ten miles from here) & for tasking the wrong road once. If the chauffeur had known the road it would have been very comfortable but as it was I had to keep my eye on the map all the time to warn him of level crossings etc. The I.G.C. is not quite satisfied by the position of the Directors, mentioning that they should be with him and not with Cavan. Except the D.M.S. (who is with him & the A.D.V.S.) who he thinks should be with Cavan.[85] Cavan on the other hand says that Lawson only wants to get rid of Newlands (D.M.S.) because he doesn't like him.[86] Personally I think this question should be solved if the number of Directors & assistant directors were reduced & then it would soon be found out where they must go to carry out their work best I must say I should have though the directors of supplies & ordnance stores should be with the I.G.C. but I have no wish to reopen the question which has already been decided by the Army Council, but just give you the chat. I put my foot in it over one matter Lawson is very touchy about anyone interfering with his round when I was there at the W.O.; Tim told me to tell Cavan that the Army Council had decided that Cavan's suggestion that Brassey should be an area commander at Genoa was not approved & that Schletter (who has been appointed) would probably appointed. I told Lawson, who would have it that Cavan had remembered Lamb from Rome & was evidently upset that Lamb was Lawson's selection! That he (Cavan) would not have him of course I never dreamt that Lawson did not know about it.

One has to be weary I have been caught once or twice already because Cavan does not tell his staff what he has written. The ribbon for the Italian medal about which you wired me is a case in point.

Cavan has not told the A.D.M.S. the whole story. Cavan is not very happy about Fanshawe but I won't repeat it here as I'm writing to Tim about it.[87] When I saw Cavan at noon today he told me all about Montouri conference of which you know a good deal already. It is rather a shock & very disappointing to find Montouri solemnly making promises which at a moment's inspection show to be impossible. The inference is that Diaz realises that he has been didilled by the Austrians & finding that he cannot now quickly turn on the original offensive & is trying to put up a show quickly. The fact remains it was proposed to exploit the limited offensive already arranged for (now to be carried out on the 18th) by advancing the British right to M. CATZ where they would presumably be French troops in touch with us but the main business was push up about 14 Divisions between the VAL FRENZEL (which is impossible) and GALLIS WOOD (west of Gallis) & spread out to right & left – here I believe Montouri spread his hand out as if he was swimming – and pinched Gallis Wood (which is full of guns) & spread out over the country to the right Bosche tactics gone mad. Montouri even spoke of bringing up an additional 14 Division in a week!

As you know Cavan refused to do this I here. In addition to the arguments, you know he pointed out that he had no artillery arrangements for the support of our attack on M. GATZ as that place had originally been part of the French objective. Montouri then proposed putting in the Italian brigade to take M.GATZ. Cavan asked what artillery they would have to which Montouri replied 'They must attack without' or words to that effect. Cavan of course told him his idea of moving up these divisions in a word was impossible & Bandy (Gregianis chief of staff) described it after as 'alfragrante' I don't like Gregianis behaviour over this business considering the fuss he made originally when he was to have been left in M. GATZ, how he got Cavan to agree to come forward to support his left and finally now the operation was to have been carried out in one day instead of three to suit hit him, it is very ungracious that he did not now come forward and say that he thought the task asked of the British was too much. He admitted to Cavan that he quite saw his point of view and that had he been in Cavan's place he would have done the same but I understand that MAESTRE used to act in a much more friendly manner.

You will see from the above how important it is for Cavan to have an army & so have more say. It is unsatisfactory that a Corps commander should be placed in a position of having to refuse to do what his army commander tells him. That is one reason why your appearance in the theatre at this time would be very valuable.

If you want me during the battle my address will be CONE de FONTE. The TONALI show comes off on the 16th inst.[88]

14.6.18

My dear Henry

I have not seen the arrangements about the Americans I only know what you told me at Versailles. The 100 Divisions is a good business we shall be in a better position to talk when they come.

Cava says Montouri is quite pleased with his papers & that any more extended offensive is off for the moment. This fever is playing the devil with the troops. It leaves the men so weak that the battalions have to be carried about in lorry's instead of marching, in some cases practically the whole of the 48th Division HQ Staff was down with it but they are all about again now looking rather the worse for wear.

I am going out for a walk with Wardrop tomorrow I am amused I don't know what we are going to see or why.[89] Possibly he is trying to make up because when I want his final news, he said they were all busy. He was fussed about something I just said 'I only came to see if there was anything I could do for you'.

I had a great mountain walk today wish you could have been there. I see my brevet is in the papers today thanks so much for it. It was a great surprise when I was told about it. Poor Dick Crichton is very sad to get nothing. He feels he ought to have got something for missing the Cambridge course I am writing to Tim about it.[90]

23.6.18

My dear Henry

I got down all right in the Rolls & I hope it got back in time. It should have done. There was a state of pandemonium at the station, everyone leaving Paris I wonder when you will finish your meeting & what decisions will be got to. It seemed rather hopeless I should awfully like to know what they decide to do with the Americans, everyone appears to want something different.

It was good seeing you but Du Cane was a bore getting in the way just at the wrong time![91] Things seem pretty critical I hope you will have your way. This old train shakes as you see, I thought I would tell you or you might think it was drink! I wonder next time I come here will it be Bordeaux or by sea via Marseilles! I shall look forward to your visit.

P.S. I think it would be a good thing if people at home and at Versailles adopted a less suspicious attitude regarding the Italians I must say when I came here & Tit Willow and others said cheerily 'Hullo how are the Ice-creamers' it jarred on me.[92]

17.6.18

My dear Henry

I will not describe the fight even if I could for fear of overlapping.[93] What a pity our offensive never came off it would have been a sitter I'm afraid, however, that Commando Supremo took another point of view. They say 'Now see how wise we were not to attack because if we had we should have been in a bad position to meet the attack on the PIAVE'. They did not appear to realise that by adopting this attitude that at once put the Austrians on a higher plane than themselves. For they acknowledge that whereas they have been put off attacking by the mere threat of an Austrian attack, yet they credit the Austrians with the desire and ability to carry out an offensive even though they were being heavily attacked themselves.

In this connection Babington was saying to me on the 10th 'This would never have happened if Cavan had an army.' You will have gathered also from communications you have had from GHQ that Cavan feels his helplessness in this matter. He, or at any rate Gathorne Hardy is anxious to meet any eventuality. It is a delicate situation but it would be a great thing if it could be done.

Cavan is weakening about having an army because he thinks the mixture of Italian & British troops would be unsuccessful. He is I think disheartened & the attitude of the Italians towards training we have tried to give them, and he fears he might get a Corps commander like ALFIEU, which would be hopeless & wishes that an army had been made up of British & French, so that the commander of the army could have had some influence with Commando Supremo.

Now to the battle. Deserters have given information as to the attack & the divisional commanders came down to GHQ on the morning of the 14th June & got their instructions. You must remember that we had been told on previous occasions that the enemy was going to attack at a certain time but nothing happened. Not that precaution's were not taken, but 6th Army issued no instructions to suspend the offensive preparations, consequently we had the curious situation that a party of 50 gunners were actually preparing a battery position in no-man's land when the enemy barrage opened. More than this the 70th Brigade on the right, continued up to 11pm on the 14th to form dumps on no-man's land. Next day they found that they had run out of ammunition & wished they had formed their dumps behind instead in front.

The artillery was rather in a state of transition, also the trench mortars which had formed part of the protective barrage of the 23rd Division had moved away to act offensively for the 48th Division & so weakened the barrage of the 23rd Division. I'll tell you all this to show you the disadvantages of the situation.

The hostile bombardment was not very heavy but it was quite serious. Anyway it was rather the bombardments we know. It hardly disturbed the wire or trenches & in some places it missed our front line altogether. Roads were heavily damaged and a good many casualties were caused on them. In this country it takes a long time to get from place to place unless you can motor everywhere & also I did not like leaving my car where it might get cut off by a chance shell hitting a tree. Walking across country takes a long time as it is hilly & wooded. This must account for the extraordinary fact that though I did not stay long at any one place (ate lunch walking!) I had little to show for my day. I left here before 8am and got back 9pm. During that time I visited GHQ twice, saw Dick Crichton twice and his advance report centre at Lime de Friuti, and visited 2 divisional HQ's, 2 brigades and one battalion commander I looked in at the Heavy artillery for a few moments also. The further forward I got the more cheery I found everyone. They said the Austrians were good targets in their long dark coats, and if you know the range were excellent 'running men'. Tonight I was told the 23rd Division calculate they can see 750 corpses close to the trenches.

We have had very bad luck with the weather. There have been thick clouds on the high ground PAU, LIMA Di FONTIQE. This has handicapped our armies and artillery. The artillery proved very successful & Cavan is very pleased with them. They established O.P's in trees on the lower slopes below the clouds and got some excellent targets. Wardrop told me they got into the batteries in the open & saw guns & ammunition flying in the air.

The prisoners I saw looked miserable & half starved of course prisoners never look their best but I have never seen such a rotten lot as this.

Considering the trouble we have had with the fever Divisional staffs suffered especially I think it is a very fine performance having given the Austrians such a hiding & I hope they will remember their taste of real rifle & machine gun fire.

Prisoners continue to roll up & we have now got 1,052 & 4 Divisions who attacked us have been so roughly handled that they had to be relieved. As regards the Italians it is very difficult to get at the truth. In the mountains I think all is well. Possibly fighting in mountains suits the Italians best especially as their best troops are Alpine. On the Piave things are not quite so good. One has to balance what one gets from different sources. To give an idea of the sort of thing. Yesterday I went to the 3rd & 8th (Late 2nd) Armies & 11th & 23rd Corps (both 3rd Army) I got a good impression, though one or two things were unsatisfactory. When I get to Delme-Radcliffe he was quite enthusiastic about what the Italians had done & warned me that Garthorne-Hardy did not take quite the right vein. This morning Garthorne-Hardy (who is in bed with a carbuncle) took a gloomy view & said the Italians (as he always said) didn't fight in defence, that you could not believe what they said, that the staff work wasn't good enough for a counter attack to succeed, that they had taken their guns back & would not shell the bridges & finally that

Delme-Radcliffe's information was most unreliable. The C in C took a very steady view & said it was a great thing that the Italians were fighting every yard. It is of course quite possible that the <u>satisfied</u> attitude of the Italians may be the Valour of Ignorance but considering avoidable venture on either side there should be no course for anxiety.

I was once again dissatisfied with my trip yesterday. Formalities have to be gone through which take time I left here soon after 8am to get to 3rd Army HQ (Duc de Aosta) at 12.30 which was opportune as he asked me to lunch. He talks English, as you probably know but I find him difficult to talk to. Incidentally he does not believe in the American soldier because he says you cannot improvise an Army. So he thinks that the war must end next year! I don't think I need to go into details about his point the situation is still very unstable but might not been too critical. I saw a captured order giving objectives for the Austrian cavalry! I then went to 8th Army (Gen PENELLAS). Luckily he spoke French so I did not to use the interpreter as I had at the 11th & 23rd Corps. He seemed to me to have a grip on the MONTELLO situation & explained how he had brought up the 55th Division & 13th Division (the latter by lorry) to put in the counter attack (30 Battalions).

The 55th Division was to swing parallel to the roads which cross the MONTELLO from south to north. The 13th Division was to make for NERVESA. Cavan says this plan is perfectly sound but we subsequently heard that it was carried out in a different manner & the 55th moved close to the Piave & soon the forward slopes where they got slated with artillery & the counter attack failed & came back. Now the Austrians have enlarged their gains & have got about ¾ quarters of the Montello. The Italians hold approximately the Corps line which I have shown roughly in red. Probably they are not quite so far forward on the right. Both sides are now moving up reserve divisions & the balance should be in favour of the Italians. It is interesting to note that the Italians abandoned their Tonale offensive & have brought down 2 Divisions from these parts.

There is a gain some Austrians were in a bad way west of the Piave. They captured a pigeon loft & though they would send a message by one to their own people. The bird of course went the other way & the despairing message fell into Italian hands.

Cavan has been given the Italian Croix de Guerre I don't quite know what they call it. The Czech-Slav enthusiasts have a slight rebuff – as the 12th Austrian Division which was considered to be so unreliable that it had to be relieved (they fought they would desert en-masse) have been at the fore-front of the battle & fought well! Cavan this afternoon explained his views to me, which coincide very much with yours. He says we ought to attack in France. Meanwhile we must attack in Italy. He suggest bringing to Italy in the most unostentatious manner sufficient Divisions to total, with what we have here 6 British, 6 French, 4 Americans. The Italians should then take over the mountain sections & the allies fight in the plains. He anticipates great results from such an offensive.

I forgot to mention communications. As one cannot bring cable in the rocks the lines get cut & communication goes. It is hard to put over this difficulty. If they lay the lines across country by different routes the linesmen's duty would be too great. At present large number of lines are laid along the roads which are heavily bombarded so the lines get cut.

The following might interest you

23rd Division	17 officers	400 men
48th Division	69 officers	839 men
Heavy Arty	7 officers	130 men
	93 officers	1369

Prisoners captured 1052.
Number of men suffering from fever.

	In C.C.S.	In Convalescent Camps
June 11th	1840	311
12th	2145	193
13th	1940	100
14th	1653	44
15th	1253	nil[94]

19.6.18

My dear Henry

Gathorne Hardy has gone to hospital with his carbunckle. It has been very painful but he is better. Cavan will be lost without him.

Yesterday I went round with the chief engineer doing the left of our line to where the CESNA-ASSIAGO crosses the GHELPAC. The trenches have not been knocked about much on the left but square where the GHALPAC runs E to W the trenches have been obliterated. This was one of the chief points of entry. The men were salvaging equipment etc in no-man's land. They tell that the Austrians were well equipped for the fight nearly everything was new. They appeared to have carried a large amount of stick grenades & the country is strewn with them.

All day I was crossing over the news & wondering how the Piave was getting on. When I got in was told the joyful news that the bridges over the Piave had gone. There appear to have been some remaining S of Ponti de Piave but round the Mortello they had all gone and have not yet been replaced.

The Italians did not intend attacking till tomorrow morning but they took advantage of their luck and attacked at 3pm today & made progress capturing 700 prisoners & 200 M.G. companies. The latter are important, on one front they fought well. I hope they will finish off the job & complete the discomfort of the Austrians.

In the south Cap D'Argive continues to be captured and re-captured but on the whole the advantage lies with the Italians. I saw a captured order of the day issued by the Austrian regimental commander which is of interest. He holds forth about the end of trench warfare & getting the enemy into the open 'the Italian command will be obliterated by the thunder of the Austrian artillery. It will be no use sending reinforcements to any one place, they will be wanted everywhere as we shall attack all along the line.' He ends up saying 'Forward to VERONA where 100 years ago the founder of this illustrious Regiment defeated the combined Italian & French Armies.'

Another order was captured giving orders for the withdrawal & I am inclined to think that the withdrawal took place after it became evident that the attack on the front was only successful at one point. The men attacked with vigour at the same time which strengthened the Austrian determination to carry out their orders.

Today I had an interesting round with Wardrop. He showed me country I did not know well & showed me some guns. He is very pleased with the 9.2 howitzer. Then we went to a Hill in Sq h.44. & then to Hill 971 in SQ 34. We counted 25 dead Austrians still requiring burial. It is not often a BGRA can go out into no-man's land in daylight to see the result of his barrage. He was able to note mistakes & I hope correct them. The effect of our fire along the hostile front near CANOVE are very marked. There is hardly a vestige of wire left.

I think a big raid might be very successful I hear our airmen brought off a star turn today. 3 of them met 9 Austrians & brought down 6, one of which fell just in front of the King.

We are very bucked by the German repulse at Rheims.

It would be a great thing if you could come out & talk over things with Cavan & Diaz. Cavan feels he would like he would like to put his view forward so as to influence Diaz, I think, but in his present position he cannot do so. He is all for attacking as soon as possible.

Fanshawe has gone so that is finished.[95]

30.6.18

Soon after I came back I visited the lines of communication. First I went to Cremona where I stayed the night. Major McTurk & Colonel Smyth RE came to dinner & next day they took me round the establishments at Cremona, hospital, veterinary hospital, remount squadrons. Cremona is a nice little town & the Hotel Roma quite better than anything we can produce in Vincenza. The Cathedral is made to a very good proportion, I went to the tower whence you get a very good view of the country which is very flat I passed through Verona, Mantova, & Picenzia all most picturesque. After lunching in Cremona having finished my morning inspection I went on with Captain Parke & met Colonel Williams in Voghera & saw some similar establishments there & then went on to Tortona where I stayed with the IGC, Sir H. Lawson he was very kind & hospitable. Next day I saw all the establishments at Arquarta, General Strick taking me round.[96] It rained all day we saw the reinforcements camp, ordnance stores, supply workshops etc all very interesting. General Lawson has gone since I was there & now General Strick is IGC with temporary rank of major general. After tea I went to see the arms dumps & then work back to Thiene visiting the establishment along the way & sleeping a night at Sermione on Lake Garda where there is a rest station. However a wire came to me at the ammo dump (Rivalta) & I had to come back to Tortona at 8pm & motored 285k getting there at 2.45am. Diaz had been considering launching some minor offensives & Cavan had objected to what he wanted having insufficient artillery. The French general to my mind did not back Cavan sufficiently strongly though he told Cavan he agreed with him. Anyway Montouri (Commanding 6th Italian Army) was quite pleased with Cavan's letter putting forward his objections to the proposals.

A few days after my return (15th June) the Austrians attacked all along the left of our front to the sea. On our front he penetrated the line of the 48th Division but found himself in a wired pocket & made little progress. We counter attacked in the evening & again in the morning & it was then all over. We captured about 800 prisoners, our total losses were about 1,350. The Austrians relied I believe on the bombardment being exemplary but it was nothing of the sort & they failed to get through our uncut wire. On the Piave they had some success. They got part of the Montello & got a footing on a considerable front north of the Capo site. There was fighting for several days some villages changing hands several times. However, there was a lot of rain & the Piave rose & washed away nearly all the bridges. The Italians hammered away & on the night of the 22/23 June the Austrians withdrew & the battle was an end. Subsequently the Italians continued their attacks to recapture a portion of their line to the West of the Bienta, which were still in German hands. On the 29 June they captured 800 prisoners.

Henry Wilson came out to see Cavan & Diaz, he arrived in Turin on the 23rd where I met him in his saloon & we were very comfortable. His visit was a great success I did not see much of him but on his last day 27th June he took me into Venice. We did not have perfect weather but it did not rain until after we were coming back so we had little to complain of. Delme-Radcliffe came with us.

On the 28 June Hereward Wake came through & stayed the night, he had been on a trip to Macedonia from Versailles & was on his way back with his report.[97] He is very enthusiastic about getting the Bulgarians out of the War he says that will take out Turkey & Austria I wonder. I took him on the 29th to Cima di Fonte & to Cima Eckar whence we could see the shells bursting on Col Rosso & where the fighting is taking place. Hereward went off by the 9pm train.

1.7.18

My own darling

I had a good day today I went up Mount Grappa with an Italian officer. It was a lovely day & we got good views though the distant views were not so good. It is quite cold up there, my fingers got quite white. We stopped to have lunch (provided by my Italian friend) Frangialli at that moment we met a gunner major who started off by abusing my friend for not saluting him! However, he was easily appeased & told us we could eat our sandwiches in his hut.

Then he complained that those in uniform on the plain got all the decorations whilst those in the hills got none. Finally he said that officers 3 years junior to him were being promoted over his head because they had been to the staff college I asked why he hadn't been there & he said he had not the inclination preferring horses & riding so I suggested that those who had taken their profession seriously deserved to get on but I don't think he understood as his English was not very good. On my return I went & saw Cavan & had a chat. He is very divided, gives his opinion but never by any chance asks mine.

The Prince of Wales has got out of going home for the silver wedding and has gone off to Venice for the day on the strength of it.

1.7.18

My dear Henry

RI went up M. Grappa today & had lunch I got splendid views. It strikes me that it will be a big undertaking to continually improve the Italian positions in this region but it is a strong position as it stands. You know they want to take M.PRASSOLAN – M.PERTICO – COEDELLA BERRETTA – Col CAPRILE.

I could not see the latter from M. Grappa but my information was that in order of gaining ground on this front should be to take,

1. M.SPINUCCIA – M. SOLAROLO – M. PRASSALAN – M. PERTICA.
2. Take Col DELLA BERRETTA + Col CAPRILE.

A more intimate knowledge of the ground might show that this is not sound but I think if you commence at BERRETTA the approaching troops will get taken in badly by artillery fire from both flanks.

I saw Cavan this evening I know he is writing to you but I may as well repeat what he told me. He is very pleased with the results of the last Italian fight on M.Val Billa & Col Del Rosso etc. He says it is the best thing the Italians have done yet. It went well throughout and the troops fought well. The relative casualties are significant Austrians 2,000 odd captured Italians casualties 500. The Austrians now have little to show for their great offensive moreover they lie in their communiqués. They claim the 'thrust against M.SISEMOL broke down under our fire'. The French never 'thrust against SISEMOL'. They occupied a small place near BERTIGO & sent some patrols to take trenches they found unoccupied but they never attempted to go near SISEMOL. There have been some little fuss apparently the Italian 12th Division did not care for the 48th & were very suspicious of their actions during the battle. This must come to MONTOURI'S ears so he had Cavan and GREGARIUM to lunch and after he gave them a lecture on what Cavan described as PLATOON TACTICS. He told them all the things they ought to do. Cavan assured him all was being done but that he would go straight away to see his divisional commanders & find out exactly how many men were being employed on the works in question. Accordingly he did so & found all was being done as it should be. He wrote and told Montouri so but before he could get the letter to Montouri, he came round & saw him again & lectured him for <u>an hour</u>, as to what could happen if the Germans attacked etc, etc. Cavan was very bored can't you see him! The result has been that Montouri has sent 3 company's of sappers to help the 7th (left Division).

Cavan is thinking of taking a month's leave in August I don't know if he mentioned it to you but it would be a very good thing if you suggested to him later on. I shall probably go to Val SAGARINO & Val GRIDICANIA this week I shall stayed at SEMIONE (GARDA). Hope you saw Hereward.[98]

2.7.18

My own darling

It is too annoying the signals muddled my letter for the Kings Messenger so it has not gone. If only I had known Dick could have taken it but the clerk didn't tell me till after dinner. Bridge arrived to today & has gone off again very sudden. If you see him thank for bringing me your letters & say I was sorry not to see him, as I had to go off on an expedition I had planned.

Today I finished up with an English speaking officer at Army HQ & we motored up to the mountains to the HQ of his Division. His battalion was close so off we went to find him but he was with the moles! They then suggested I should have lunch with the divisional HQ & that he should be brought there. He arrived during lunch having had his & sat and watched us eat, always an awkward business, alas I did not know he had fed & though perhaps it wasn't etiquette for a 2 Lt to feed with his commander so I did not at first ask him if he had had lunch. We weren't a great success together as his French was bad & he did understand mine! After lunch I went off with 2 officers & saw some of the ground the Italians have been fighting over near Val Della. They really have done well today they captured a lot more prisoners at 3 different points on their front.

3.7.18

My own darling

I have seen so much today I wish you could see. The Italian officer with me is not a success, he is nice but I can't make him understand anything in English, he is supposed to be an interpreter I have to repeat everything twice & then often have to give it up or translate it into French. We had intended to start at 8.30am but at 6.45am Boyd reported that he had broken something in the carburettor but could get it repaired. He got it repaired but it broke again so I wired the S.M.T.O. & he sent down a motor with a Sgt Major, a fitter & an electrician & a new carburettor & we got off at 10am. We went to one of the Italian Army HQ's & got there at 11.30am. Here I presented a letter from Delme-Radcliffe, he has given me a bundle of letters some of them for people I cannot possibly meet!

After leaving we went through Verona & up the valley of the Adige it is lovely. You suddenly come to what looks like an impossible barrier of rock but the road, railway & river just manage to squeeze through. Then you have rocky mountains on each side for miles. We called in at Corps HQ & got an officer to go with us, so we dropped Heywood off for the time being. We went up the valley for a bit then turned off as usual up a zig-zag road & eventually we had a good view of the country. We came down a new road we were the first motor car down it! Now I am at rest camp, we got here at 8.45pm, a Captain Radcliffe, an Australian is running it. He is very full of himself but a good fellow. After dinner he took me to the village, such a quaint place with water all round it. We went to a hotel where there was a topping piano, the pianist used to accompany George Bowlby but in spite of that is first class & played some Chopin for us & Radcliffe sang. He has a fine voice, and used to sing he tells us for his master's voice. He sang a song I had not heard 'Harvest', the words are fine, we had a lot of songs. I am quite alright now my toothache went as suddenly as it came.

4.7.18

My own darling

I have written a long letter to Henry, which takes time. We were off this morning at 8.45am & motored along Lake Garda, then we left the lake & climbed & climbed up the mountainside though with less zig-zags than before which are a bore. Just as you are looking at a bit of country you are suddenly whisked round & nearly fall out of the car & fall over the next fellow & are switched away from what you are looking at. We met our Captain guide again at 12 & walked up a high mountain overlooking the end of a lake & looking right away north. They are seldom free from clouds but today was perfect & was worth many wet days. The beautiful blue of the water was gorgeous, you don't get it elsewhere. We had our lunch up there from sandwiches they prepared at Sermione where I am staying. I caught them out they are not very good at map reading although they are very much at home with the names of places they know. The mountain flowers are so lovely & wild, forget me knots & many alpine flowers as you see in rock gardens. It is a bit early for them but some were in a mass of bloom, there is still some snow on top of the mountains I was in. We looked down on to the towns of Riva, Rovereto & Arco, coming down I met such a nice man a brother of a man who had taken me round with Hardress-Lloyd only a few days ago. He would have been with me today but he was away on another duty & so could not come. We got back at 7.15pm & that only with a struggle, it takes a long time to get about. You can't hurry over mountain roads & I spend my time telling my driver to go slow. I had a dip before dinner, it is only a question of going out of the door & there you are I was not in for more than 2 minutes that was quite enough.

4.7.18

My dear Henry

Only a strong sense of duty coupled with the possibility of losing my job, enabled me to write to you tonight I am staying at the Officers Club Semione – Col Garda. It is a lovely spot and after a good dinner & after a really good glass of brandy I began to feel it is a dolcha for Vietta. I have had the most glorious day today up in the mountains between LAGAVINIA Valley & Lake Garda. I hardly know where to begin telling you though I fear I have little of military interest I shrink from describing the towns & scenery because you always seem to know everything I think you must be very old! We went through BARDOLINI – Garda where the streets can only get about by going through house & churches. Caprino – Ferrara & all along the side of Monte Baldo de Havene. From there we walked to the top of ALTIMISSIMO. The muleteers were Czechos (I never can spell it) & severe difficulty arose as no one could understand. Eventually it was discovered that one of them knew a little German! I was very lucky – very seldom do they get a clear day on ALTISSIMO but today was perfect. To the left we could see Lake LEDRO & the PONALER river running to Garda. This country looked quite impossible to attack over. Then RIVA & the DROAD Valley of the ADIGE where lies ROVENTO. It struck me as a possible operation to take this mass of hills but I assumed the rocks were full of tunnels & machine gun. The Italian position is a very strong one and they have several lines of defence all admirably sited but it is unnecessary to bore you with the details.

The Czeck-Slav Division is in the front and on the slopes of M.BALDO & in the valleys that run from the ADIGO they were ideal training grounds which they are making full use of. I could not help thinking what a nice spot it could be for us in really hot weather. It is cheerful in ALTISSIMO & there is still snow there. The blue of the lake looked at from ALTISSIMO is most beautiful.

Yesterday I arrived at 1st Army HQ PECOLI GIRALDI at 11.30. A dangerous hour I begged the old boy to let me go as we were late but he seemed to think it should save time for us to lunch with him so there was nothing for it. The old boy is deaf which I didn't discover for some time & I thought he didn't understand my French! He wore black elastic boots & black puttees! A queer figure. We went to XXIX Corps HQ at BORGETTO in the Val LAGANIVA where we got a nice officer to guide us. We went into the hills East of Val up to the Val Valento to PASSA BINOLO not far south of COIN ZUGUA. We could not get to the latter as we were too late but we did pretty well as we saw the VALLARISA. The strength of the positions impressed me & I am glad to find they realise that if the flanks hold they need not fear an advance down the valley. They are improving the defences to meet such a case. On July 2nd I went to the Italian trenches opposite SISEMAL, just to the right of the French & so called COSTALIMGA redoubt, which was captured by the Austrians on June 15th & it gave the Italians some trouble to get it back. It is not a redoubt but a system of trenches.

They are all very enthusiastic over their attacks. I mention this to bring out a contrast. I lunched at the HQ 14th Division. This division had just completed the capture of the Val Bella. The officer who commanded and his French stokes (or stokus as they call it) batteries were actually having lunch there also. In spite of this I noticed the very serious look in the divisional commander's face when it was suggested that Germans might come here. My own opinion is that you can't count on the Italian moral <u>if</u> Germans come here. I am sure we must stiffen the Italians with more British and French divisions. Incidentally the ordinary Italian commander has no conception of the position in France & cannot understand why we can't send division here from France.

Many thanks for your last letter I have thought a bit over the problem of winter fighting. Small coup de mains are possible & were done last year but the difficulty is communications & supply. Troops carrying out even these small enterprises have had to undergo great hardships in these accounts. It would be a good plan however to get people thinking of it for if once the idea catches on a solution will be found, but it requires very high organisation.

I go tomorrow to see Val Gruidicanica & have to stay somewhere in the mountains. It is too far to do it from here. My car was the first car to come down the road from Pasa Buolo yesterday – my chauffeur was naturally frightened I think![99]

7.7.18

Edolo

My dear Henry

I have now visited VAL GRUIDICANICA, Val Cammenica & Val Valtelline, everything was fixed for me to stay and as it is somewhere on the Adamillo it will be interesting & I have decided to stay I don't propose writing much tonight, but I must tell about the General PICCIONE. He commands the 55th Division, which has 8 fighting battalions & altogether 5,000 Alpini. He has a front of 50 kilometres I am quite sure he is a good man. Yesterday went in the teleferics,[100] we got into buckets, the two of us together, they looked as if they wouldn't hold a decent sized dog, climbing up mountains etc. He had a word for all his officers & the men love him. The work was all going well & it is obvious he sees to it all. His officers all beamed when he appeared. He really might have been a British general. He strapped one man for not having his cap on straight & got fussy with some officers because empty cartridge cases had not been collected, and cursed some men for using a telephone by day, and was annoyed with one man for trotting his horses down a hill. Coming down in the snow it got very steep & he bent down and slid on his bottom & me after him – when he got to the bottom of the hill he apologised for being so young 'one behaves like a child here', he said. He is 53. He has had lots of experience in mountain warfare & knows every trick. He ran the last Tonali offensive which was no small undertaking & has given the Italians very important ground. This command, as he commands so many troops & he has such a large front, that he should be a Corps commander. He has the same staff as any other Divisional commander.

8th July I asked General Piccione about his command. He has 3 regiments (Brigades) of Alpini. Total 18 battalions & in addition he has 15 other battalions – territorial's etc. 70,000 men & 12,000 animals all told including horses, mules, donkeys & dogs. We had a splendid day. We left here about 6am motored to Val deli Avis about 15 kilometres up the OGLIO from here (Edolo). We went up by teleferic's to PASSO di BRIZIO on the ADAMELLO Plateau. Here we got into sleighs, one in each & each pulled by 3 dogs. Here also we saw the arrival of the first mules to walk up the whole way. There were some donkeys there before but they had come up by teleferic, can' you see them!

The dogs took us about 4 kilometres to LOBBA ALTA I did not care much for the sleigh, they are slow & I got very cold. Luckily the General brought a closh for me. All the country up here is the most perfect skiing ground. You (or at any rate) I never saw lovely stretches of virgin snow, with not a rock, slopes of every degree. The Alpini gave us an exhibition of skiing.

We had a great lunch & at the end we had champagne (over 9,000 ft up). Demi-sec – I wondered what it can be like when it ceases to be sec I was terrified when the General got up & made a very touching speech, 'Here where the snow is the symbol of purity of one's aims I drink to the health of your King & success of your aims etc'. It was my turn then & I just managed it – but not more. After lunch the General went off to see about some gun positions & I went off to LOBBIA MUZZO & LOBBIA BASSA. Part of the way being on the west line (with our feet in it) only 2 kilometres from the Austrians.

Today & 2 days ago I have seen the ground over which they attacked CIMA ZIGOLEN, CIMA PRESENTA 7 MONTICELLO. It was wonderful performance all up in the snow. They marched in the snow by night & lay out in it & attacked at dawn.

Two days ago I went to PIA DI LAGO SCURA north of where I was today & walked along the back of the mountains to PIA DI CASTELLACCIO. Then down the slopes to Lighi PRESENA & through the PASSO Del MONTICELLO northwards to the PASSO del TONALE. The Tonale is very strong now the Austrians attacked on the 13th June but got badly knocked.

21.7.18

On the 4 July I went off to visit the 1st & 2nd Italian Armies I visited the great valleys.

> Lacarina (Adige)
> Guidicara (Chiese)
> Camonica (Aglies)
> Va Tellina (Adda)

It was intensely interesting I stayed two nights at Sermione (British Club) on Lake Garda from which I did each side of Lajoina. The scenery is superb, the colour of the Lake is wonderful when viewed from the top of Alt Esimo. Captain Talucchi (29th Carpo) came with us & proved an excellent guide. The Cechoslovak Division is on the slopes of Mount Baldo holding the front. They look to be a fine body of men. On the 7th Army front we stayed the night at Breschia after having been up the Guidicaria. We had lunch & diner with General Sagromozo 14th Corps that day & he had us up Mount Pallone we got a fair view though the weather was none too good, we motored up the top almost. Then we spent 3 nights with General Piccone commanding the Italian 5th Division at Edola in Val Camonica. A fine soldier I am sure & a perfect host, he made excellent plans for our visit. The first afternoon he took me to Ponte de Castellaccio & Ponte de Lago Scursor. All were 9,000 ft up in the snow I saw the success of some good Italian coup de main & was very much impressed with the skill & endurance necessary to carry them out. We slithered down in the snow having gone up in a telefenic I went off to the Vallellina where I met General Rosacher who commands 75th Division he is not the active & energetic man like General Piccone is but he was very kind. He took me to the Stelvio Pass & along the Val Garia & so down again to the Valo Caininicia. We saw the five peaks of Mount Cinfinale, there I also met Scothi who knows Henry. The last day was the most interesting in many ways, we went in a telefenic to the Adamello plateau up the Anio Valley.

The next trip was 2 days to the Piave between the old & the new it was fearfully hot there though the second trip was done in the motor & was pleas-anter. Both days we walked in great heat for 2 hours or more. Captain Green came with me the second time I was accompanied by Lt. Revel of the 3rd Army. Almost all of the country is flooded now with just the roads left high above the water. Yesterday I visited General Monesi commanding the 12th Italian Division on our immediate left.[101]

21.7.18

My own darling

I left England on 1st June, 7 weeks ago yesterday, that is quite a long time ago. I think the Bosche must be sick at his failure I hope we keep calm & don't make a too much of it, we have a lot to do before we can begin to crow. Anyway it is very good. I got up yesterday early & had breakfast at 6.30 & went off with General Monesi, a divisional commander. He walked me about his mountains till 11am. There were the usual caves for guns &men & paths cut out of the sides of rock. All very interesting & we got good views too. He is a regular buffoon & never ceases talking & he mimics everything motor cycles, shells, aeroplanes. He cannot talk unless he explains everything. He took me back to lunch of course he has a nice snug little HQ tucked away in a corner of a mountain. He would not make a road up to it because he wanted to keep the Italian guns away. We were a big party at lunch including his staff, his artillery commander an old man with a cheeky boyish face & one of his brigade commanders with whom I have to dine with tonight. There is an English speaking officer there, his name is Raspauli or something like it, his mother was American & he was at Eton. He looks quite English & like a good type of Etonian. We had a good lunch and ended it with champagne, not so sweet. After drinking the health of England to which I replied with the Italian Army!!

After lunch I went off to see Holmes, he commands Anthony's battalion & is a temporary commander of a brigade.[102] We had a long chat he told me Garnett has a brigade!! Fancy him & not Norman. Holmes discussed Anthony, apparently he is quite useless.[103] Very brave but no use as an officer, he knows nothing at all about war if it was not for his pluck the men would do nothing for him. At the same time he has been very uppish, saying he is a Captain.

Then I went to see Pelly commanding another brigade where I had tea & got back at 7pm.[104] Stanley (Lord Derby's son) & Ward (Sir E. Ward's son) came to dinner, they are both at GHQ. We heard last night that General Piccorne has had a success in the mountains where I was so I have sent a wire to congratulate him. Yesterday I was in a pass with a sheer drop of several hundred feet at the side and no rail! I should hardly think the Italians are strong enough to put up an offensive now. The Austrians have more divisions.

I am so glad Minshull Ford has a division I will write to him I only wrote a few days ago to thank him for his letter.[105] I expect the difficulty about me will be the usual one I have been away from France for 9 months now, therefore thought to be quite ignorant & unfitted for a division! I don't worry but I agree there will be little for me to do in the winter here & I am sure Tim will pull me out soon.

25.7.18

My own darling

I took Colonel Brion out this morning, he is always appreciative and grateful we had a bad day as there were clouds about but I managed to show him something.[106] We got back at 3pm, as he has to leave GHQ at 4pm. He has a hot trip in front of him as he has to go to Rome & Tarranto. I went up to GHQ & had a chat with PT I also saw Alexander,[107] he rather annoyed me! Tomorrow I must be up early as I start at 6.45am for Verona to attend a French lecture I understand they will feed us after I don't like the look of this state I see the Coventry men are out. Very bad I hope the government will be strong I see Cassel has resigned the Judge Advocate Generalship.[108]

I don't suppose that Henry thinks the Germans will put in a big attack on us I think they are about done for this year as regards anything big.

26th July 18. We had a great show today I had to be at Verona for this lecture. It was very good. The lecturer discussed the recent French failures & successes & compared them and then conclusions, which I think sound. Towards the end I found him hard to follow I think he took less trouble about being distinct. I saw several friends including General Piacentino. He says they all talk about my visit & that I must go back. He says that his attack was a great success. He says it from his command post in the snow. He says he will probably come & stay with me, which will be grand, but it will be an undertaking &

I will have to make a programme for him to get some of the divisions to give him lunch etc.

Then I saw 1st Army commander, he hadn't got elastic side boots on today! And the commander of the 29th Corps and the Besangleri I dined with the other night. After the lecture we drove round the town in torrents of rain. It is a wonderful old place & so picturesque with the river going through it I think I told you once it is as broad as the Thames. It is nothing like it! At 12 we lunched with the French general who runs the French schools. About a 100 sat down nearly all Italians. Of course I was terrified that there would be speeches & was making one up but I was thankful to say there were not any. I made several new friends at lunch, Bridge came in my car. He had gone with Dick in the French liaison officer's car. The Frenchmen left Dick to go home with someone else & remained in Verona to get his photo taken. Carling is sleeping here tomorrow night en route to England, he is going on leave.

27th. I'm at the British mission, Delme Radcliffe is away & I am sitting at his table & this will go by Bridges tonight. My car is being overhauled so I liked to get another but they are very scarce so I went with Dick to GHQ & then came on here with him. He is moving around his schools & will put me up. I have been raking my brains I have met a Major Wakefield who is here. His face & name were familiar & now I am sure he was adjutant of one my battalions in 46th Division I think he can't have spotted me either as he has never mentioned 46th Division to me.

28.7.18

My own darling

Carling arrived all right & went off to Vincenza yesterday & came back for dinner. He is a calm old thing, Dick says the war has improved him & he seems to enjoy himself here. He came up to my room after & helped me with some work I was doing. He & I went up to the tower as the atmosphere is so clear today & we get a lovely view. I have discovered that I can see Mount Grappa & Mount Pasintio from this house. Its Sunday, Mordant has just be in, he is in great form as he is off on leave I wish they would give him a Division I am sure he would do very well, he is very sound and a great fighter.

I am having dinner with your friend Major Barne tonight.[109] Tomorrow I go to Verona for this lecture I have had no exercise lately so will try & take Dick out this afternoon, as he wants to go & see some hills near Vicenza. Good news today of the Bosch retiring, the morale effect will be good I expect Henry will be delighted.

I think Winston has rather bungled the state business with a little care & tact he could have arranged it without causing trouble, but of course there is always the other side, no doubt he feared that explanations might have been taken as a sign of weakness.[110] Cavan comes back on Tuesday, and I suppose Delme Radcliffe will come too!

Dick had had a good stay & the only one he can remember so he tells everyone. An Australian & American were discussing their experiences, 'Last

Xmas' said the Australian 'I spent in Bethlehem', the American replied, 'I guess those Sheppard's did watch their flocks that night'.

3.8.18

The storms are terrific I have seen I have had another day with General Monesi (the correct spelling) I met him at 7am & we walked round the trenches & galleries which overlook the junction of the valley of the Val de Assi & Val de Asties. We got to his HQ about 12.30 & I had lunch with him.

Two days I went over to Verona where the French have an officer's course in progress. A Lt.Colonel Fawry lectured on recent fighting in France he was very good. He showed the failure of the French 6th Army when attacked on the Chemin des Dames in May & the success of 4th Army General Gouraud when attacked in Champagne in July 15th 1918. He then tried to explain to us the failure in one case & the success in the other. We had lunch both days with General Grange who runs the school. There were about 100 officers present at lunch I should say. The second day Major Mitchell was with me & we walked round Verona, which is an interesting town. A few days after I lunched with Delme Radcliffe & met my cousin Eugenio Niccoline, he is a nice old man & I am going to stay with him at Prato (Tozcana). Another day I went to visit General Correlli commanding 2nd Beissinge Brigade, his HQ is at Aisiero. He is a very nice man but was suffering from an old wound & so was not energetic. We went part of the way to the Italian positions under Ciunoni in a telefenic & then next on mules. General Correlli nearly got killed by a stone, which came down the hill & just touched the mule on the leg.

9.9.18

We have lived since the Austrian Offensive more or less in a state of suspense or perhaps to be more accurate since the allied success in France we prepared for an offensive on the Anapo plateaux but General Diaz would not fix the date & time dragged on. He wanted tanks & gas shells from the French & they did not seem anxious to grant.

General Cavan was worried by our inaction affirming that we should either attack or send troops to help France. Accordingly he sent me home on the 11th April to see Henry Wilson before the Versailles conference, which appeared likely to take, place & I was back on the 20th on which date Cavan wanted to go on leave. Before I started the offensive was decided on & we were put on a week's notice. When I got to England I found there was to be no conference chiefly I believed because Clemenceau & Lloyd George had had a row at the last one? Henry went off to Ireland for a few days & I got a few days leave I saw little of Henry and came back again leaving London on the 24th August I stayed one day at Versailles with Tit Willow.

I got back on the 28th but in the meantime a meeting was arranged between Diaz & Foch. Cavan being anxious that there should be no delay on account of the shortening days sent me off to see Henry before the meeting. However, Henry turned out not to be coming over to see Diaz so that fell through. I saw

Diaz but failed to get anything out of him & came back leaving Paris on the
2nd September. I was disappointed by the results of my mission but it could
not be helped. When I got back to Italy I found that Diaz was not coming
back till Sunday (eventually he came back on Saturday instead) & that he had
sent no orders. Finally when he came back everything was off & the C in C
decided to go on leave on 11th September. Personally I am glad there is to be
no offensive there has been too much talk of it & it is a very big undertaking
also the season is too far advanced to get any real value out of its success.

27.9.18

On 13th September I started off on a trip, which in a way turned out, to be
quiet eventful I went to Tarranto first on duty to stay with General Clove,
commanding the base there. I stayed one night & went on the next day &
stopped the night of the 17th at Baglione Hotel, Florence. Next morning
I went on Prato arriving at 9.30, there Eugenio Nicollin[111] met me & also
Berta his daughter with whom I struck up a great friendship whilst I stayed
with them at San Matino. Partly because she talked English but partly because
she liked walking, we were a great deal together.

2.10.18

My own darling

I went round some of the Brigade HQ's & ended up with General Charing
having lunch with me. The Brigade major there, Bedwell I am told is a
brother-in-law of Tim Harrington. I got back here at 3 to be met by great
excitement. First of all Gathorne-Hardy could not go to Genoeve with
me then General Badoglio wanted to see me 'urgentissimo' at Commando
Supreme so off I went. I can't why he sent for me, but I presume it was because
Delme is away I had after that to see Gathorne, so I got to dinner with him
soon after 8, & we agreed to do our trip by starting early this morning. I got
up at 6 & Gathorne called for me & off we went to meet Major Hailey & an
Italian Officer beyond Verona. The Italian did not turn up. Hailey told me
that Piccone was so anxious to see me last night that on the way in Piccone's
car they ran off the road into Lake Garda & were lucky they were not both
drowned. Piccone went back to his HQ dressed as a British Staff Captain!!

We had a pretty good day in the Val Lagarmia & got a good view. It is a
lively valley I must take you there someday but I am afraid it won't be in
a Rolls Royce! Dick comes back on the 4th I hear. My French is so much
better now & I hope if I stick to it, it may improve.

3.10.18

My own darling

We have a dinner tonight Major General Kay & General Byron and a Major
Findley from the British Mission.[112] Last night a man from the Italian Mission
came over for dinner about this business Badoglio saw me about. Tomorrow
night a Major Whittaker (RAF) is coming to dinner & he is bringing an

Italian artist to draw my picture! He did such a good job of Col Joubert. If it is a success they can photocopy it for me & let me have copies. I am off this morning to look at some bridging material with one of my sappers & then go to GHQ. Send my letters off by KM & after that wait till C in C returns on the 10th before knowing when I am to return home.

I forget if I told you the Italian mission can get Lorenzo here in 4 days I very much doubt it but it doesn't very much matter if they don't. However I think it will be useful to me. I have wasted all day over this blessed thing of Badoglio's I am so sorry that the one time they wanted my help I have failed them. It was not altogether my fault, but the result is just the same whether it is or not.

I had lunch with the Italian mission today the Colonel can't speak English, which seems strange, but there are two nice fellows who speak English well. They are a very large party. They live in a nice old villa with the usual terraces. It was so nice today in the sunny terraces. The only time I have really felt warm today. Major General Radcliffe has been ordered to France. He wrote to me to get something done for him but I had not done anything when I got his letter.

Dinner quite a success, two cheery gunners & and a Major Findley from the British mission. The gunners by the way were both brigadiers. Now I have to arrange to go off with Colonel Bridge to the Piave.

4.10.18

My own darling

6.45pm Just in I motored over 270 kilometer's going right down to the mouth of the Piave, we met some nice people & had lunch with the brigadier. The poor man has been suffering from fever for months & can't get rid of it. My French was not good today! Perhaps Bridge puts me off, he is a great linguist. He never knew Italian before he came here and now speaks quite well.

Tomorrow I go out with Bridge again, not so early this time I leave at 7am and hope to get back for lunch. Boots have turned up too! News seems scarcer now. What a lot of prisoners the British Army have taken in the last 2 months, it makes me very proud of them I have just seen 4th Army has taken another 3,000 Germans.

5.10.18

My own darling

I am dining with the 23rd Division I wish I wasn't as I am so sleepy! Dick is back and looks well he seems to have spent his leave in the garden cutting down trees & digging potatoes. I was up at 6am & started off at 7am I picked up Captain Henderson & went to an Italian Division. We had a great deal of delay there where we picked up a guide, who turned out not to know his way! We went along the Brenta Valley. It is a fine valley with high steep rocky sides, mountains on each side. There is a large amount of villages in the valley & the Brenta is a fine river too. We got to the OP we wanted too & then came down after seeing what we wanted. I met an interesting man yesterday, his father (Italian) was Josse Pasha, a great explorer who was with Gordon. The men has written his father's memoirs and published them in English under the title 'Seven Years in the Egyptian Sudan', it might be interesting.

I am so glad to see we have taken Aubers Ridge, a very important place. I sat under it all the first winter with the 38th Division. Not quite so cold today but chilly I have given up khaki drill altogether now.

I am very proud of the fact that I have been through 4 years of war & have not got a single foreign decoration I am so sorry to see that Colonel Bridge has been killed. He was Brigade Major RA in 46th Division a really first class man. Apparently Philip Game is to replace Kerr Dick is fuming at his being kicked out. At the age of 55 he isleaving the Navy & is to become a 2Lt in the Guards MG Corps – madness I call it.

6.10.18

My own darling

I have to go to see the C in C. It is one bore of this place that it takes 40 minutes to get to GHQ. However, the advantages outweigh the disadvantages. A great dinner last night with the 23rd Division. There was a band and after dinner they had a private programme with the cinema which was good. They have a very good Italian cook too. Old PT & Cecil Howard came to tea yesterday. PT being the divisional commander flying his flag on the motor. PT is an imposing figure with his large moustache & he has a great row of medals I think he has four foreign decorations, he is a fine man. His Division carried out a great raid the other night capturing 150 prisoners with very little loss. In 11 weeks that Division has captured 600 prisoners which is good. I haven't seen the C in C yet.

8.10.18

War Office did not approve of my going home, they suggested I should wait till Cavan comes out again on the 10th. This has one advantage from my point of view it made it necessary for me to settle down to work again. Consequently I became once more energetic I visited the Val Sugana again, this time with Gathorne Hardy & Hailey & Major Lowe & I went to the Biente Valley with Captain Henderson.

Events began to move apparently Foch pushed the Italians a bit. That & Bulgaria going out of the war decided the Italians to start an offensive. Cavan was wired to come back & arrived on the 6th October & so I had to start on the 7th with letters. Cavan is to have an Army of 1 British & 1 Italian Corps. There really appear to be no signs that the Germans are beaten. The glorious record of the British army in the last two months in France & Palestine makes one really proud of our country. The Germans have lost 250,000 prisoners & over 2,600 guns in France in those months. A few days ago there was news that they had asked for an armistice to discuss terms of the peace recently enumerated by President Wilson. There is however small chance of the allies allowing an armistice.

13.10.18

My own darling

I suppose I might as well wait PT is ringing Corps up again. The Corps said before dinner that they had not received the thing from the Army. It is all so hopeless isn't it.

Such a wet day, we had a conference at 9.30am a revival of what I used to do long ago we are to have them 3 times a week. Then I went up the line with sandwiches & an apple. It came on to rain at about 1.30pm & it rained off & on for the rest of the day. Have just heard that all the Corps are in bed but the clerks say my leave has not reached them so I asked if I could have 10 days leave.

14.10.18

My own darling

The General has said I am not to leave until the papers come through & that they haven't left Corps yet. It is maddening & couldn't be worse if there was a regular conspiracy against me.

Later.

At last I have got word & I am to go off tomorrow so that is it.

15.10.18

My own darling

We had tea in Turin & are now together in the sleeper I have had a wire to say I must go to Vicenza instead of Padova so I suppose I will have to go to the old house which is drafty I hope the letters will go better now I posted today and one yesterday by bag from Versailles. The KM leaves HQ Tuesday, Thursday & Saturday & arrives London Friday, Sunday & Tuesday I can't make out why you did not get the letters I take such care as you can imagine to catch the KM. I shall get busy about it when I get back. Riggiones 4 days was a myth.

We are on our way to Modena. We were about an hour late. The scenery is lovely the colours in the valley are very fine. At Versailles they were simply gorgeous bright reds and yellows, the chestnuts were golden, whole avenues of them. Hereward and I went for a walk after tea & he took me into the gardens of the Trianon Palace. It is a sweet little square block a house & on the grounds there is a sort of model farm (or rather it was) where Hereward says Marie Antoinette used to go & play at being a dairy maid. There is one big-gish building & a lot of tiny picturesque cottages. The grounds are so nice & full of nice trees. He thinks Henry right to close Versailles.

16.10.18

Raining like the deuce country flooded & we are moving today I am afraid I shall have to leave Dick which I hate, the grounds are nice and we have hills close by to walk up but I feel I shall have to move to GHQ as soon as they get a place for me at present they are in too chaotic a state to take me. No electric light here which is a bother. I find there is a great deal of exception taken to the wording of the first few lines of LG's last message to Haig 'I have just heard from Marshall Foch etc' I am sorry for this as I am sure that Henry helped to write it. It is hard to avoid displeasing people.

17.10.18

General Headquarters

British Forces, Italy

Cavan has just told me he has written to Henry to say he does not want me anymore. First because he thinks I am wasted here, second because he says I am reticent & do not tell him Henry's view & he has to dig information out of me! As I told him he hardly gave me a chance as we went to lunch almost at once & I told him I did not do it consciously. Thinking it over I think, That he expects too much in the way of policy from Henry.

That I am bad at picking up 'chat' & that cannot be mended. Some fellows go & come back with all sorts of gossip which may be routine and quite valueless but creates a good impression others like myself do not pick up much.

Henry has told me so many secrets in recent years that I have got into the habit of not telling what he tells me consequently I am not sure what I can tell Cavan I am thinking all the time how much I ought to tell.

Cavan of course been very nice about it I then asked Henry to let me know what is to happen as I presume he will keep me here now & the uncertainty is bad for work.

17.10.18

My own darling

I have been thinking again about Cavan & me. He hates to have failed of course but I felt all along I was not a success I don't think I have ever been in sympathy with Cavan like I used to be with Rawly, TC & Bingo. I always found it difficult to express myself to him. He always seems to make me feel I was not telling him what he wanted to know. You remember from the first he said he did not feel the need for an liaison officer & then he did not take me into his mess, thank goodness. Then I think he expects Henry to tell him things he has not even thought of himself. How can he expect Henry at this moment to be seriously considering the future use of British Divisions in Italy! Yet he seemed to think I ought to have been able to tell him this. I am amused because they got rid of poor Williams because he never told them anything, but in his case based it on his not being in sufficient touch with Henry. They can't say that of me so they think I know a lot or won't tell! Cavan was very nice about it he said he had written to Henry to say he thought my talents were wasted here & also I am not suitable for the job as I am reticent. He says it is a very good thing to be but not for a liaison officer! He says Henry always writes 2 lines & ends up saying 'Mary will give you all the gossip' & that then I tell him nothing & that he has to drag it out of me I can only say that there are some men who make one open out & that Cavan is not one of them I have of always tried to tell him all I know but it doesn't come out as it should. Well there it is I have failed & there is nothing to be said Dick is much more upset than I am! I don't care a bit, except for the uncertainty & I told Cavan I thought I was a waste of money. He says with 3 KM a week he does not require me & that if he wants to send an officer to Henry personally he could send one of his staff.

Don't worry for me Baby I'm not worrying in the least I knew I could not go on here indefinitely. What Tim will put me into I don't know but I have asked him to put me in as a Brigadier or in any rank he likes. I have told Henry all the above but if you see him tell him I lunched with Cavan again today. Then I went to see the Italian Corps HQ & finally had tea with the 7th Shoubridge was out.

You might impress on Tim if you can that a definite decision is what I want. Henry may decide that he wants me here apart from what Cavan wants, in any case I ought to be told quickly as one cannot work without an object.

18.10.18

My own darling

Well I am laid up with flu![113] Cold has never quite gone & had turned to a sore throat. Last night I could not sleep easily in the night because my feet were so cold & in the latter part of the night I was so hot I couldn't sleep either! No one had a thermometer so I got up and motored to a Doctor, a man called Captain Bainbridge. He found my temperature was 100 so off I went to bed. He has given me a powder (which hasn't worked yet) aspirin & sweating mixture. I have been sleeping & sweating I have had no lunch only milk soda & now have had a little tea. Don't worry about me darling I am not at all bad. The Doctor comes again tomorrow morning to see me. Great news today Lille gone & Belgium cavalry nearing Bruges I wonder where the Bosch is off to?

19.10.18

My own darling

Much the same today Doctor has just been & found the temperature the same. He is delighted I came to him at once & say I won't be long bad. My throat is ever so much better I may eat what I feel inclined for I had been rather starving but he says that it is not necessary. Cavan has sprained his ankle jumping a ditch I wonder what Henry will think about Cavan letter about me & how soon he will move me.

Eggs are almost impossible & Heywood tells me they cannot give him all the milk he wants as they want it for a dog! I have slept a good deal today & had a good sweat after lunch. The difficulty is there is no way to dry the wet things. Also there are no pillows in the house at all. However I jog along alright & am not too bad. Poor Henry will be worried about me.

20.10.18

My own darling

The doctor has been I thought I was better but he says not & that I must go to hospital I think he is quite right as I probably require nursing & I am tired of nursing myself! Now what worries me is my letters & also I shall have to send them by post which will take longer. I have to go back to near Thiene. Darling I am afraid you will be worried but I don't think there is any need because my temperature has never been high.

21.10.18

My own darling

Here I am packed up and no ambulance yet I am going to 24 CCS a very nice hospital. I have been there once or twice to see people I am beginning to feel a little tired & my appetite not quite so good but hospital diet will help I expect. What a business and all for a wretched microbe!

22.10.18

My own darling

My temp was over 102 last night I had such a nice night, sister such a nice kind face & soft voice, middle aged. Really I didn't find my first night in hospital particularly restful. The stove went out 3 times & it seemed to me the sister was always rushing at me with medicine, she says she only did it three times & the amount of hot drinks I had in the night was tremendous, milk, lemonade, chicken broth, and so on. The Doctor examined my lungs very carefully & says that they are quiet all right I have got rather a head this morning & this eternal sweating is tiresome I had 3 changes of pyjamas last night I really think I ought to give a donation to the British Red Cross. I don't have meals yet, only lots of drinks thrown at me when anyone thinks I ought to have one.

I feel good for nothing today I don't know if I ought to have given in but I felt I wanted to sleep. The doctor said I had best do as I was inclined. They are very full here so I don't see much of the hospital staff & Heywood comes in very useful. We had great work over the washing this morning I've still got a head which is wearisome after 5 days & everything tastes so vile I feel sometimes as if I am going to be sick

23.10.18

Yesterday my temperature was 104 & today it is down to 102 which is a great joy. They gave me a pill which rather disturbed me last night I think the bedpan is the most disgusting unsanitary business imaginable I should hope they could invent something better. I feel a bit better today but very slack still & heady but not quite such a lot of noises in my head. Heywood has just washed & shaved me. I wonder if I will get any letters or papers today I have had nothing since moving here.

I am feeling so much better just now I think I am perfect in the head. Food taste better & the head is better & migraine seems to have gone away. Perhaps

Dick will be coming this afternoon I keep wandering what my fate is to be & whether they would give me a Brigade in France. I shall write some letters this afternoon Heywood does the floor with beeswax. I am looking forward to the time when I can have a nice cool long drink. Everything I get here is hot & not so much as a bit of toast for solid. I am dozy & keep dropping off to sleep. It is a lovely bright day I went out for an hour this morning.

24.10.18

My own darling

I'm sick of medicine I have just has a most horrible concoction that appears to leave your mouth full of white & is extraordinary salty. Stopping in bed does not appear to improve my writing. I spent a very hot uncomfortable night & I was very surprised to find this morning that my temperature had dropped from 104 to 99.4. However that may be I felt good for nothing & let Heywood shave & wash me. Just as I was brushing my hair I said to Heywood I was going to be sick he offered a little tray about the size of a saucer. Luckily I spotted the basin & got him to take the sponge out just in time I was fearfully sick regular torrents. The doctor didn't like it I think he said it very often happens with flu I hope it doesn't happen again to me.

1.11.18

After two days at home I came out again arriving by train at Corps. We moved that day to Battagna, south west of Padua. On the 1st I went down with flu & after 2–3 days in bed & getting no better I went to the casualty clearing station near Thiene. My temperature ran up to 104 for 2 days & then went down with a bang & I got rapidly better.

The Italian offensive in the Piave in which the British took part whilst I was hospital went well. Today we are told that the Turkish has signed an Armistice giving us control of the Dardanelle's. Also officially the Austrian plenipotentiaries are at Command Supremo now. In the meantime we have had innumerable notes passing between USA & Germany I am told today the allies have decided in their terms of the armistice which practically amount to the laying down of arms I wonder if Germany will accept Austria going out should help her to a decision. Anyway with Turkey & Bulgaria both out times are exciting.

On the 17th Cavan had told me he had written to Henry Wilson to say that I was wasted here & also that I am too reticent to be a liaison officer.
I think he is a little hard on me in that respect as I have seldom had time to tell him. However HW does not appear to be going to remove me so I wrote to Cavan to put the case clearly to him stating that I had no chance to do otherwise.

9.11.18

I came out of hospital on the 2nd & went straight to GHQ to Lord Cavan's mess. This proved a good plan & and of course I ought to have been there all along. Anyway Lord Cavan was quite friendly. On the 3rd Lorenzo &

I went over the Piave by pontoon bridge & went through Vayallo – Sacile
to Polyenigo where we met General Basso commanding the Italian XVIII
Corps under Cavan's command.

From there we went to XIV British Corps HQ at Pordenone & came back
we crossed the Livenza by pontoon bridge & trestle which had a chink in it
& my motor would not go round it had backed & manoeuvred a great deal.

At Priale we crossed the Piave (It is close to Nervesa) on that day the
armistice was signed & hostilities ceased on November 3rd at 3pm. The total
captures at that time amounted to 450,000 prisoners & 7,000 guns.

It is wonderful to think that if it had been for the two British divisions
who forced the Piave (7th & 23rd) the Austrian disaster could not have taken
place. The Italians on our left failed to cross & had to cross behind the British
& swing to their left of the Piave. They fought well enough & the whole
front loosened. The British 48th Division was left on the Asiago plateau &
subsequently attacked & took 30,000 prisoners & 700 guns only losing 200
casualties.

On the 4th Lorenzo & I went to Padova & left about 7pm I for England &
he for Florence I lunched at the British Embassy on my way through Paris.
Lord Derby, Lady Pembroke, Lady Victoria Primisore, Major General Sir
Philip Nash, General sir Charles Ellis, Captain Bullock, Colonel Sheffington
Smith, General Sackville West & a sailor & Sir Charles Montague. They were
extraordinarily friendly. When I got home I found the delegates were coming
to see Foch.

On the 9th we heard that the delegate who was coming back was stopped
by the Bosche machine gun fire & eventually had to be sent by aeroplane. The
part played by the British Army in the fighting in France as in other countries
is truly wonderful. Since August 8th we have captured 200,000 prisioner's as
many as France & America put together & we continue to be successful.

8.10.18 [Out of order and repeated from October]
War Office did not approve of my going home, they suggested I should have a
wait till Cavan comes out on the 10th. This has one advantage from my point
of view. It made it necessary for me to settle down to work again consequently
I became at once more energetic I visited Loyumma again this time with
Guthrie, Hardy & Hailey I went to the lower Piave with Colonel Bridges &
major Lowe & I went to the Biente valley with Captain Henderson.

Events began to move apparently Foch pushed the Italians a bit. That and
Bulgaria going out of the War decided the Italians to start an offensive. Cavan
was aired for to come back & arrived the 6th October & so I had to start
home on the 7th with letters. Cavan is to have an Army of one British & one
Italian Corps. There really appear to be signs that the Germans may be beaten.
The glorious record of the British army in the last two months in France &
Palestine makes one feel very proud of our country.

The Germans have lost 250,000 prisoners & over 2,600 guns in France in
these months. A few days ago there was news that they asked for an armistice

to discuss the terms of the peace enumerated by President Wilson. There is however small chance of the allies allowing an armistice.

1 November 1918
[Sadly there appear to be missing entries after this date]

NOTES

1 Major General Alister Grant Dallas CB, CMG (1866–1931). 16th Lancers. Brigadier General IV Corps. GOC 53rd Div. at Gallipoli, Egypt and Palestine. Retired 1922.
2 General Sir Julian Hedworth George Byng (1862–1935). GOC Third Army. *See* Jeffrey Williams, *Byng of Vimy* (London, 1983).
3 General Sir Hubert de la Poer Gough (1870–1963). He was replaced on 27 March 1918 by Sir Henry Rawlinson. An official enquiry that had been promised was never held. *See* Farrer-Hockley, *Goughie* (London, 1975). See also Ian F.W. Beckett & S. Corvi (eds), *Haig's Generals* (Pen & Sword, 2006), for a good all-round view of commanders.
4 Brigadier General W.J. Webb-Bowen, GOC 8th Inf Bde. He had been wounded 2 April 1918.
5 Major General C.J. Deverell, GOC 3rd Div. since August 1916.
6 Brigadier General Bertie Drew Fisher (1878–1972). 17th Lancers. Later Lieutenant General Southern Command 1939–40.
7 Lieutenant Colonel George Kendall Priaulx DSO, KRRC. Killed in action, 24 March 1918.
8 Lady Joan Mulholland remarried in 1922 the same Frederick Rudolph, 10th Earl of Cavan; Victor Gilbert Lariston Garnet Murray Kynnynmond Elliott, 5th Earl of Minto; Mabell Countess of Airlie, her husband was killed at Diamond Hill 1900.
9 Major Douglas Stewart Davidson DSO, MC, Royal Scots Fusiliers.
10 Hon. Sir Derek Keppell, Master of the King's Household 1912–1936 (1863–1944); Mrs Alice Keppell, mistress to King George VII, was his sister-in-law.
11 Major Clive Wigram, Equerry to King George V.
12 Major General Charles 'TW' Sackville-West was a major ally of Henry Wilson and had replaced Rawlinson at Versailles.
13 Lieutenant Colonel Sis Albert 'Bertie' Gerald Stern KBE, CMG. He was one of the principal people involved with the development of the tank from its foremost days.
14 Bentinck Major Lord Charles Cavendish DSO, Queen's Royal Lancers.
15 IWM: Wilson Papers HHW 73/1/12; Lieutenant General Earl of Cavan took command of GHQ Italy at noon 10 March 1918 from General H.C.O. Plumer.
16 IWM: Wilson Papers HHW 2/32A/2.
17 General Armando Diaz (1861–1928). He took over command of Italian CGS from General Cardorna.
18 IWM: Wilson Papers HHW 2/32A/2.
19 Brigadier General Charles Delme-Radcliffe CVO, CB, CMG (1864–1937). Chief of Italian Mission since 1915. He had been military attaché to Rome 1906–11.
20 Lieutenant Colonel Arthur Frederick Carlisle Williams DSO. Liaison Officer from War Office to Italy, 11 March to 19 April 1918.
21 IWM: Wilson Papers HHW 25/4/18.
22 Brigadier General Hon. J.F. Gathorne-Hardy (1874–1949). GS at GHQ Italy. In 1927 he was promoted Lieutenant General Northern Command.
23 Lieutenant Colonel T.R.C. Howard, GS 47th Div.

24 IWM:Wilson Papers HHW 2/32A/3.

25 IWM:Wilson Papers HHW 2/32A/4.

26 'Wullyites'is a reference to General Sir William Robertson who had been replaced on
    18 February 1918 by General Sir Henry Wilson.

27 Major General Hugh Montague Trenchard (1873–1956). GOC RFC in France, left to
    become Chief of the Air Staff in London 18 January 1918. He returned to France to take
    command of the Independent Air Force.

28 Major General Thomas Herbert Shoubridge, GOC 7th Div. This division moved to Italy in
    November 1917.

29 IWM:Wilson Papers HHW 2/32A/7.

30 IWM:Wilson Papers HHW 2/32A/8.

31 Brigadier General Walter William Pitt-Taylor DSO, RB, BGGS XIV Corps (1878–1950).

32 IWM:Wilson Papers HHW 2/32A/9.

33 *See* Rupert Godfrey (ed.) *Letters from a Prince* (LittleBrown, Great Britain, 1998); these are
    a collection of letters from Edward Prince of Wales (later King Edward VIII) to Mrs Freda
    Dudley-Ward between March 1918 and January 1921. The opening chapters concern his
    time in Italy in 1918.

34 General Luca Montuori, GOC Italian Second Army.

35 IWM:Wilson Papers HHW 2/32A/10.

36 King Victor Emanuel II of Italy.

37 Lieutenant Colonel Charles Hamilton Mitchell (1872–1941). GSO 1 (Intelligence).
    Canadian Officer GSO 3, 1st Canadian Div. 1915. GSO 2 (Intelligence) Canadian
    Expeditionary Force. BGGS Intelligence British GHQ Italy 1918. After the war he returned
    to Toronto University and became Dean of Engineering.

38 Lieutenant C.J. Goldsmit, GSO 3 British Mission with Italian GHQ November 1917–18.

39 Brigadier General T.S. Lambert, GOC 69th Bde.

40 Lieutenant Colonel H.R. Sandilands, GSO 1 23rd Div.

41 Major General Sir J.M. Babington, GOC 23rd Div.

42 Brigadier General H. Gordon, GOC 70th Bde.

43 55th Div. was part of V Corps, First Italian Army under Lieutenant General Count
    Pecori-Giraldi (Trentino).

44 Lieutenant General Giardino, GOC Fourth Italian Army.

45 Brigadier General Gerald Carew Sladen, GOC 143rd Bde, 48th (1st South Midland) Div.

46 *Degoutant:* 'disgusting'.

47 Major General Sir Frederick Barton Maurice (1871–1951). DMO between December 1915
    and April 1918. Maurice wrote a letter to the London newspapers accusing Lloyd George's
    government of deceiving both Parliament and the country about the strength of the British
    Army on the Western front in 1918. This caused a great scandal and the ensuing debate left
    Lloyd George in a far stronger position than before. Maurice was at once retired from the
    army and refused a court martial or inquiry. *See* Nancy Maurice (ed.) *The Maurice Case*
    (London, 1972).

48 Lieutenant Colonel O.C. Mordaunt, AD Signals, British Forces Italy.

49 IWM:Wilson Papers HHW 2/32A/12.

50 Lieutenant Colonel William Basil Charles Bridge married Arianna Maria Charleton 1906.

51 Lieutenant Colonel Philip B. Joubert de la Ferte (1887–1965). 14th Wing RAF. Later Air
    Chief Marshal.

52 IWM:Wilson Papers HHW 2/32A/13.

53 General Alfrieri, Italian Minister of War.

54 General Montuori, Italian II Corps.

55 General Montuori, Italian II Corps.

56 Newton Diehl Baker (1871–1937). He was the US Secretary of State for War 1916–1921
    under President Woodrow Wilson.

57 IWM: Wilson Papers HHW 2/32A/16.

58 Brigadier General T.S. Lambert, 69th Bde, 23rd Div.

59 Colonel Charles A. Court Repington, *The Times* correspondent. He had served in the Rifle Brigade at the same time as Henry Wilson. They fell out regarding a divorce case that cited a court and this led to end of his military career. For a well-balanced view of these events see Jeffery pp. 48–53.

60 Major William Roper Caldbeck was serving with the Bedfordshire Regt, he had studied law at Trinity College, Dublin.

61 Lieutenant Frank Popkin Glover, 13th RWF.

62 TNA: *see* W.O. 374/50002; refers to General R. Hutton Davies who committed suicide.

63 Lieutenant Colonel G.H. Barnett, AA & QMG 48th Div.

64 Brigadier General T.S. Lambert, 69th Bde, 23rd Inf Div.

65 General Badoglio, Deputy GIGS.

66 Sir Percy Zachariah Cox (1864–1937). Made an honourable major general in 1917. Chief Political Officer, Indian Expeditionary Force.

67 Major General W.C.G. Heneker, GOC 8th Div.

68 Lord Milner, Secretary of State for War.

69 Sir Philip Kerr (later Lord Lothian) (1882–1940). He was a key figure in the Liberal Party and became part of Lloyd George's 'Garden Suburb'. He was a foreign policy expert and played a crucial role in the negotiations over the Treaty of Versailles. He became British ambassador to the USA in 1939 but died suddenly the following year.

70 Major General John DuCane, XV Corps Commander.

71 General T.H. Bliss, a US delegate to Versailles, Chief of Staff to General Pershing the US Commander.

72 Captain Hon. Visct. V.B. Duncannon TF. Personal Secretary to Field Marshall Henry H. Wilson 19 February 1918.

73 Lord Derby in 1915 introduced a scheme to reconcile the demands of the army with that of industry by calling up certain groups of men, as they were wanted, and taking single men first. It was replaced in 1916 by conscription. He later became British ambassador in Paris.

74 John Thomas Davies was the Private Secretary of the Prime Minister Right Hon. David Lloyd George.

75 General John J. 'Black Jack' Pershing, C in C American Expeditionary Force (AEF).

76 Marechal Ferdinand Foch, Commander of all Armies fighting the Germans.

77 Monsieur George 'the Tiger' Clemenceau (1840–1925). The French prime minister.

78 Signor Orlando, the Italian prime minister.

79 Baron Sonnino, the Italian foreign minister.

80 Major General Sir J.M. Babington, GOC 23rd Div.

81 Major General T.R.C. Hudson, CRA XIV Corps.

82 IWM: HHW 2/32A/17.

83 IWM: Wilson Papers HHW 2?32A/15A.

84 Lieutenant General Sir Henry Merrick Lawson RE (18591933). IGC November 1917 to July 1918.

85 Lieutenant Colonel H.S. Mosley, ADVS.

86 Major General Sir Foster Reuss Newland, Director of Medical Services (18621943).

87 Lieutenant General Sir Edward Arthur Fanshawe RA (18591952). He.was GOCV Corps and was removed from command after the German Spring Offensive March 1918. In August 1918 he was given command of XXIII Corps but was then transferred to Garrison the Firth of Forth.

88 IWM: Wilson Papers HHW 2/32A/19a.

89 Brigadier General Alexander Ernest Wardrop (18721961). BGRA GHQ Italy. Later Lieutenant General GOC Palestine 1921, QMG India 1930 and GOC Northern Command 1933.

90 IWM: Wilson Papers HHW 2/32A/19b.

91 Lieutenant General Sir John Philip Du Cane, British Representative with Marshal Foch (18651947).

92 IWM: Wilson Papers HHW 2/32A/14.

93 The Battle of Asiago took place between 15–16 June 1918; it later became known as the Third Battle of the Piave. *See Official History of the War, Military Operations Italy 191518* (HMSO, 1949), Chapter XV, pp. 194220.

94 IWM: Wilson Papers HHW 2/32A/20.

95 IWM: Wilson Papers HHW 2/32A/21.

96 Brigadier General John Arkwright Strick, Base Commandant, IGC 4 July 1918 to end of the war.

97 Lieutenant Colonel Sir Hereward Wake KRRC.

98 IWM: Wilson Papers HHW 2/32A/22.

99 IWM: Wilson Papers HHW 2/32A/23.

100 This is a very small type of cable car mainly used to ferry supplies.

101 12th Div. was part of XXVI Corps, First Italian Army.

102 Major (later Lieutenant General) William George Holmes DSO & Bar, acting CO of 1st Bn RWF till October 1918. He went to live in the USA when retired, died 1969.

103 Captain D.B. Anthony MC & Bar, served 1st Bn RWF. He received the Italian Al Valoire for the same action he was awarded his second MC (for a raid on the Asiago Plateau, 7 April 1918, where he was wounded).

104 Brigadier General R.T. Pelly, 91st Bde, 7th Div., served until the Armistice.

105 Lieutenant Colonel J.R.M. Minshull-Ford RWF, DSO, MC (1881–1948).

106 Colonel Brion CIGS, French Tenth Army.

107 Brigadier General H.L. Alexander, DA & QMG at GHQ at this time.

108 Sir Felix Maximilian Schoenbrun Casell, Judge Advocate General 1915–34 (1869–1953).

109 Lieutenant Colonel W.B.G. Barne RA, GSO 1, 7th Div. until Armistice.

110 W.S. Churchill had become Minister of Munitions. It is difficult to assess his comment but there were a number of disputes regarding pay & profiteering at this time. He also persuaded Lloyd George to threaten workers with conscription. Churchill did spend a great deal of time in France and, although outside the inner War Cabinet, did have direct access to Haig and saw himself as very much the man on the spot. *See* Roy Jenkins, *Churchill, A Biography* (New York, 2001), Chapter 18.

111 It would appear that this was his second & third cousin but I am unable to be absolutely certain.

112 Major General W.H. Kay, CRA Tenth Army; Brigadier General John Byron, CRA 23rd Div.

113 There were a few influenza epidemics during 1918 in Italy. This outbreak did have an effect on the fighting and occurred in May/June and again in October. *See OH Military Operations Italy 1915–19*, pp. 181, 195, 217 and 268 for a fuller picture of it effects.

Epilogue

The importance of the correspondence of Major General Price-Davies VC to historians and other interested parties can clearly be seen from the brief outline of his career during the Great War.

When the British Expeditionary Force arrived in France in August 1914, it soon found itself hurriedly moving north to engage the sweeping forces of the German Army moving across Belgium. As the British Divisions met this invading army, it became involved in a life or death struggle for its own existence. The speed and depth of these early battles, and the subsequent retreat during the fast-moving early months of the war, put a huge strain on the way commanders at all levels communicated with each other. As a result, officers like Captain Price-Davies VC had moved from the MOD across to France as 'Liaison Officers'. As mobilisation had been carried out rapidly, he was posted to work with 2nd Division in dealing with communications between the Divisional HQ and 1st Guards, 5th and 6th Brigades, which was commanded by Major General C.C. Munro. His correspondence during the first two years of the war gives an insight as to how difficult the work of a liaison officer was to say nothing about how dangerous it was. Equally complex was how quickly circumstances changed during this period and how often the officer had to interpret the meaning of orders passed on to a senior officer who was actually fighting the battle. Captain Price-Davies VC's letters and diary entries reveal how demanding his work was and how important these messages were in the days before radio communication was available.

At the end of 1915 he is promoted to brigadier in one of the New Kitchener Army Divisions. His first encounter with 113th Infantry Brigade, 38th Welsh Division is at Winnal Down, just north of Winchester, and he takes command of them as they move across to France. This is a very different experience, as although he has a few regular officers, the vast majority of junior officers are new to the military life. His correspondence reveals his deep frustration over the way the brigade is used during the nearly two years he is in command. The division takes part in the battle for Mametz Wood during the early stages of the Somme battle. The following year it takes part in the battle for Pilckem Ridge and Langemarck, the opening battle of the Third Battle of Ypres.

During the final year of the war, he is posted to Special Duties as a major general at British GHQ Italy. Here we see how difficult coalition warfare was and how efforts were made to overcome the problems these circumstances posed. The new and very different topography of warfare on this front compared to France necessitated a study of new methods and skills required by British forces. He is also in close liaison with the new CIGS, Henry Wilson, his brother-in-law, about both the tactical and strategic problems of this front. His relationship with Lord Cavan, the commander of British forces in Italy, is explored in some detail, as well as his interaction with the Italian commanders. His letters finish unexpectedly, late in November 1918 while he is in Versailles on his way to England on leave.

Overall, his correspondence reveals a deeply sensitive man who was more than ever aware of his own abilities whether they were positive or otherwise. His background ensured that he was well founded in the world he had chosen and he had all the social skills of this period. The list of people that he encountered during these war years shows how comfortable he was in this world, while at the same time reflecting on the nature of these meetings. The journey he took during these momentous years also reflects how the old Edwardian Army that had started the First World War became a much more integrated and capable military machine at the end of it.

Bibliography

Unpublished Primary Sources
Imperial War Museum
Department of Documents
Major General L.A.E. Price-Davies VC, CMG, papers
Field Marshal Sir Henry H. Wilson CB, DSO, papers

National Army Museum
Templer Study Centre
Major General L.A.E. Price-Davies VC, diaries 1914–18

National Archives, Kew (Public Records Office)
CAB 45/133 Price-Davies letter to General Sir James Edmonds regarding the Somme Battle. For the History of the Great War, Military Operations
W.O. 95/2539 38th (Welsh) Division War Diary December 1915 – July 1916
W.O. 95/2540 38th (Welsh) Division War Diary 1916–1919
W.O. 95/2551 113th Infantry Brigade War Diary November 1915 – June 1916
W.O. 95/2552 113th Infantry Brigade War Diary July 1916 – February 1917
W.O. 95/2553 113th Infantry Brigade War Diary March 1917 – December 1917
W.O. 95/4194 G.H.Q. Italy 1917 – 1918
W.O. 374/8825 Lt Colonel C.G. Blackader pension file

Royal Welsh Fusiliers Museum
The Royal Welsh Fusiliers Officers 1914–1918. Researched carried out by Mr Tyler
R.W.F. Battalion Files World War One, Colonel N. Lock O.B.E

Printed Primary Sources
Harts Army List 1906 (Three volumes)
The Monthly Army List, August 1914 (Two volumes)
The Monthly Army List, July 1916 (Three volumes)
The Half-Yearly Army List December 1922
The History of the Great War, Order of Battle of Division, Part 1. The Regular British Divisions. Major A.F. Becke (H.M.S.O., 1935)

Order of Battle of Divisions, Part 3A and 3B. New Army Divisions. Major A.F. Becke (H.M.S.O., 1938)

Order of Battle Part 4. The Army Council, G.H.Q.s, Armies and Corps 1914–1918. Major A.F. Becke (H.M.S.O., 1945)

Jeffery, K., *The Military Correspondence of Field Marshal Sir Henry Wilson 1918–1922* (Bodley Head for the Army Records Society, London, 1985)

Sheffield, G. and Bourne, J. (eds), *Douglas Haig, War Diaries and Letters 1914 –1918* (Weidenfeld & Nicolson, London, 2005)

Oxford Dictionary of National Biography

The VC and DSO Book: The Victoria Cross 1856–1920

The VC and DSO Book: Distinguished Service Order 1886–1915

The VC and DSO Book: Distinguished Service Order 1916–1923

The Register of the Victoria Cross (Trowbridge, England, 1981)

Military Operations France and Belgium 1914, Volume 1 (H.M.S.O., 1923)

Military Operations France and Belgium 1914, Volume 2 (H.M.S.O., 1925)

Military Operations France and Belgium 1915, Volume 1 (H.M.S.O., 1927)

Military Operations France and Belgium 1915, Volume 2 (H.M.S.O., 1928)

Military Operations France and Belgium 1916, Volume 1 (H.M.S.O., 1932)

Military Operations France and Belgium 1916, Volume 2 (H.M.S.O., 1938)

Military Operations France and Belgium 1917, Volume 1 (H.M.S.O., 1940)

Military Operations France and Belgium 1917, Volume 2 (H.M.S.O., 1948)

Military Operations France and Belgium 1917, Volume 3 (H.M.S.O., 1948)

Military Operations Italy (H.M.S.O. 1949)

The Welsh Academy Encyclopaedia of Wales. Co-editors John Davies, Nigel Jenkins, Menna Baines, Peredur L. Lynch (University of Wales Press, Cardiff, 2008)

Who's Who 1920 (A. C. Black Ltd, London)

Who's Who in Wales 1933 (Reynolds & Co Ltd, London)

Secondary Sources

Atkinson, C.T., *The Seventh Division 1914 – 1918* (Rowe Ltd, Wiltshire, 1927)

Callwell, Major General Sir C.E., *Field Marshal Sir Henry Wilson GCB, DSO: His Life and Times Volumes 1 & 2* (London, 1927)

Griffiths, Llewellyn Wyn, *Up to Mametz* (London, 1931)

Griffiths, Llewellyn Wyn (author) and Riley, Jonathan (editor), *Up to Mametz and Beyond* (Barnsley, 2010)

Hughes, Colin, *Mametz – Lloyd George's 'Welsh Army' at the Battle of the Somme* (Gliddon Books, 1990)

Munby, Lt Colonel J.E., *A History of the 38th (Welsh) Division* (H. Rees Ltd, London, 1920)

Thompson, Mark, *The White War* (Faber & Faber, London, 2008)

Wilks, John and Wilks, Eileen, *The British Army in Italy 1917–1918* (South Yorkshire, 1998)

Index

If you enjoyed this book, you may also be interested in…

Somewhere In Blood-Soaked France

THE DIARY OF CORPORAL ANGUS MACKAY, ROYAL SCOTS, MACHINE GUN CORPS, 1914–1917

From the heat and dust of the Dardanelles to the mud of the Western Front, Corpor
Angus Mackay had one constant companion, his diary. He wrote of the battles an
campaigns he fought in, names that would go down in history: Gallipoli, the Ypr
Salient, the Somme and Arras. Serving in the 1st/5th Battalion (Queens Edinburg
Rifles) Royal Scots and later the 88th Brigade Machine Gun Corps, he left a reco
of one man's extraordinary and tragic war

9780752464466

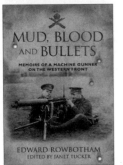

Mud, Blood and Bullets

MEMOIRS OF A MACHINE GUNNER ON THE WESTERN FRONT, EDWARD ROWBOTHAM, I
JANET TUCKER

It is 1915 and the Great War has been raging for a year, when Edward Rowbotha
a coal miner from the Midlands, volunteers for Kitchener's Army. Drafted into t
newly-formed Machine Gun Corps, he is sent to fight in places whose names w
forever be associated with mud and blood and sacrifice: Ypres, the Somme, a
Passchendaele. He is one of the 'lucky' ones, winning the Military Medal for brave
and surviving more than two-and-a-half years of the terrible slaughter that left nearl
million British soldiers dead by 1918 and wiped out all but six of his original compa

9780752456201

The Final Whistle: The Great War in Fifteen Players

STEPHEN COOPER

This is the story of 15 men killed in the Great War. All played rugby for one Lond
club; none lived to hear the final whistle. Rugby brought them together; rugby l
the rush to war. They came from Britain and the Empire to fight in every thea
and service, among them a poet, playwright and perfumer. Some were decorated a
died heroically; others fought and fell quietly. Together their stories paint a portrait
miniature of the entire War.

9780752479354

Trench Talk: Words of the First World War

PETER DOYLE & JULIAN WALKER

One of the enduring myths of the First World War is that the experience of
trenches was not talked about. Yet dozens of words entered or became familiar
the English language as a direct result of the soldiers' experiences. This book looks
how the first-hand and second-hand experience of the First World War changed
English language, adding words that were both in slang and standard military use, a
modifying the usage and connotations of existing words and phrases. Illustrated w
material from the authors' collections and photographs of the objects of the war,
book will look at how the words emerged into everyday language.

9780752471549

Visit our website and discover thousands of other History Press books.

www.thehistorypress.co.uk